W9-AWM-874

BRIDGES TO
LITERATURE

McDougal Littell
A HOUGHTON MIFFLIN COMPANY
Evanston, Illinois • Boston • Dallas

READING • LITERATURE • VOCABULARY

Author

Jane Greene Literacy Intervention Specialist; Reading, Writing, Language, Evaluation Consultant to schools nationwide; author of *LANGUAGE! A Literacy Intervention Curriculum*. Dr. Greene established the underlying goals and philosophy, advised on the tables of contents, reviewed prototypes, and supervised the development of the assessment strand.

English Language Advisor

Judy Lewis Director, State and Federal Programs for reading proficiency and high-risk populations, Folsom, California; Editor, *Context*, a newsletter for teachers with English learners in their classes. Ms. Lewis reviewed selections for the program and provided special guidance on the development of EL notes.

Consultant

Olga Bautista Reading Facilitator, Will C. Wood Middle School, Sacramento, California. Ms. Bautista provided advice on reading, pacing, and EL instruction during the development phase and reviewed final prototypes of both the Pupil Edition and Teacher's Edition.

ISBN-13:978-0-618-08734-1

ISBN-10:0-618-08734-6

Copyright © 2002 by McDougal Littell, a division of Houghton Mifflin Company.
All rights reserved.
Printed in the United States of America.

Warning: No part of this work may be reproduced or transmitted in any form or by any means, electronic or mechanical, including photocopying and recording, or by any information storage or retrieval system without prior written permission of McDougal Littell Inc. unless such copying is expressly permitted by federal copyright law. With the exception of not-for-profit transcription in Braille, McDougal Littell Inc. is not authorized to grant permission for further uses of copyrighted selections reprinted in this text without the permission of their owners. Permission must be obtained from the individual copyright owners as identified herein. Address inquiries to Manager, Rights and Permissions, McDougal Littell Inc., P. O. Box 1667, Evanston, IL 60204.

Teacher Panel

Katherine S. Barg, Teacher
Central Middle School
San Carlos, California

Claudette Burk, English Department Chairperson
Tetzlaff Middle School
Cerritos, California

Susan Busenius, Core Teacher
Valley View School
Pleasanthill, California

Deborah Dei Rossi, Teacher
Cunha Intermediate School
Half Moon Bay, California

Lana Fenech, Teacher, Technology Coordinator
Borel Middle School
San Mateo, California

Joy Martineau, Language Arts Teacher
Warner Middle School
Westminster, California

Annie Muchnick, Literacy Coach
Garvey School
Rosemead, California

Joanne Nash, English Teacher
Sunnyvale Middle School
Sunnyvale, California

Patricia Radotich, Teacher
Woodbridge Middle School
Woodbridge, California

Frances Rubin, English Teacher
Emerson Middle School
Los Angeles, California

Sue Sermeno, Grade Level Coordinator
North Park Middle School
Pico Rivera, California

Margaret Williams, English Language Arts
   Chairperson
Carmenita Middle School
Cerritos, California

Teacher Reviewers

Lillie Alfred, Teacher
Altgeld School
Chicago, Illinois

Tracy Arrington, Teacher
George W. Curtis School
Chicago, Illinois

Stephanie Gates, Teacher
Miriam G. Canter Middle School
Chicago, Illinois

Regina Gooden-Hampton, Teacher
Kipling Elementary School
Chicago, Illinois

Student Reviewers

Aunyetta Crosby, Detroit, Michigan
Phimy Danh, Long Beach, California
Julie Daniels, Sacramento, California
Maria Fraga, Sacramento, California
Eduardo Obeso, Detroit, Michigan
Erik Quirk, Encinitas, California

Michael Roett, Tallahassee, Florida
Michelle Schmitt, Tallahassee, Florida
Barbara Schwenk, Weston, Massachusetts
Renee Sevier, Long Beach, California
Shane, Lincoln, Massachusetts

BRIDGES TO
LITERATURE

Level II

Some selections available on the Reading Coach CD-ROM

No Turning Back

Fiction

Sometimes a decision you make or an action you take can't be undone. Like the characters in this unit, you may face a moment that changes your life forever.

These works are all **fiction**—stories created from a writer's imagination. Fiction has four main elements:

- **Plot:** what happens in the story

- **Characters:** the people or animals the story is about

- **Setting:** where and when the story takes place

- **Theme:** the writer's message about life or human nature

Baseball
SAVED US

by Ken Mochizuki

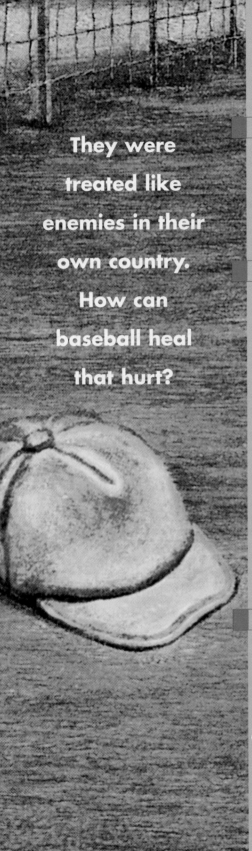

They were
treated like
enemies in their
own country.
How can
baseball heal
that hurt?

Connect to Your Life

What do you know about the game of baseball? With a classmate, write these column headings: *Field, Equipment*, and *Baseball Skills*. Fill in as much as you can under these headings.

Key to the Story

Baseball Saved Us is an example of **historical fiction**. This is fiction set in the past that often tells about actual people and events.

The story takes place during World War II. In 1941, Japan bombed the U.S. naval base in Hawaii. Soon after, the United States entered World War II.

People were afraid that Japanese Americans would turn against the United States. As a result, the U.S. military forced 110,000 Japanese American citizens to move to places called *detention camps*. Decades later, the U.S. government apologized for making citizens live in these camps.

Vocabulary Preview

Words to Know
barracks
bleachers
glinting

 Reading Coach CD-ROM selection

One day, my dad looked out at the endless desert and decided then and there to build a baseball field.

He said people needed something to do in Camp. We weren't in a camp that was fun, like summer camp. Ours was in the middle of nowhere, and we were behind a barbed-wire fence. Soldiers with guns made sure we stayed there, and the man in the tower saw everything we did, no matter where we were.

As Dad began walking over the dry, cracked dirt, I
10 asked him again why we were here.

"Because," he said, "America is at war with Japan, and the government thinks that Japanese Americans can't be trusted. But it's wrong that we're in here. We're Americans too!" Then he made a mark in the dirt and mumbled something about where the infield bases should be.

infield bases
four bases arranged in a square around the pitcher

Back in school, before Camp, I was shorter and smaller than the rest of the kids. I was always the last to be picked for
20 any team when we played games. Then, a few months ago, it got even worse. The kids started to call me names and nobody talked to me, even though I didn't do anything bad. At the same time the radio kept talking about some place far away called Pearl Harbor.

Pearl Harbor
U.S. naval base located in Hawaii

One day Mom and Dad came to get me out of school. Mom cried a lot because we had to move out of our house real fast, throwing away a lot of our stuff. A bus took us to a

place where we had to live in horse stalls. We stayed
there for a while until we came here.

This Camp wasn't anything like home. It was so
hot in the daytime and so cold at night. Dust storms
came and got sand in everything, and nobody could
see a thing. We sometimes got caught outside,
standing in line to eat or to go to the bathroom. We
had to use the bathroom with everybody else, instead
of one at a time like at home.

We had to eat with everybody else, too, but my big
brother Teddy ate with his own friends. We lived with
a lot of people in what were called
barracks . The place was small and had no
walls. Babies cried at night and kept us up.

> **barracks**
> (băr′ əks)
> *n.* houses built
> for military
> purposes

Back home, the older people were always
busy working. But now, all they did was
stand or sit around. Once Dad asked Teddy
to get him a cup of water.

"Get it yourself," Teddy said.

"What did you say?" Dad snapped back.

The older men stood up and pointed at Teddy.
"How dare you talk to your father like that!" one of
them shouted.

Teddy got up, kicked the crate he was
sitting on, and walked away. I had never
heard Teddy talk to Dad that way before.

> **REREAD**
> How is Teddy
> changing? Why?

That's when Dad knew we needed baseball. We got
shovels and started digging up the sagebrush in a big
empty space near our barracks. The man in the tower
watched us the whole time. Pretty soon, other grown-
ups and their kids started to help.

THINK IT THROUGH
The narrator's dad wants to build a baseball field. How does
the daily life in Camp lead to his decision?

FOCUS

Find out how the narrator performs in one of the early ball games.

We didn't have anything we needed for baseball, but the grown-ups were pretty smart. They funnelled water from irrigation ditches to flood what would become our baseball field. The water packed down the dust and made it hard. There weren't any trees,

but they found wood to build the
bleachers . Bats, balls and gloves arrived in
cloth sacks from friends back home. My
mom and other moms took the covers off
70 mattresses and used them to make
uniforms. They looked almost like the real
thing.

bleachers
(blē′ chərz)
n. outdoor stands
or benches for
watching games

    I tried to play, but I wasn't that good. Dad said I
just had to try harder. But I did know that playing
baseball here was a little easier than back home. Most
of the time, the kids were the same size as me.

    All the time I practiced, the man in the tower
watched. He probably saw the other kids giving me a
bad time and thought that I was no good. So I tried
80 to be better because he was looking.

    Soon, there were baseball games all the time.
Grown-ups played and us kids did, too. I played
second base because my team said that was the
easiest. Whenever I was at bat, the infield of the other
team started joking around and moved in real close.
The catcher behind me and the crowd for
the other team would say, "Easy out." I
usually grounded out. Sometimes I got a
single.

REREAD
How do you
think the
narrator feels?

90   Then came one of our last games of
the year to decide on the championship. It was the
bottom of the ninth inning and the other team was
winning, 3 to 2. One of our guys was on second and
there were two outs.

    Two pitches, and I swung both times and missed. I
could tell that our guy on second was begging me to
at least get a base hit so somebody better could come
up to bat. The crowd was getting loud. "You can do
it!" "Strike out!" "No hitter, no hitter!"

100   I glanced at the guardhouse behind the left field foul line and saw the man in the tower, leaning on the rail with the blinding sun glinting off his sunglasses. He was always watching, always staring. It suddenly made me mad.

glinting
(glĭn' tĭng)
adj. sparkling

REREAD
How would you feel in the narrator's place?

    I gripped the bat harder and took a couple of practice swings. I was gonna hit the ball past the guardhouse even if it killed me. Everyone got quiet and the pitcher threw.

110   I stepped into my swing and pulled the bat around hard. I'd never heard a crack like that before. The ball went even farther than I expected.

    Against the hot desert sun, I could see the ball high in the air as I ran to first base. The ball went over the head of the left fielder.

    I dashed around the bases, knowing for sure that I would get tagged out. But I didn't care, running as fast as I could to home plate. I didn't even realize that I had crossed it.

120   Before I knew it, I was up in the air on the shoulders of my teammates. I looked up at the tower and the man, with a grin on his face, gave me the thumbs-up sign.

THINK IT THROUGH
What are two surprising things about the narrator's victory?

FOCUS
The war ends and the families leave Camp. Read to discover how the narrator performs in a game back home.

    But it wasn't as if everything were fixed. Things were bad again when we got home from Camp after

the war. Nobody talked to us on the street, and nobody talked to me at school, either. Most of my friends from Camp didn't come back here. I had to eat
130 lunch by myself.

REREAD
Why do you think the narrator's family is treated this way?

Then baseball season came. I was the smallest guy again, but playing baseball in Camp had made me a lot better. The other guys saw that I was a pretty good player. They started calling me "Shorty," but they smiled when they said it.

By the time the first game came around, I felt almost like part of the team. Everyone was laughing and horsing around on the bus. But as soon as we got out there, it hit me: nobody on my team or the other
140 team, or even anybody in the crowd looked like me.

When we walked out onto the field, my hands were shaking. It felt like all these mean eyes were staring at me, wanting me to make mistakes. I dropped the ball

Baseball Saved Us **11**

that was thrown to me, and I heard people in the crowd yelling "Jap." I hadn't heard that word since before I went to Camp—it meant that they hated me.

My team came up to bat and I was up next. I looked down. I thought maybe I should pretend to be sick so I wouldn't have to finish the game. But I knew that would make things even worse, because I would get picked on at school for being a chicken. And they would use the bad word, too.

Then it was my turn at bat. The crowd was screaming. "The Jap's no good!" "Easy out!" I heard laughing. I swung twice and missed. The crowd roared each time I missed, drowning out my teammates, who were saying, "C'mon, Shorty, you can do it!" I stepped back to catch my breath.

REREAD
What do you predict will happen next?

160   When I stepped back up to the plate, I looked at the pitcher. The sun glinted off his glasses as he stood on the mound, like the guard in the tower. We stared at each other. Then I blocked out the noise around me and got set. The pitcher wound up and threw.

I swung and felt that solid whack again. And I could see that little ball in the air against the blue sky and puffy white clouds. It looked like it was going over the fence.

THINK IT THROUGH

1. What happens at the end of the story? Why is this important to the narrator?
2. How do you think baseball "saves" the narrator?
3. What good things does baseball do for the families in Camp?

THE DAY THE SUN CAME OUT

by Dorothy M. Johnson

In the Old West, pioneers struggled to start a new life. Some, like Mary, even risked their lives in order to survive.

Connect to Your Life

What do you know about the problems the pioneers faced as they traveled West? With a partner, list the hardships that made the journey so challenging.

Key to the Story

In **historical fiction,** the setting often influences the plot in some way. This story of the Old West takes place during the mid-1800s in the Rocky Mountains. At that time, 350,000 pioneers traveled west in search of a better life. One in 15 died along the way. The story is told from an 11-year-old boy's point of view. His mother has died. Now the rest of the family is going west.

Vocabulary Preview

Words to Know

desperate	savoring
grudging	sedately
endured	

We left the home place behind, mile by slow mile. We were heading for the mountains, across the prairie where the wind blew forever.

At first there were four of us with the one-horse wagon and its skimpy load. Pa and I walked because I was a big boy of eleven. My two little sisters walked until they got tired. Then they had to be boosted up in the wagon bed.

That was no covered Conestoga, like Pa's folks
10 came West in. It was just an old farm wagon, drawn by one tired horse. It creaked and rumbled westward to the mountains, toward the little woods town where Pa thought he had an old uncle who owned a little two-bit sawmill.

Two weeks we had been moving when we picked up Mary. She had run away from somewhere that she wouldn't tell. Pa didn't want her along. But she stood up to him with no fear in her voice.

"I'd rather go with a family and look
20 after kids," she said, "but I ain't going back. If you won't take me, I'll travel with any wagon that will."

REREAD
Read Mary's words aloud, letting your voice show her feelings.

Pa scowled at her, and wide blue eyes stared back.

"How old are you?" he demanded.

"Twenty," she said. "There's teamsters come this way sometimes. I'd rather go with you folks. But I won't go back."

"We're prid'near out of food," my father
30 told her. "We're clean out of money. I got all I can handle without taking anybody

teamsters
(tēm' stərz)
people who work with teams of horses to haul loads

else." He turned away as if he hated the sight of her. "You'll have to walk," he said.

So she went along with us. She looked after the little girls, but Pa wouldn't talk to her.

THINK IT THROUGH

What reasons does Pa give for not wanting Mary to join them?

FOCUS

What problems does the family face?

On the prairie, the wind blew. But in the mountains, there was rain. When we stopped at little timber claims along the way, the homesteaders said it had rained all summer. Crops among the blackened
40 stumps were rotted and spoiled. There was no cheer anywhere. The people we talked to were past worrying. They were scared and desperate.

> **desperate**
> (děs′ pər ĭt)
> *adj.* suffering from extreme need

So was Pa. He traveled twice as far each day as the wagon. He ranged through the woods with his rifle. But he never saw game. He had been depending on killing a deer. But we never got any deer meat except as a grudging gift from the
50 homesteaders.

> **grudging**
> (grŭj′ ĭng)
> *adj.* unwilling

He brought in a porcupine once. And that was fat meat and good. Mary roasted it in chunks over the fire, half crying with the smoke. Pa and I rigged up the tarp sheet for a shelter to keep the rain from putting the fire clean out.

The porcupine was long gone, except for some of the dried-out fat that Mary had saved, when we came

to an old, empty cabin. Pa said we'd
have to stop. The horse was wore
60 out. It couldn't pull any more up
those hills in the mountains.

At the cabin, at least there was a
place to stay. We had a few potatoes
left and some cornmeal. There was
a creek that probably had fish in it,
if a person could catch them. Pa tried it for half a day
before he gave up. To this day I don't care for fishing.
I remember my father's sunken eyes in his sad face.

He took Mary and me outside the cabin to talk.
70 Rain dripped on us from branches overhead.

"I think I know where we are," he said. "I figure to
get to old John's and back in about four days. There'll
be food in the town. They'll let me have some
whether old John's still there or not."

He looked at me. "You do like she tells you," he
warned. It was the first time he had admitted Mary
was on earth since we picked her up two weeks before.

"You're my pardner," he said to me, "but it might
be she's got more brains. You mind what she says."

80 He burst out with bitterness. "There
ain't anything good left in the world. Or
people to care if you live or die. But I'll get
food in the town and come back with it."

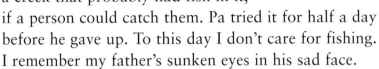

REREAD
What do Pa's
words tell about
him?

He took a deep breath and added, "If
you get too all-fired hungry, butcher the horse. It'll be
better than starvin'."

He kissed the little girls goodbye. Then he plodded
off through the woods with one blanket and the rifle.

THINK IT THROUGH
What is the family's worst problem? What is Pa's plan to solve it?

The cabin was moldy and had no floor.

90 We kept a fire going under a hole in the roof, so it was full of blinding smoke, but we had to keep the fire so as to dry out the wood.

The third night, we lost the horse. A bear scared him. We heard the racket. Mary and I ran out. But we couldn't see anything in the pitch-dark.

In gray daylight I went looking for him. I must have walked fifteen miles. It seemed like I had to have that horse at the cabin when Pa came or he'd whip me.

REREAD
Why is the loss of the horse so important?

100 I got plumb lost two or three times. I thought maybe I was going to die there alone and nobody would ever know it. But I found the way back to the clearing.

That was the fourth day. And Pa didn't come. That was the day we ate up the last of the grub.

The fifth day, Mary went looking for the horse. My sisters cried. They huddled in a blanket by the fire, because they were scared and hungry.

I never did get dried out, always having to bring in 110 more damp wood and going out to yell to see if Mary would hear me and not get lost. But I couldn't cry like the little girls did, because I was a big boy, eleven years old.

It was near dark when there was an answer to my yelling. Mary came into the clearing.

Mary didn't have the horse. We never saw hide nor hair of that old horse again. But she was carrying something big and white that looked like a pumpkin with no color to it.

120 She didn't say anything, just looked around and saw Pa wasn't there yet, at the end of the fifth day.

"What's that thing?" my sister Elizabeth demanded.

"Mushroom," Mary answered. "I bet it hefts ten pounds."

"What are you going to do with it now?" I said. "Play football here?"

"Eat it—maybe," she said, putting it in a corner. Her wet hair hung over her

130 shoulders. She huddled by the fire.

THINK IT THROUGH
The family's situation has changed. How has it gotten worse?

FOCUS
Discover why the narrator begins to hate Mary.

My sister Sarah began to cry again. "I'm hungry!" she kept saying.

"Mushrooms ain't good eating," I said. "They can kill you."

"Maybe," Mary answered. "Maybe they can. I don't set up to know all about everything, like some people."

"What's that mark on your shoulder?" I asked her. "You tore your dress on the brush."

140 "What do you think it is?" she said. Her head was bowed in the smoke.

"Looks like scars," I guessed.

"'Tis scars. They whipped me, them I used to live with. Now mind your own business. I want to think."

REREAD
What do you learn about Mary's past?

Elizabeth cried, "Why don't Pa come back?"

"He's coming," Mary promised. "Can't come in the dark. Your pa'll take care of you soon's he can."

She got up and looked around in the grub box.

150 "Nothing there but empty dishes," I growled. "If there was anything, we'd know it."

Mary stood up. She was holding the can with the porcupine grease.

"I'm going to have something to eat," she said coolly. "You kids can't have any yet. And I don't want any crying, mind."

It was a cruel thing, what she did then. She sliced that big, solid mushroom and heated grease in a pan.

The smell of it brought the little girls out of their
160 bed. But she told them to go back in so fierce a voice that they obeyed. They cried to break your heart.

I didn't cry. I watched, hating her.

I endured the smell of the mushroom frying as long as I could. Then I said, "Give me some."

"Tomorrow," Mary answered. "Tomorrow, maybe. But not tonight." She turned to me with a sharp command: "Don't bother me! Just leave me be."

170 She knelt there by the fire and finished frying the slice of mushroom.

If I'd had Pa's rifle, I'd have been willing to kill her right then and there.

She didn't eat right away. She looked at the brown, fried slice for a while and said, "By tomorrow morning, I guess you can tell whether you want any."

The girls stared at her as she ate. Sarah was chewing on an old leather glove.

endured
(ĕn dŏŏrd')
v. put up with; past tense of *endure*

REREAD
Why do you think Mary won't let the others eat?

180   When Mary crawled into the quilts with them, they moved away as far as they could get.

    I was so scared that my stomach heaved, empty as it was.

    Mary didn't stay in the quilt long. She took a drink out of the water bucket and sat down by the fire and looked through the smoke at me.

    She said in a low voice, "I don't know how it will be if it's poison. Just do the best you can with the girls. Because your pa will come back,

190 you know. . . . You better go to bed. I'm going to sit up."

REREAD

What is Mary waiting for?

    And so would you sit up. If it might be your last night on earth and the pain of death might seize you at any moment, you would sit up by the smoky fire, wide-awake, remembering whatever you had to remember, savoring life.

    We sat in silence after the girls had gone to sleep. Once I asked, "How long does it take?"

savoring

(sā′ vər ĭng)
adj. enjoying and appreciating fully

200   "I never heard," she answered. "Don't think about it."

    I slept after a while, with my chin on my chest.

THINK IT THROUGH
What do Mary's actions show about her?

FOCUS
A new day is beginning. Read to find out what happens to Mary.

    Mary's moving around brought me wide-awake. The black of night was fading.

"I guess it's all right," Mary said. "I'd be able to tell by now, wouldn't I?"

I answered gruffly, "I don't know."

Mary stood in the doorway for a while, looking out at the dripping world as if she found it beautiful.
210 Then she fried slices of the mushroom while the little girls danced with anxiety.

We feasted, we three, my sisters and I, until Mary ruled, "That'll hold you," and would not cook any more. She didn't touch any of the mushroom herself.

That was a strange day in the moldy cabin. Mary laughed and was gay. She told stories. And we played "Who's Got the Thimble?" with a pine cone.

In the afternoon we heard a shout. My sisters screamed and I ran ahead of them across the clearing.
220 The rain had stopped. My father came plunging out of the woods leading a pack horse—and well I remember the treasures of food in that pack.

He glanced at us anxiously as he tore the ropes that bound the pack.

"Where's the other one?" he demanded.

Mary came out of the cabin then, walking sedately. As she came toward us, the sun began to shine.

> **sedately**
> (sĭ dāt′ lē)
> *adv.* in a slow, dignified way

My stepmother was a wonderful woman.

THINK IT THROUGH

1. What does the last line of the story tell you?
2. What can you infer, or figure out, about Mary's character? What clues tell you this?
3. In what ways does Mary show the toughness necessary for pioneer life?

RETOLD BY JULIE LAWSON

THE DRAGON'S PEARL

A MAGIC PEARL BRINGS A BOY AND HIS MOTHER GOOD LUCK. BUT THE PEARL HAS MORE POWER THAN THEY KNOW!

Connect to Your Life

Have you ever found something valuable by accident? Tell a partner what happened afterwards.

Key to the Folk Tale

A **folk tale** is a story in which the characters are ordinary people or animals that act like people. The stories usually teach lessons about life. Magic often plays a key role, as it does in *The Dragon's Pearl*.

In Chinese folk tales, dragons are water gods. Each spring they bring life-giving rains to the land. They also reward people who please them and punish those who anger them.

Vocabulary Preview

Words to Know

drought	pierced
scorched	flourished
craved	

 Reading Coach CD-ROM selection

The Dragon's Pearl **25**

FOCUS
Read to learn how a young boy and his mother survive in ancient China.

In the faraway days of cloud-breathing dragons, there lived a boy named Xiao Sheng who loved to sing.

Not that he had much to sing about. He toiled from dawn till dusk cutting grass and selling it for fuel or fodder . In that way, he was able to earn just enough money to buy food for himself and his mother.

fodder
(fŏd' ər)
food for animals

Still, Xiao Sheng was a good-natured boy.

"Good-bye, Mama," he said each day. "Who
10 knows what the gods have in store for us. Today may not be the same as yesterday."

But each day was the same. Off Xiao Sheng would go, thinking how lovely the river looked in the early morning sun. He wished he could fish from its banks or swim in its cool water, but there was never time. With only his song for company, he cut the grass and carried it to the village to sell. At sunset, he made his way home for a bowl of rice, a cup of tea, and a welcome sleep. And each day was the same.

THINK IT THROUGH
What does Xiao Sheng do all day?

FOCUS
Will Xiao Sheng's luck change? Read to find out.

20 Then came a terrible drought . Day after day the sun beat upon the land. Streams no longer sparkled in the hills. The river burned like fire along its scorched banks.

drought
(drout)
n. time of little or no rain

scorched
(skôrcht)
adj. burned on the surface

As always Xiao Sheng sang to lift his spirits, but he was worried. He scanned the sky for a sign of the rain-bringing dragons, but there was never a trace, not even the silkiest wisp of a cloud. Farther and farther into the hills he went, searching for grass that was not shriveled and dead.

REREAD
Why is Xiao Sheng worried?

30

One day, as he reached the crest of the highest hill, Xiao Sheng gazed upon a splendid patch of rich, green grass. Eagerly he cut the whole patch and hurried to the village, where he sold it for more money than he had ever received before.

When he returned the next day, he discovered the grass had grown back.

"Thank you!" he said, bowing to whatever gods were responsible for his good fortune. Once again he
40 cut the grass and rushed off to the village.

The same thing happened on the third day and on the fourth. Each morning the grass that had been cut had grown back as green and lush as ever.

An idea came to Xiao Sheng. "This must be magic grass," he said. "And if it grows so well here, why not anywhere? I'll plant it at home and save myself a long journey each day."

THINK IT THROUGH
What good luck has Xiao Sheng had? What do you think will happen when he moves the grass?

FOCUS
The boy makes several amazing discoveries. Read to learn what they are.

Next morning he began to dig up the grass, carefully moving the earth and roots to the tiny plot
50 of land beside his hut.

Back and forth he went, digging and transplanting one small bit at a time. He was almost finished when he noticed something shimmering, deep in the earth. He reached for it—and gasped. For in his hand, glowing like a rose-colored sunset, lay a pearl.

He raced home, crying for joy.
60 "Mama! See what the gods have given us!"

His old mother beamed. "This pearl will bring us a fortune. But let's keep it for a while before we lose sight of its beauty."

Xiao Sheng agreed, and he watched his mother hide the pearl in their near-empty rice jar. Then he went back
70 to his planting.

"How wonderful it will be," he said. "Tomorrow I'll cut the grass right here. Maybe I'll have time to catch a fish for supper."

But it was not to be. Early next morning, Xiao Sheng rushed outside—only to find that his grass had withered and died.

"What have I done!" he cried. And he
80 cursed himself for disturbing the earth, for destroying the rich, green grass, for being too happy and tempting the gods.

In the midst of his tears a thought struck him.

> **transplanting**
> (trăns plăn′ tĭng)
> moving a plant to another place

> **withered**
> (wĭth′ ərd)
> dried up

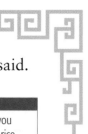

"Perhaps I should have planted the pearl," he said. And he dashed off to the rice jar.

What a sight met his eyes! The jar was now brimming with rice, and on top of the rice lay the gleaming pearl.

REREAD
Why do you think the rice has multiplied?

"A magic pearl!" his mother exclaimed. "Let's put it in our money box and see what happens."

They placed the pearl beside the one coin in the money box, and in no time the box was brimful of gold.

"Ah!" the old woman gasped, running her fingers through the coins. "You were right, my son. Today is not the same as yesterday!"

How they rejoiced! Their oil jar overflowed, their rice jar was never empty, and the money box was always full. While the neighbors prayed for rain, Xiao Sheng and his mother sang for joy and blessed their precious pearl.

THINK IT THROUGH
In what way does the pearl change the lives of the boy and his mother?

FOCUS
Will the pearl continue to bring joy to Xiao Sheng and his mother?

Their friends were not blind to their good fortune. Day after day they saw Xiao Sheng playing in the village or dreaming by the river. He brought home fish and no longer went into the hills to cut grass. He had always been a happy boy . . . but now!

"Have you ever seen such a smile?" the villagers said. "And how well his old mother looks! Surely the gods have favored these two."

The villagers were not angry or jealous, because
wealth did not make Xiao Sheng and his mother
selfish. They gave generously to everyone
who had shown them kindness in the
past. Their poor drought-stricken
neighbors were thankful.

REREAD

If you were a villager, how would you have felt?

Well, most of them.

One night, two men burst into the hut demanding
food and money. "We know you have a box of gold
coins," one rough fellow shouted. "Give it to us at
once." The men pushed the old woman aside and began
to tear the hut apart, searching for the money box.

"Stop!" cried Xiao Sheng in alarm. "I'll give you
some money." He pulled the box from its hiding
place, but no sooner had he done so than the bigger
man grabbed it and opened it.

"What have we here!" he bellowed, holding up
the pearl.

Xiao Sheng snatched it from his hand. "You can
have all our money, but you can't have the
pearl."

The ruffian lunged toward the boy.
Quickly Xiao Sheng popped the pearl into
his mouth. The man grabbed him by the
shoulders and shook him while the other
beat upon his back. "Spit it out!" they yelled. "Spit it
out or it will be the worse for you!"

ruffian
(rŭf′ ē ən)
tough person

Afraid for her son, the old woman began to wail.
Poor Xiao Sheng was so confused by all the shaking
and shouting that he gulped—and swallowed the pearl!

THINK IT THROUGH
What problem has the pearl caused?

140 An intense heat seared through him, as if he had swallowed a ball of fire. He grabbed the teapot and emptied it in one gulp. Then he rushed to the water jar. Ten, twenty, thirty cups he drank, trying to put out the fire. But even after the jar was empty, he craved more water.

craved
(krāvd′) v. needed very badly; past tense of *crave*

His mother and the two men watched helplessly as he rushed outside to the riverbank, threw himself down, and began to drink.

"Stop!" his mother begged.

150 But he would not and could not stop. Before long, Xiao Sheng had drunk the river dry. And still the pearl burned inside.

The sky darkened and a fierce wind swept along the riverbanks. Lightning crackled. The 160 roar of thunder shook the earth and made it tremble. The villagers clutched one another, gaping at the blackness overhead. Xiao Sheng's mother rushed to his side and clasped him tightly.

"Come inside," she pleaded.

But even as she spoke, a great change was coming 170 over the boy.

The Dragon's Pearl **31**

Xiao Sheng began to grow—first his legs, then his body. The scales of a fish rippled along his back and the antlers of a deer appeared on his head. His hands became the talons of a hawk and his neck stretched like a snake. As he moved, he felt the twisting and coiling of a serpent's tail, and when he opened his mouth, his mother saw the gleaming pearl.

talons
(tăl′ ənz)
claws

She stared, amazed. In front of her very eyes, her
180　son had become a dragon!

THINK IT THROUGH

In your own words, describe how the boy changes.

Xiao Sheng no longer needed to search for wisps of cloud. Throwing back his mighty head, he breathed cloud after cloud and sent them billowing into the sky. As the villagers watched, the clouds burst open and the rain came streaming down. "It's over!" they cried. "Xiao Sheng has ended the drought!" They raised their smiling faces to the life-giving rain and praised the beneficent dragon.

190 Xiao Sheng sang as the rain poured into the thirsty earth and filled up the river. As he turned toward the river, his mother clung to his legs, trying to hold him back. Gently he freed himself from her grasp. Again and again she flung herself upon him. Again and again he set himself free.

Into the river he went, but his mother's cries pierced his heart and he could not keep from looking back. Each time he turned, his massive body cut into the river's edge, sculpting the banks with his
200 last farewell.

Alone by the river, the mother of Xiao Sheng wept as her son disappeared beneath the surface of the water. And still the rain poured down, washing away her tears.

The villagers were kind to Xiao Sheng's mother and honored her as they honored her son. Each morning they tossed a few grains of rice into the river as a gift to Xiao Sheng, Most Honored and Precious Dragon.
210 Every evening his mother sat on the riverbank, giving him the news of the day. She told him how the crops flourished and

beneficent
(bə nĕf′ ĭ sənt)
kind

pierced
(pîrst)
v. touched deeply; past tense of *pierce*

sculpting
(skŭlp′ tĭng)
shaping

flourished
(flûr′ ĭsht)
v. grew very well; past tense of *flourish*

how lush the countryside was, now that the drought was over. She spoke of the strange manner in which the rain fell—how it poured on all the fields except on those of the two wicked men. Those men finally left their dry, barren land in disgrace and were never seen again.

Sometimes a dragonfly landed softly on her shoulder, or a bright orange carp splashed its tail right at her feet. This made

220

carp
(kärp)
large fish

her smile, for she knew these to be glimpses of her son. And sometimes when the waters lapped the shore she could hear a light, tinkling sound, as clear and bright as the jingling of golden coins. This, too, made her smile, for she knew she had heard Xiao Sheng singing, "Today is not the same as yesterday."

As long as she lived, she watched for him every spring when dragons rise up from the rivers and
230 breathe clouds to rain upon the earth.

Today in China, the River Min still flows through the province of Szechuan. If you stop by that river to watch sunlight dance upon the water, you will see the banks carved by the dragon's tail.

And if you listen very carefully to the rippling of the water, you may even hear the dragon singing.

THINK IT THROUGH

1. How does the dragon end the drought?
2. How does the boy show his mother that he still cares for her?
3. What powers does the pearl seem to have?
4. Do you think that in this story all the good people are rewarded and all the bad ones punished? Why or why not?

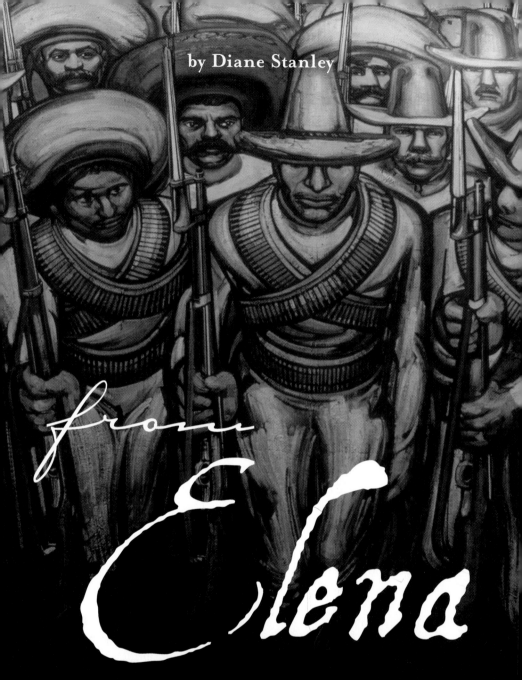

by Diane Stanley

from

Elena

War. No food. Lack of work.
Sometimes events force people to leave
the homes they love. For some of them,
there is no turning back.

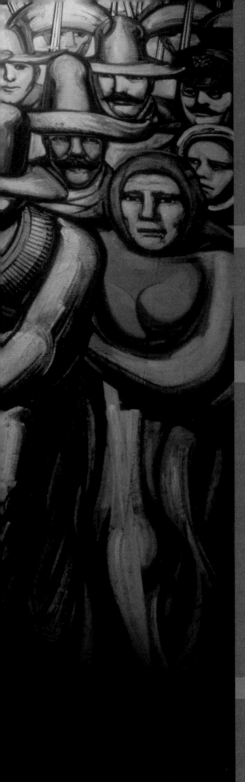

Connect to Your Life

How important is your home and community to you? How might you feel if you were forced to leave it and go to a new land? Discuss your opinions with your classmates.

Key to the Novel Excerpt

Elena is an example of **historical fiction**—fiction that is set in the past. This novel is based on the life of a real person and her family. You will read an excerpt, or a part, of the novel.

In telling the story, the writer changed some events and added details from her imagination. She also changed some of the names. For example Mamá's real name was María. In the story, she is called Elena.

This part of the novel is set in the early 1900s during the Mexican Revolution (1910–1920). Pancho Villa was a famous Mexican bandit who became a leader of the revolution.

Vocabulary Preview

Words to Know

notorious   refugees
condolences   barrio
detain

 Reading Coach CD-ROM selection

from Elena **37**

Time passes quickly when you are busy and happy. It is not human nature to stop and say, "I must remember this moment, for such a time may not come again." We take happiness for granted. We think there will always be a tomorrow and it will be the same as today. Great changes take us by surprise.

REREAD
How does this passage hint at what might happen in the story?

In the year 1910, when I was about five years old, my father had to go to Guadalajara on business. He went there once or twice a year. It was nothing unusual. As he mounted his horse, my mother went out to say good-bye. "Be careful," she told him. She was worried about who he might meet on the road. We had heard talk of a revolution. There were said to be rough soldiers and armed campesinos about. They were dangerous men. But Father just squeezed her hand and smiled. "I will be careful," he said.

campesinos
(käm' pě sē' nôs)
peasants or farmers

Father was joined by several villagers who were making the trip with him. They waved to us and headed off across the rugged countryside, for there were no proper roads. It was just at the end of the rainy season and the path was wet. About an hour after they left, the ground under Father's horse suddenly gave way, creating a landslide. Down they plunged into the ravine below.

The villagers raced back for help, and many men hurried off with ropes to haul my father up to safety.

They brought him to our house and laid him on the bed. The doctor came and dressed my father's wounds. As he was leaving, we asked the doctor, "Will he live?" He shrugged his shoulders. "Who can tell?" he said. "Perhaps Pablo knows. It is a gift some Indians have."

My mother stood and watched the doctor walk away from our house. "He is right," she thought to herself. "Pablo knows." So she went into the darkened room and knelt down beside the bed. She took his big hand and gently stroked it.

40 "Husband," she whispered, "how is it? Do you think you will recover?"

For a long time he did not look at her and he did not answer. At last he turned his head and spoke. "No," he said. Then in a weak but steady voice he told her what he knew. He named the very day and hour in which he would die. He said there would be war and that she and the children must leave their home.

REREAD
What is unusual about Pablo's answer?

"You will always be in my heart," he
50 said. He never spoke again.

Three days later, at the very hour he had spoken, my father died.

THINK IT THROUGH

What great change happens to the family? What other changes does Pablo predict?

FOCUS

Find out how the family reacts to Pablo's death.

Mother went crazy with grief. She ran weeping into the patio, and with a big stick began to swing wildly, knocking down her beautiful flowers. Then she opened all the cages and let the birds free.

After that, my mother grew quiet. Though she went on caring for us just as before, that *chispa,* the bright spark that was always a part of her, went out. Papá's
60 absence filled our house with emptiness. I could not really understand what had happened, because I was so young. It seemed to me that Papá had just gone to where I couldn't see him—perhaps he was in the next room. I kept expecting him to walk in our door one day and make everything good again. But he never came, of course, and in time I understood that he never would.

I remember that it was warm and beautiful at that time, the skies a brilliant cloudless blue, day after day.
70 It was as if nature were mocking us.

THINK IT THROUGH
What details tell you how deeply the narrator and her mother, Elena, miss Pablo?

FOCUS
Discover how Elena reacts when Pancho Villa and his soldiers take over the town.

One day I was playing upstairs with my brother Luis. I heard the loud clop-clop of horses on the stone pavement outside—not one, but many horses. So I ran to the window to see. Looking down, I saw our street transformed into a river of sombreros. The revolution had reached our little village—it was the army of Pancho Villa riding by!

With a gasp, Mother pulled me away from the window, for Pancho Villa was a
80 notorious man. It was true that he was fighting to help free Mexico from the dictator Porfirio Díaz and that he wanted

sombreros
(sŏm brār′ ōz)
large, wide-brimmed hats

notorious
(nō tôr′ ē əs)
adj. well-known for bad deeds

Photo of a wall mural showing Mexican revolutionaries and their leader Emiliano Zapata
(Inset) Pancho Villa, a leader of the Mexican Revolution

to give back to the *campesinos* the land that had been stolen from them. He was, in fact, on his way to becoming a genuine folk hero, the Robin Hood of Mexico. But it was also well known that he had once been a bandit and that his men were just as bad as the government soldiers. Neither army respected the law. Wherever they went, they stole from the people, killed anyone who challenged them, and left burned villages in their wake. What would happen to us?

REREAD
How might you feel about Pancho Villa if you were the narrator?

Mother knelt down and gathered us in her arms. She understood in a flash that everything that had happened to her before had been for a reason. The books she had read, the hard numbers she had conquered, the battle she had won over her marriage—all this had made her strong. Now she had no father and no husband to help her. She had, instead, great courage and determination. Had there not always been wars? And in every country and every age, brave men and women had faced terrible dangers. She could do it, too—God had put it into her heart. We saw this understanding pass across her face like a ripple of light. "Children," she said urgently, "we must find Esteban."

REREAD
Why has Elena's strength become so important?

110 She knew that soldiers often took older boys and forced them into the army. My brother was sixteen.

None of us had seen him for hours. We searched the house for him, but he wasn't there. A book lay open on his bed. He had put it down and gone off somewhere. Maybe he was out in the streets among all those men. Maybe they had already taken him. At last María found him—up on the roof watching the soldiers. Boys are so foolish sometimes!

We made a hiding place for him in a kitchen cabinet, behind the big clay pots. Then Mother had 120 another thought—the horses. They were sure to steal the horses. But maybe if they found the stable empty, they would think the horses had already been seized. They would certainly not think to look for them in the kitchen, so she brought the horses in there, too.

Before my mother could hide anything else, there was a loud knock on the door. We could hear deep voices laughing and talking outside. Mother hesitated a moment, wondering what to do. Then she sent us into the back room. We did as we were told but opened the 130 door a crack so we could see what happened. Mother took a deep breath and opened the door.

THINK IT THROUGH
What steps does Elena take in order to protect her family, especially Esteban?

FOCUS

Read to find out who is at the door and what the person wants.

There stood four or five soldiers, rough men who smelled of sweat and horses. The man in front was stout and wore a huge drooping mustache. *Bandoleras* crossed his chest. We had seen his face before, on a government poster. It was Pancho Villa himself!

"Señora," he said, "is this the house of Pablo, the famous maker of sombreros?" It was the last thing she expected to hear.

140 "It is," she said, "I am his widow."

"Then please accept my sincere condolences," said the leader of the rebel army, bowing slightly. He paused for a moment and then added almost shyly, "And the hats? The fine hats? Are there no more left?"

> **condolences**
> (kən dō′ lən sĭz)
> *n.* statement of sympathy and concern

My mother actually smiled. "Excuse me a minute," she said. She went to a cupboard in her bedroom and
150 returned with one of Father's beautiful silver-trimmed sombreros. "This is the last one," my mother said.

Pancho Villa was delighted. He put it on right away and actually paid her for it. Not only that, he posted a guard outside our house. As long as
160 Villa's army was there, we were not harmed.

THINK IT THROUGH

What is surprising about Pancho Villa's actions?

FOCUS _____

Find out why Elena and her family leave their village and
what new problem she must solve.

"Pablo was surely watching over us this day," my
mother told us later. "But it may not always be so.
Before your father died, he told me there would be
soldiers. He told me we must leave our home. I
wonder how I could have forgotten it."

"You were sad, *Mamacita,*" María said.

When the *Villistas* had gone, Mother went to the
plaza and opened the shop to the people of the
village. She emptied the store of everything, taking
170 down great bolts of manta and giving them to people
who had nothing. We took only our money, some
clothes, and food for the journey. We were leaving
behind our aunts and uncles, our little
house, the furniture, the pictures, the
pots and pans and dishes. We said
goodbye to the friends of a lifetime.

REREAD
What sacrifices
must the family
make so they
can leave?

Everyone urged us not to go. "It is not
proper for a woman to travel unprotected like that,"
they said. "It is not safe."

180 "The world is changing around us," Mother
answered. "We must change, too."

We left the village early in the morning. When we
reached the train station, we found that it was packed
with frantic, pushing people. It seemed as though
everyone in Mexico was trying to get on that train.
Mother and María managed to make it inside. Then
before Esteban got on, he handed Luis and me in
through the window, along with the basket of food.

We were lucky to have benches to sit on. Most of
190 the people were in boxcars or crowded in the aisles.

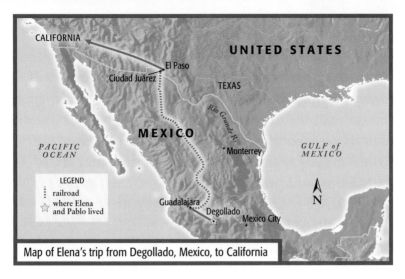

Map of Elena's trip from Degollado, Mexico, to California

For five days the train chugged north. Through the open windows came soot, dust, and flies. I had worn a beautiful lacy white dress for the trip. Soon it was damp with sweat and covered with dirt.

When we reached Ciudad Juárez, we faced a new problem. What were we to do with Esteban? He was tall, almost a man. The soldiers at the border crossing would not treat him as a child. They might detain him for days, together with the rough men from the train. They might take him for the army.

200

"I think the answer will come to me," Mother told us. "We must be patient."

So we waited while she thought, but it was not a good place to be. The town was rough and lawless. With thousands of refugees pouring in, desperate to flee homes that were no longer safe, thieves and pickpockets roamed the streets. Hotels and shops charged ridiculous prices that people had to pay, because they had no other choice but to starve or sleep in the streets. For days we ate nothing but fruit.

210

detain
(dĭ tān')
v. stop from leaving

refugees
(rĕf' yoō jēz')
n. people who flee a country to find protection from war or political oppression

Mother befriended a Chinese fruit seller who was honest and kind. One day she told him our problem. He smiled, for he knew exactly how to help us. Every day he crossed the border with his fruit wagon. We could dress Esteban in the man's clothes and straw hat. He would pretend to be

220 the fruit seller's helper.

That afternoon we went over the bridge to El Paso together, Mother and the three of us walking along next to the fruit wagon. The cost was one penny each. At last we were safely in the United States.

THINK IT THROUGH

What problems does the family face? How do they solve their problems?

FOCUS

Elena decides to move her family to California. Read to find out what their life is like there.

We headed for California because we had a cousin, Trinidad, who lived there. We didn't have his address,
230 though. In fact, we didn't even know what town he lived in. So we went to San Francisco, which was famous. We made our way to the barrio, where many people from Mexico lived. We asked everyone we met there, "Do you know our cousin Trinidad?" No one did. And besides, we didn't like it there. It was damp and cold. In Los Angeles, no one had heard of Trinidad, either. We were happier there, because the

barrio
(bä′ rē ō′)
n. mainly Spanish-speaking neighborhood in a U.S. city

240   weather was warmer. But the city was too big, not like our lovely little village in Mexico. We heard about a place called Santa Ana. There were lemon and orange and walnut groves there and good schools for the children. So that is where we went and that is where we stayed. We never did find Trinidad.

    By then, we had spent most of our money. So Esteban got a job picking fruit. Sometimes he was gone for weeks, living in the camps near the farms. When he came home he was sore and tired. He didn't laugh and
250 play with me the way he had before.

    Mother ran a boardinghouse, which was hard work. She did the cleaning, made the beds, mopped the floors, and scrubbed the bathtub. She washed and ironed the boarders' clothes. After all that, she went into the kitchen and cooked mountains of rice and beans and tortillas and enchiladas for them to eat. We all sat down to dinner together at a long pine table. Sometimes the boarders were very nice and became
260 our friends. Some even came from the same part of Mexico as our family had. It made me feel like I wasn't so far from home.

> **boarding-house**
> private house where meals and rooms can be rented

    María and I did what we could. We hung the laundry out on the clothesline, and we brought it back in if it rained. We helped wash the dishes and changed all the sheets once a week. And we looked after little Luis.

    But Mother said that our real job was to get an education. School and
270 homework always came first. When we were done with that, she said, we could help. I felt bad sometimes, sitting in a chair with a book in my lap while Mother was never still, always

> **REREAD**
> Why is education so important to Elena?

bustling about at her chores. She did it with a good spirit, though. If I said to her, "You work too hard, *Mamacita*," she would just shake her head and smile.

"And what is so bad about work?" she would say. "Work is how I take care of my family. Work is how I keep busy. Work is

280 how I am useful. It is not so bad."

REREAD
What do you learn about the way Elena views herself and the world?

THINK IT THROUGH

Compare Elena's life in the United States to her life in Mexico. Which do you think she prefers?

FOCUS

Read to see how the children and their mother adjust to life in California.

At school we learned to speak English and heard all about George Washington crossing the Delaware and Thomas Jefferson writing the Declaration of Independence. We wrote essays on the American Revolution and the American Civil War, and one day it dawned on me that Americans had suffered in terrible wars just as we had. And not long after that, I realized that Americans weren't "they" anymore. After all, we wore American clothes, read American

290 books, knew American songs, and ate American candy. We had all become *real* Americans—all of us, that is, but Mamá.

She never quite knew what she was. Part of her was still back in Mexico and part of her was with us in California. Sometimes in the evening, after the dishes were done, we all went out on the porch to sit and enjoy the cool night air. At

REREAD
Do you think that Elena's feelings are common among people who come to the United States from other lands?

those times, Mother liked to
300 talk about the old days. She
told us about growing up in
her father's great house in the
beautiful mountains of
Mexico. She talked of her
gentle sisters who sang so
beautifully to the guitar. She
remembered her own little house full of flowers and
birds. But she especially loved to talk about Father—
how they fell in love first and got to know each other
310 later, how he was such an artist, making beautiful
sombreros, and how he knew things it was impossible
to know, yet he knew them just the same. I had been
so small when Father died, I could scarcely remember
him. Those stories gave him back to me.

In all those years she talked only of happy times. It
was much later that we learned what had happened in
our little village. Only when we were grown—strong
and full of hope—did we find out that it was gone,
burned to the ground by the soldiers. And when we
320 heard about the people who had died, people we had
known, then we understood what our mother had done.
With her courage and daring, she had saved us all.

THINK IT THROUGH

1. What words would you use to describe the
   narrator's mother? Support your answer with
   evidence from the story.
2. How does the narrator judge her mother? Do you
   agree with her judgment? Why or why not?
3. Do you think Elena would return home if she
   could? Give details to support your opinion.

City Scenes

Unit 2

Poetry

In poetry a few words express many ideas, images, and feelings. Poets choose words for their sounds and meanings. The poems in this unit will help you explore the sights and sounds of the city.

Poets use many tools to create their poems. Sometimes they use **rhyme,** words that end in the same sound. They may also use **rhythm,** or a pattern of beats. **Imagery**—words and phrases that appeal to the five senses—is also important in poetry. As you read poetry, notice how sounds and word pictures work together.

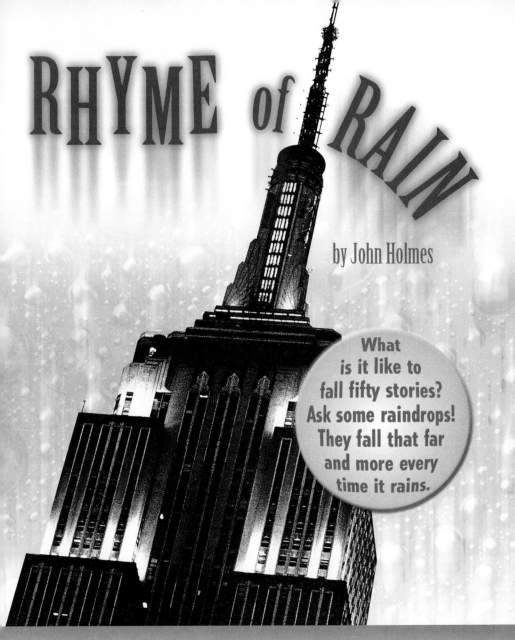

RHYME of RAIN

by John Holmes

What is it like to fall fifty stories? Ask some raindrops! They fall that far and more every time it rains.

 Reading Coach CD-ROM selection

Connect to Your Life

Think of the tallest building you have ever been in. How did you feel when you looked down? Discuss with your class how heights make you feel.

Key to the Poem

This poem tells a story. It has a plot, a setting, and characters. Listen for the **rhyme**, sounds repeated at the ends of words, and the **rhythm**, a pattern of strong and weak syllables.

Vocabulary In line 4, **Empire State** means the Empire State Building in New York City.

RHYME of RAIN by John Holmes

"Fifty stories more to fall,
Nothing in our way at all,"
Said a raindrop to its mate,
Falling near the Empire State.

5 Said the second, "Here we go!
That's Fifth Avenue below."
Said the first one, "There's a hat.
Watch me land myself on that.
Forty stories isn't far—

10 Thirty seven—here we are—
Twenty, sixteen, thirteen, ten—"
"If we make this trip again,"
Said the second, "we must fall
Near a building twice as tall."

15 "What a time to think of that,"
Said the first, and missed the hat.

THINK IT THROUGH

1. Who is talking in this poem? What are they doing while they're talking?
2. What does one raindrop plan to do in lines 7–8?
3. What finally happens in the last line? How did you react to what happens?
4. Which words rhyme in the last two lines? Clap to the rhythm of the strong syllables in those lines.

PIGEONS

by Lilian Moore

Some cities seem to have more pigeons than people. Why do these birds like cities so much?

Connect to Your Life

Have you ever watched a group of pigeons walking around? What were they doing?

Key to the Poem

 Reading Coach CD-ROM selection

With **personification,** a poem can describe an animal or object as if it were a person. You may never think of pigeons in the same way again!

Vocabulary In line 10, a **hedge** is a row of bushes. In line 11, **commutes** means "travels regularly from one place to another."

PIGEONS by Lilian Moore

Pigeons are city folk
content
to live with concrete
and cement.

5 They seldom
try
the sky.

A pigeon never sings
of hill
10 and flowering hedge,
but busily commutes
from sidewalk
to his ledge.

Oh pigeon, what a waste of wings!

THINK IT THROUGH

1. According to the poem, how are pigeons like city people?
2. What does the last line of the poem mean when it says "what a waste of wings"?
3. What message does this poem have for some people?

CITY

by Langston Hughes

Big cities have a certain
look during the day—bright,
busy, alive. But how do they look at night?

Connect to Your Life

Do you prefer being
downtown in the morning
or at night? Explain why.

Key to the Poem

To describe something, a poet may use a
metaphor. A **metaphor** compares one thing to
another without the word *like* or *as*. This poem
describes a city by comparing it with two other
things. Find out what the city is like in the
morning and at night.

 Reading Coach CD-ROM selection

CITY   *by Langston Hughes*

In the morning the city
Spreads its wings
Making a song
In stone that sings.

5 In the evening the city
Goes to bed
Hanging lights
About its head.

THINK IT THROUGH

1. What is the city compared to in lines 2–4? How do the two things look or act alike?
2. What is the city compared to in lines 6–8? How do the two things look or act alike?
3. How does the poem make the city seem alive?

The City Is So Big

by Richard García

The Brooklyn Bridge: Variations on an Old Theme (1939) Joseph Stella. Oil on canvas, 70" × 42". Collection of Whitney Museum of American Art, New York Photograph Copyright © 2000: Whitney Museum of American Art.

In the city, everything moves: trains, elevators, and even stairs. But what if they moved by themselves?

 Reading Coach CD-ROM selection

Connect to Your Life

Have you ever ridden on an escalator, or moving stairway? Have you ridden in elevators? How did you feel on these rides?

Key to the Poem

Poems can give you **images,** or pictures, of what they are about. In this poem, the words tell you what a big city looks like. The words can also create a **mood,** or feeling, for the reader. What does this poem make you see and feel?

Vocabulary In line 2, **quake** means "shiver."

The City Is So Big by Richard García

The city is so big
Its bridges quake with fear
I know, I have seen at night

The lights sliding from house to house
5 And trains pass with windows shining
Like a smile full of teeth

I have seen machines eating houses
And stairways walk all by themselves
And elevator doors opening and closing
10 And people disappear.

THINK IT THROUGH

1. What image does line 2 give the reader?
2. What mood or feeling do lines 2 and 7–10 create? What images help create this feeling?
3. How is the feeling about cities in this poem different from the feeling in the poem "City" on page 57?

In the Inner City

by Lucille Clifton

Orchard Street (1972), David Levine. Watercolor, 11″ × 14″. Collection of the Artist.

In the "inner" city, buildings and cement
take the place of trees and grass.
But there are playgrounds—and kids.

Connect to Your Life

What do other people think of the neighborhood you live in? Do they like it or dislike it? Discuss why you agree or disagree with their opinions.

Key to the Poem

A poem may have a strong **theme,** or message about life. The poet wants you to understand something about life. "In the Inner City" gives a message about people who live in the inner city. It tells how they feel about where they live.

 Reading Coach CD-ROM selection

In the Inner City *by Lucille Clifton*

in the inner city

or

like we call it

home

5 we think a lot about uptown

and the silent nights

and the houses straight as

dead men

and the pastel lights

10 and we hang on to our no place

happy to be alive

and in the inner city

or

like we call it

15 home

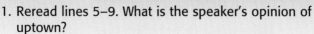

THINK IT THROUGH

1. Reread lines 5–9. What is the speaker's opinion of uptown?
2. According to the poem, how do the people in the inner city like living there? How do you know?

Sheer Fear

Nonfiction

What scares you the most? Fear can be triggered by a scary animal, a disaster, or the unknown. These nonfiction articles explore many kinds of fear.

Nonfiction is writing about real people, places, and events. There are several kinds of nonfiction.

• **True accounts** describe actual events but read more like stories. They often contain dialogue and colorful description.

• **Informative articles** give facts about people, places, or things.

• **Interviews** record people's answers to questions about their lives. Interviews are often written in a question-and-answer format.

By Don L. Wulffson

FORTY-FIVE SECONDS INSIDE A TORNADO

A tornado hits, destroying everything in its way. What would it be like to be caught in the path of such a storm?

Connect to Your Life

What do you know about tornadoes? How might it feel to be caught in one? Share your ideas with a partner.

Key to the Article

A tornado is an unpredictable force of nature. This is a **true account** of two men who were caught in a tornado that hit Waco, Texas. You will learn exactly what the men saw, heard, and felt. Through their experience you will come to know the power of nature.

Vocabulary Preview

Words to Know

wake	devastated
rubble	pale

 Reading Coach CD-ROM selection

As Ira Baden and Roy Miller work, what is unusual about the weather?

It was an overcast morning in May. Ira Baden gripped the steering wheel tightly as his car sped along a Texas highway. He and Roy Miller were on their way from Dallas to Waco. There they had a job installing automatic doors on the Amicable Life Building.

The men had no way of knowing it, but they were on their way to a disaster. They were headed into a living horror, a tornado. That very afternoon it would strike Waco. In its wake would be

10 left a horrible path of destruction. As many as 114 would be dead. More than 500 would be injured. Two square miles of the city would be turned into a mass of twisted rubble.

wake
(wāk)
n. trail

After a long and tiring drive, Baden and Miller arrived in Waco. They made measurements and talked over their plans. Miller began removing the old doors. Down in the basement of the Amicable Building, Baden worked on the new doors. Around

20 four o'clock they were ready to be installed.

rubble
(rŭb′ əl)
n. broken bits of something that is destroyed

Baden and Miller lugged the doors upstairs. They figured how they would set them in place. At the same time, they noticed that people passing in the street seemed quite worried. Everybody was talking about a storm that was coming. The men went to work installing the doors. But it was hard for them to concentrate on the job. The air was strangely heavy and still. It seemed to be pressing down on them. Although it

30 was only afternoon, the sky was as black as night.

REREAD
What signs show that a storm is coming?

"Have you ever seen weather like this?" Miller asked Baden.

"No," he said. He looked up at the dark sky and shook his head. "I don't like the looks of it. It's really strange."

THINK IT THROUGH

Describe the weather on the day the tornado hits.

FOCUS

Read to find out how the tornado begins.

The men tried to put aside their fears. They kept working on the doors. It seemed like a good idea to get them up as fast as possible. All of a sudden it
40 began to rain. The drops weren't hitting the street. They were flying sideways!

With the rain came an odd roaring noise. The noise became unbearably loud. Then, above the roar, Baden heard the sharp tinkling of breaking glass. He turned in time to see a mailbox flying by. It passed just inches from his head. One pink leg from a store dummy skittered along the asphalt. Half of a store-front sign did somersaults through the air.

> **asphalt**
> (ăs' fôlt')
> tar mixture used
> to pave streets

50 The wind was overwhelming. It was like nothing Baden had ever known. He grabbed hold of a railing. For the first time he was really scared. The wind terrified him. He was afraid that he would be torn from the railing and sucked up into the black sky.

As he clung to the railing, a powerful force began to move up the street. It ripped the fronts off buildings across the way as it came. One place after another simply exploded. Power lines tore loose. They

60 danced in the street, showering sparks everywhere. People leaped and jumped from the deadly lines. Cars braked and swerved away from them. One crashed through a plate-glass window.

THINK IT THROUGH
What details helped you imagine the approaching tornado?

FOCUS ───────────────
Find out what Baden sees and feels.

Baden tried to get inside the door of the Amicable Life Building. The force of the wind was too great. It had him glued to the railing. He couldn't move. From the corner of his eye he could see Roy Miller plastered against the wall of the building. The man was holding onto the wall with his fingertips.

70 Baden put his head against his chest. He felt suffocated. The air had been torn from his lungs. Gasping, he blew in and out. It did no good. He could not catch his breath. All the air in the world seemed to have been sucked up into the tornado. Ira Baden was sure he was going to die.

Baden looked up. He could see the ugly, swirling tip of the tornado. It dipped and swayed down the street. It demolished one spot and left another untouched. It completely missed the Roosevelt Hotel but reached

80 beyond to level a movie theater. A second later the tip caught the Dennis Building and tore away the top four floors. The pieces whirled upward and came apart in the air. Then they crashed down in the same

spot. Roofs were popping off buildings. Giant walls collapsed into the street. Cars leaped upward and flew away like airplanes.

In the middle of this 90 shrieking nightmare, a man suddenly rushed past Baden through the half-finished doorway. Baden shouted for him to stop. The man yelled back that his wife was in the building across the way and he had to get to her. As he stepped off the curb, 100 the wind picked him up. As he screamed, it carried him away. He just disappeared.

Right after that, the wind tore the roof and a wall from the building on the other side of the street.

The top picture shows the Dennis Building before the tornado hit. The bottom picture shows it after the tornado.

The place looked like a cross-section drawing. Baden could see a man standing beside his desk. He walked 110 to the crumpled edge of the floor and looked over the side. Then he turned and ran to the back wall. He opened a door to what had been a hallway a few seconds before. Then he stepped out into empty space. He was carried up and away by the tornado. Baden never saw him again.

THINK IT THROUGH

What are three amazing events that Baden witnesses?

At last the twister began to move away. It was headed southwest, zigzagging off through the city. Baden eased his grip on the railing and looked around. The cars parked on his side of the street were hardly scratched. Those across the street were something different altogether. They had been thrown around and squashed like bugs. That whole side of the street had been devastated.

The blowing rain continued. It filled the ruined avenue with water. But in spite of the downpour, a crowd of survivors began to gather. Miller put his arm around Baden. Open-mouthed, the two men looked at each other. Then they joined the gathering crowd in the street.

Most of the people were in a daze. Their eyes were blank and their limbs trembled. Some of the people were injured. Others had most of their clothes blown off. One woman put her head on the shoulder of a pale, bloodied policeman. She wept silently.

> **devastated**
> (dĕv′ ə stā′ tĭd)
> v. completely destroyed; past tense of *devastate*

> **pale**
> (pāl)
> adj. without much color, as if ill

This photograph shows Waco after the tornado.

While he was standing there with the crowd, Baden realized that he still had his glasses on. The tornado had flattened him against a railing. It had picked up cars and blown them away like leaves. It had turned whole buildings into great dusty piles of bricks. Yet his glasses, incredibly, still sat untouched upon his nose.

REREAD

Why do you think the writer tells about Baden's glasses?

Baden and Miller went to the nearest scene of destruction. They helped to search for survivors. It seemed like a miracle each time they found someone alive beneath the heaps of rubble. The rescue work went on all night. Fire fighters, the National Guard, and others arrived to help.

By morning, Baden was so tired he could hardly stand. Roy Miller was as pale as a ghost. It was clear they could do no more. Behind the Amicable Life Building, Baden found his parked car. He and Roy Miller headed back to Dallas through the battered remains of Waco. In all, Baden had been face-to-face with the tornado for no more than forty-five seconds. But he would never forget those few moments. They would remain etched in his memory for as long as he lived.

THINK IT THROUGH

1. How did Baden and Miller help others after the tornado moved on?
2. What details did the writer use to help you understand the power of a tornado?
3. What one thing do you find most memorable about Baden and Miller's account? Why?

Maybe you or someone you know has a fear of heights. Where does this fear come from?

Trapped by
FEAR

from *The Contemporary Reader*

Connect to Your Life

What are you afraid of? Have you ever tried to get rid of a fear? Discuss your special fears with a partner.

Key to the Article

Informative articles often appear in magazines and newspapers. This informative article explains why some people have unhealthy fears. It also tells about ways these people can be helped. The title of each section tells what that part is about.

Vocabulary Preview

Words to Know
panic
phobia
coping

> Read to find out how some people react to crossing a bridge.

The Mackinac Bridge is the largest suspension bridge in the world. The bridge runs from one part of the state of Michigan to another. A full five miles long, the bridge is built 200 feet above the water.

suspension bridge
bridge held up by large cables that run between a series of towers

Most people can drive across the bridge without any trouble. But some are afraid of heights. They are afraid to cross the bridge.

They're not just afraid—they're in a

10 panic. Sometimes they get halfway across the bridge and just freeze. They stop their cars, put their heads down, and cry. They don't move until help comes.

panic
(păn′ ĭk)
n. sudden fear that cannot be controlled

This happens five to ten times a day during the summer, when there is heavy traffic on the bridge. A professional bridge driver is sent to take the stopped car across.

WHO IS AFRAID?
It's hard to tell who will be afraid to cross the bridge. Sometimes it's a man, other times a woman. It can be

The Mackinac Bridge links upper Michigan with lower Michigan.

20 a young person, but just as often it's an older adult. At times, a person on a motorcycle can't get across. Sometimes even truck drivers have to ask someone to take their rigs across. The panic hits—they feel dizzy or they can't breathe—and they just have to stop.

The bridge is safer than most roads. Eighty million cars have crossed it, and only one car has ever driven off it. It happened during a high wind, in 1989. It makes no sense to fear crossing the bridge. But some people are terrified at the thought of it.

THINK IT THROUGH
Who is afraid to cross the Mackinac Bridge? How does this fear affect them?

FOCUS
Read to learn what a phobia is.

SENSELESS FEARS

30 This kind of senseless fear is called a phobia. People suffer from many kinds of phobias. Some fear heights. Others dread entering wide open places. Still others are afraid of being closed into small spaces. Many are afraid to fly in airplanes. Dirt and germs are some people's biggest fear. They don't want to touch anything, however clean, for fear of getting sick. Others are afraid of

40 animals, like cats or snakes.

A phobia is not simply a fear. A phobia is being afraid when there is really nothing to be

phobia
(fō′ bē ə)
n. strong and unreasonable fear of something

afraid of. In some people, the fear is so strong they can't do the things they want to do. There are people so frightened of open spaces that they never leave their homes.

THINK IT THROUGH
What are the results of a phobia?

FOCUS
Read to discover how phobias get started.

HIDDEN MEMORIES

What makes a person become so afraid? Most of the time, no one knows the reason. Sometimes, though, a
50 person can figure out how the fear began. Often, it relates to something that happened when the person was a small child.

One woman was terrified at the sound of running water. She went to a doctor for help. At last, the doctor figured out what had made this woman afraid. As a little girl, she had gone on a picnic with her family. Her parents told her to stay away from the river. But she went wading anyway. She fell into the river and was trapped by the water's strong current.
60 She couldn't get out. She had to stand under a waterfall for several minutes while water splashed down on her head. Her aunt found her and rescued her.

REREAD
What caused this woman's fear of running water?

The woman barely remembered this event. Yet all her life, it had made her afraid of the sound of running water.

Phobias are sometimes hard to figure out. What started as a shock from one event can become fear of many things or ideas. A small boy once scared by a dog might grow up to fear all dogs and cats. Just the sight of a fur coat could terrify him!

THINK IT THROUGH

How can childhood events lead to phobias?

FOCUS

Find out two ways people with phobias learn to survive.

GETTING HELP

How can people with phobias be helped? Like the woman afraid of running water, people can try to learn why they are afraid.

Sometimes doctors can help a person get over a fear bit by bit. A man afraid of dogs might start by patting a small piece of fur. Then he might pat a toy dog. Next, he might try standing near a dog that is tied up. With each passing week, he could stand closer and closer to the dog. When he no longer dreaded being near it, he might pat the dog. Little by little, he would shed his fear.

Many people have a fear of flying. There are even classes for people who are afraid to fly in an airplane. These people talk about their fears and work on their phobia. When the class ends, they take an airplane trip together to show they can do it.

COPING WITH FEAR

Most people just live with their phobias. They do what they must, even if they're afraid. Those who can't carry on just stay away from the things that scare them. If they are afraid to fly, they take the train.

> coping
> (kō′ pĭng)
> *n.* handling successfully

100 Sometimes people are unaware of a fear until they try something new. Many probably never know they are afraid of big bridges until they set out to cross the Mackinac. Suddenly, panic strikes. They can't breathe. They can't move. They just want to hide their eyes and cry. But they should hang on—help is on the way, both now and over the long haul.

> over the long haul
> over a long time

THINK IT THROUGH

1. How can people with phobias learn to live with them?
2. Many people have strong fears, called phobias, that greatly affect their lives. This is the main idea of the article. List at least five details that support this main idea.
3. Would reading this article help someone with a phobia? Explain.

Whatif by Shel Silverstein

Last night, while I lay thinking here,
Some Whatifs crawled inside my ear
And pranced and partied all night long
And sang their same old Whatif song:
5 Whatif I'm dumb in school?
Whatif they've closed the swimming pool?
Whatif I get beat up?
Whatif there's poison in my cup?
Whatif I start to cry?
10 Whatif I get sick and die?
Whatif I flunk that test?
Whatif green hair grows on my chest?
Whatif nobody likes me?
Whatif a bolt of lightning strikes me?
15 Whatif I don't grow taller?
Whatif my head starts getting smaller?
Whatif the fish won't bite?
Whatif the wind tears up my kite?
Whatif they start a war?
20 Whatif my parents get divorced?
Whatif the bus is late?
Whatif my teeth don't grow in straight?
Whatif I tear my pants?
Whatif I never learn to dance?
25 Everything seems swell, and then
The nighttime Whatifs strike again!

Typhoid Mary

by Henry Billings and Melissa Billings

In New York and New Jersey in the early 1900s, people are mysteriously dying. The evidence points to one person as the cause. Is she guilty of murder?

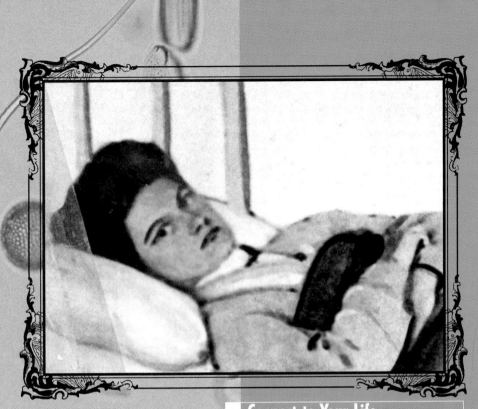

Connect to Your Life

Think about a time when a cold, the flu, or chickenpox spread through your school. How quickly did it pass from person to person? How many people became ill?

Key to the Article

This **informative article** gives facts about a real-life medical mystery. It shows that people can have diseases and not get sick themselves. Unfortunately, they may pass germs to other people without even knowing it.

Vocabulary Preview

Words to Know

condition   lunged
transferred   infamous
investigating

 Reading Coach CD-ROM selection

Mary Mallon didn't mean to kill people. For a long time, she didn't even realize she was doing it. All she knew was that wherever she went, people got sick. It was a pattern. She would be hired as a cook by a wealthy New York family. She would begin making meals. But within weeks, the family would come down with a horrible disease called typhoid.

The disease began with chills and a fever. Victims
10 often felt sick to their stomach. They developed a headache and suffered from nosebleeds. Next, they broke out with a bright red rash. They began coughing. Sometimes the fever would break and they would recover. In other cases, their condition would worsen and they would die.

condition
(kən dĭsh′ ən)
n. disease

In the early 1900s few people understood how typhoid is spread. Some people thought it came from spoiled milk. Others thought it came from garbage fumes. Only a few scientists had
20 figured out the truth: it is caused by germs that live inside the human body. These germs pass through the body when a person uses the toilet. Sometimes the germs get on a person's hands. If the person touches food before washing up, the germs can be transferred to the food. Anyone who eats the food can then come down with the disease. In the early 1900s, about one out of every five people sick with typhoid died.

transferred
(trăns fûrd′)
v. carried from one place to another

REREAD

What causes typhoid to spread?

THINK IT THROUGH

Why is typhoid such a harmful disease?

30   Mary Mallon had never had typhoid. She had always been healthy and strong. She had no reason to think she might be passing the disease on to anyone. And yet . . . no matter where she went, typhoid soon followed. Mary's reaction to this problem was simple. She ran away. Once she did stay and help nurse a family through the illness. But the rest of the time, she just packed her bags and moved on.

    In 1906 Mary got a job as the cook for Charles Warren and his family. She had been with the Warrens

40 just three weeks when one of the children got a fever. Mary knew what that meant. Typhoid had struck again. Quickly she collected her pay. Then she took off.

But this time she was followed. A man named George Soper began investigating the Warren family's illness.

investigating
(ĭn vĕs′ tĭ gā′ tĭng)
n. examining closely and carefully

THINK IT THROUGH

What does Mary do when a family she works for catches typhoid? What do you think will happen next?

FOCUS

George Soper follows Mary. Find out what he learns about her.

Soper was an expert on diseases. He knew how typhoid was spread. He figured that healthy people
50 could carry typhoid germs around without knowing it. Perhaps, he thought, Mary Mallon was a carrier of these germs. He decided to track her down. He wanted to run tests to see if her body housed typhoid germs.

Soper found Mary in March of 1907. She was working as a cook for yet another New York family. As Soper had feared, a girl in the house was already dying of typhoid. Soper went to the house. Mary was
60 in the kitchen. When Soper told her why he had come, she became furious. She picked up a huge carving fork and lunged at him. Soper managed to run away without being hurt.

lunged
(lŭnjd)
v. moved forward suddenly; past tense of *lunge*

Soon after that, Soper went to see where Mary lived. It was a dirty, smelly place. Standing in the filth, Soper understood how Mary could spread typhoid to so many people. She clearly had very poor health habits.

REREAD
Which words are clues to the meaning of *filth?*

70   Soper sent Dr. Josephine Baker to talk to Mary.
Baker worked for the city. It was her job to protect
people from health hazards. But Baker had no luck,
either. Mary simply did not believe what the doctor
told her. It sounded crazy. After all, she was healthy.
Surely she was not carrying typhoid around inside her
body. Mary just wanted everyone to leave her alone.
She wanted to go on earning a living as a cook. And
as for washing her hands after using the toilet—well,
that seemed like a waste of time and energy.

THINK IT THROUGH
| How does Mary react to the doctor Soper sends to talk to her?

FOCUS
| The government takes Mary prisoner. Read to learn why.

80   Baker and other city officials did not know what to
do. At last they decided to lock Mary up. It was a
desperate move. But no one could think of any other
way to stop her from spreading typhoid.
Baker and five police officers went to get
her. When Mary saw them coming, she
fled. After a two-hour search, she was
found crouched in a neighbor's yard.
When the police grabbed her, she began
kicking and biting. It took all five officers
90 to drag her into an ambulance. Said Dr. Baker, "I
literally sat on her all the way to the hospital. It was
like being in a cage with an angry lion."
    Mary was kept at the hospital for months. As
expected, tests showed that her body was full of
typhoid germs. That fall, she was transferred to a

hospital on a tiny island near the city. She was kept there for three years. She got a lawyer to help her fight for her freedom. She argued that it was illegal for the city to
100 hold her prisoner. Mary was right, but no judge was willing to set her free. And so she remained locked up on North Brother Island.

REREAD
What point is Mary trying to make?

THINK IT THROUGH
Why does the government keep Mary a prisoner?

FOCUS
After being on the island for three years, Mary is ready to obey the doctors. What causes them to arrest her again?

In 1910 Mary finally agreed to do what the doctors wanted. If they let her go, she said, she would never work as a cook again. She also promised to check in with them every three months. Doctors agreed to the plan. They turned Mary loose. But as soon as she was back on the streets, she vanished. For five years, no city
110 official could find her.
During that time, Mary floated from one restaurant job to the next. She cooked for hotels. She cooked in diners. She made up different names for herself. And she ran away whenever one of her customers got typhoid.
In 1915 Mary got a kitchen job at the Sloane Hospital for Women in New York City. Soon twenty-five people there came down with typhoid. One of the workers joked
120 that the cook must be the infamous

infamous
(ĭn′ fə məs)
adj. having a bad reputation

Typhoid Mary. Terrified of being caught again, Mary took off for New Jersey. But now police were on her trail. On May 27, 1915, she was arrested and returned to North Brother Island.

Mary Mallon had reached the end of the line. Health officials were not going to give her any more chances. They decided to keep her on that little island for the rest of her life. For twenty-two years, until her death at age seventy, that's where Mary stayed. In her later years, she was given her own cottage to live in. She could have visitors whenever she wanted. At mealtime, though, everyone knew what to do. They always left without eating a bite of Typhoid Mary's cooking.

130

THINK IT THROUGH

1. Why did the police arrest Mary again and keep her locked up?
2. Do you think the government was right to keep Mary a prisoner? Explain your opinion.
3. This article gives only one side of the facts about Mary. It does not give Mary's account. Do you think she felt she was a danger to others? Explain.

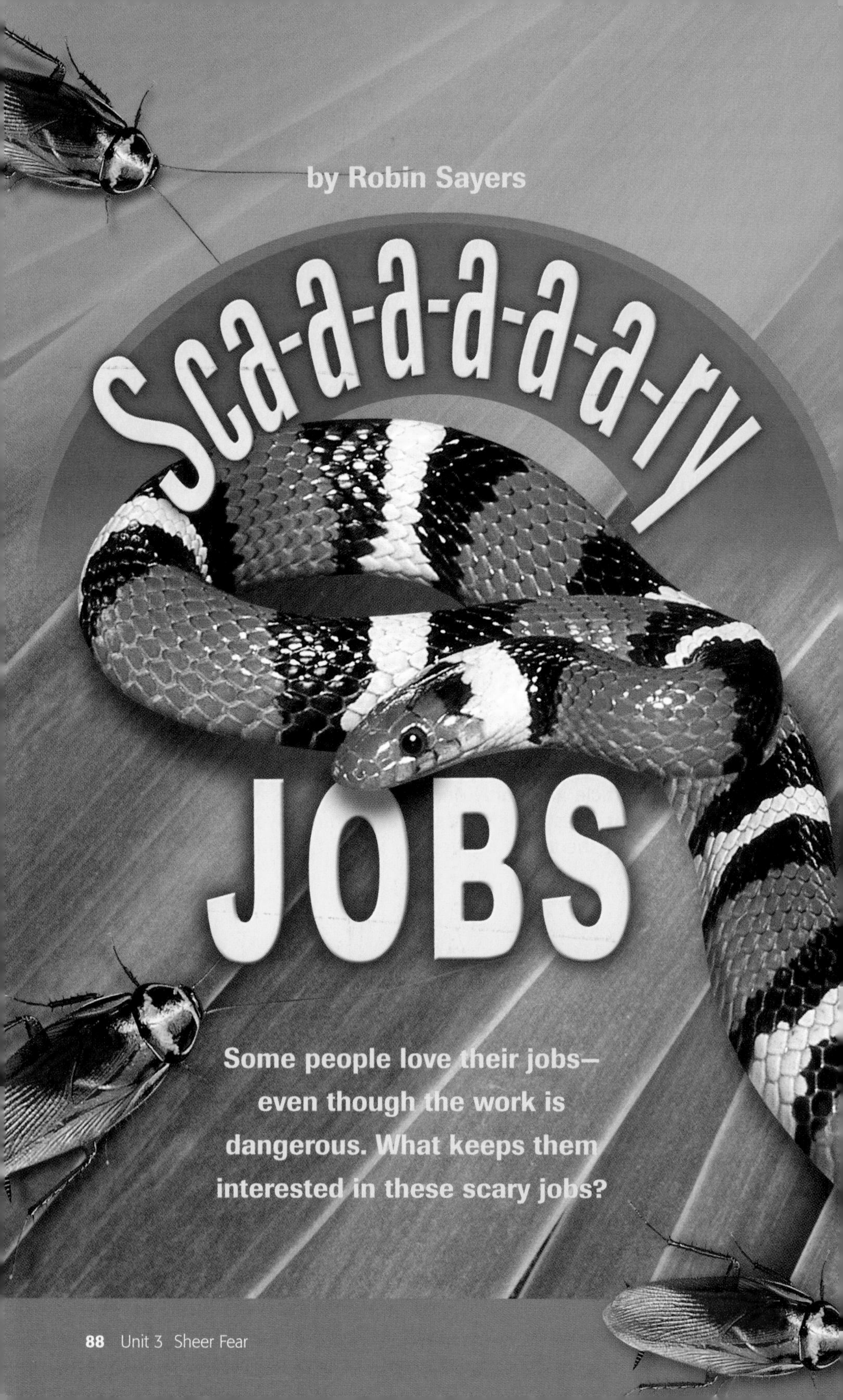

by Robin Sayers

Sca-a-a-a-a-a-ry
JOBS

Some people love their jobs—
even though the work is
dangerous. What keeps them
interested in these scary jobs?

Connect to Your Life

What kinds of jobs do you think are scary? Compare your list with those of your classmates.

Key to the Interview

In an **interview,** one person asks questions and another person answers them. In this excerpt from a *Nickelodeon Magazine* interview, reporter Robin Sayers questions two people about their scary jobs. The **Q** statements are Sayers's questions. The **A** statements are her subjects' answers.

Vocabulary Preview

Words to Know

venom	exterminator
inject	route
immune	

Bill Haast works with snakes. Find out what he does at his job.

Your life may get scary only once a year, at Halloween. Robin Sayers spoke to people whose jobs are spine-chilling all year long. Here are two of the interviews.

For Goodness Snakes!

Bill Haast runs the Miami Serpentarium Laboratory in Florida. He studies snakes—and picks them up to get their venom, which is used by researchers to develop new medicines.

venom
(věn′ əm)
n. poison

Q. NICKELODEON MAGAZINE: **How many snakes do you have in your lab?**
A. BILL HAAST: About 400, from 22 different species.

Q. How do you get the venom out of them?
A. First we pick the snakes up by the back of their
10 heads, so they can't turn around. That puts them on the defensive. Then we have them bite through a piece of rubber, which, hopefully, seems like flesh to them. The snake venom flows down a funnel and into a test tube. We take venom from each snake every two weeks.

Q. What's the deadliest snake you have?
A. Of all my snakes, the Banded Krait has the most-toxic venom.

Q. What would happen if it bit you?
20 **A.** I'm pretty well protected. In 1948, I started to inject myself with tiny amounts of cobra venom, so I would become immune to it. Then I did the same thing with venoms of other species.

inject
(ĭn jekt′)
v. force a liquid into the body, usually with a needle

immune
(ĭ myōōn′)
adj. protected against an illness

Q. Would the average person be a goner right away?

A. Not *right* away. Without treatment, the average person could be dead within 30 minutes. But anybody close to medical care would get antivenin [an antidote to snake venom], and he or
30 she would be saved.

> **antidote**
> (ăn′ tǐ dōt′)
> remedy

Q. How many snakes have you handled in total?

A. I've picked up snakes more than two million times just to collect venom.

Q. Have you ever been bitten?

A. Yes, 163 times.

Q. Does it hurt?

A. It's extremely fast. It feels like pinpricks. You can't even tell whether you've been bitten by one fang or two.

Q. What's the weirdest thing that has happened on
40 **the job?**

A. A number of years ago we got a call that some boy found a two-headed snake in a stream in West Virginia. My future wife went up there and brought it back in a cold cream jar—that's how small it was. It must have just been hatched. It was interesting. We fed it goldfish, and one of the heads would
50 always compete with the other.

Bill Haast with a small cobra. Its venom helps snake-bite victims. Don't try this at home!

Q. It really had two heads?

A. Absolutely! We raised it for about five years, but unfortunately it died. It grew to about two-and-a-half feet long.

Q. Does handling the deadliest snakes on Earth ever scare you?

A. No. I just go on as if I were playing the piano or something, because if I became afraid, I'd be a
60 nervous wreck!

THINK IT THROUGH

| What are the dangers of Haast's job?

FOCUS _____

| Read to learn what Barry Glass does for a living. Find out how he feels about the creatures he destroys.

The Verminator

Barry Glass is an exterminator who owns Big Apple Pest Control in New York City. Every day he battles roaches, rats, mice, and other pesky pests.

exterminator
(ĭk stûr′ mə nā′ tər) *n.* person who kills insects, rats, and other pests for a living

Q. NICKELODEON MAGAZINE: **Are you scared of the pests you fight?**

A. BARRY GLASS: I'm always afraid of being bitten by a rat. If you corner one, it hisses at you, *hsssssss*, and shows its teeth. Then, if it can't find an
70 escape route, it'll bite you. Luckily, I've never been bitten.

route
(rōōt) *n.* path

Q. Do you think all bugs should die?

A. I'm not a bug lover, but they've been on Earth longer than we have. They have a right to be here.

Q. What's your least favorite bug?

A. The German cockroach is my biggest enemy, because it's the most common. I tell my customers "It's gonna take the rest of my life to get rid of these guys."

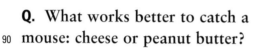

Q. Have you ever had to wrestle any animals on the job?

A. Yes. Just the other week a call came in from an art gallery. A guy went into the bathroom, looked into the toilet, and saw a live rat in there. It was big, and it was hissing. I fought it with a tool that's sort of like a garden hoe. And I won.

Q. What works better to catch a mouse: cheese or peanut butter?

A. A mouse will eat cheese, it will eat peanut butter, but the best thing is Tootsie Rolls. When you put a Tootsie Roll on a mousetrap, it gets hard, and the mouse can't pull it off. Mice like the thrill of trying to get it.

Q. Do you think cartoons make mice seem nicer than they really are?

A. Well, mice are high-strung, but they *are* cute. They play almost their whole lives, and they sleep the rest of it.

Q. Are you always on Jerry's side, or Tom's?

A. I'm on Jerry the mouse's side. Ha!

THINK IT THROUGH

1. What fears does Barry Glass have on his job?
2. In what ways are Bill Haast and Barry Glass alike?
3. If you had to pick one of these jobs, which one would you take? Why?

Close Connections

Mixed Genres

What makes a family? What does it take to be a friend? All your close connections with people teach you something about yourself and others.

This unit has four kinds of writing: a series of **poems,** an **essay,** an **interview,** and a **short story.** Each writer uses a different form to look at a different close connection.

As these works show, there's more to being a family—and a friend—than you might think!

My Man Blue

by Nikki Grimes

A man like Blue has a lot to offer. Will Damon accept his friendship?

Connect to Your Life

With a partner, talk about people who have made a difference in your life. In what ways did these people change the way you thought or acted?

Key to the Poems

My Man Blue is a series of poems that together tell a story. Each poem adds a new idea or event to the story. The speaker, Damon, talks about a man who makes a difference in his life.

Some of the poems rhyme. But most of the poems are written in **free verse,** a form of poetry that seems like conversation.

Vocabulary Preview

Words to Know

stance	jeering
disguised	callouses

My Man Blue

His leathery skin's
Like indigo ink
This rugged dude
Who some folks think
5 Looks fierce in clothes
Of midnight black.
Then there's his teeth:
One gold, three cracked.
And I suppose
10 The shades could go.
He wears them night
And day, I know.
Still, underneath
This shell, Blue hides
15 A harmless
Gentle-giant side.

THINK IT THROUGH

What details in the poem help you picture Blue? What do you learn about him?

When We First Met

My mom and me moved here without his help.
So why's this "Blue" guy stop us on the street?
His welcome is on Mom's account, I bet.
I circle, look him up and down and let

5   Him know his grin's not winning points with me.
My flashing eyes warn "Do not trespass here,"
'Cause in this family *I'm* the only man.
He nods. He understands. So I ease up.
Mom sees me eyeing Blue and lets me know

10   He's her old friend. It's safe to say hello.
She says they both grew up here way back when.
I mumble, "Well, it's news to me!" But then
I throw my shoulders back and take
   my stance.
He seems alright. I might give him
   a chance.

stance
(stăns)
n. pose or position of the body

THINK IT THROUGH
What is Damon's first reaction to Blue? Why?

Second Son

We're leaning on the stoop, see
counting wedges of blue sky
Sandwiched in between the roofs
and white clouds drifting by.

5   "Why'd you want my friendship, Blue?"
I blurt out there and then.
"I had a son named Zeke," Blue says.
"These streets became his friend.

"He needed me but by the time

10   I came, it was too late.
He'd passed the point of trusting his
old man to steer him straight.

REREAD
What happened to Blue's son, Zeke?

"Your missing daddy also left
a hole in you," says Blue.

15   "If friendship fills it, there's less chance
the streets will eat at you."

"That's cool," I say, all serious.
"But I can't take Zeke's place."
"I know," says Blue. "But your laugh sure

20   helps conjure up his face!"

THINK IT THROUGH
What words and phrases tell you why Blue wants to be Damon's friend?

Fearless

One weekend Blue and me
We storm the park.
I kill time kicking rocks
along the path
5 while Blue scouts out a tall
and sturdy tree

And urges me to loop
my fear like twine
around a branch and use
10 the rope to climb.
("Fear's useless otherwise,"
Blue says to me)

REREAD
Blue compares
fear to a rope.
How does Blue
want Damon to
use fear?

"You know I'll be right here
In case you fall."
15 Believing that is all
it takes to send
me scrambling toward the clouds
the sun, the sky.

Hey! Climbing's no big deal—
20 Next time, I'll fly!

THINK IT THROUGH
| What does Damon learn about fear?

Grounded

Asthma stole my
Weekend dose of fun
Left me glum
And wheezing while
5　The stickball game
Went on as planned
Without me.
I balled my fist
Shook it at the sky
10　And asked why I was cursed
With lousy breathing.
"Anger is a waste,"
Said Blue. "Use your lips
For something more
15　Than pouting."
He handed me a hot dog
With the works, said
"Wrap your lips 'round this,
Then tell me if it ain't
20　The perfect cure
For disappointment."
I rolled my eyes
And could've argued
Easily enough
25　But my mouth
Was kinda busy
At the time.

asthma
(ăz′ mə)
disease that
makes it hard
for a person
to breathe

THINK IT THROUGH
In what way does Blue make Damon feel better?

Read the next two poems. Find out how the friendship
between Damon and Blue is changing.

The Watcher

My favorite ball skipped off the curb
And some dumb kid disguised as me
Ran blindly after it then heard
A tire's skid and spied a rig.
5   My stubborn feet refused to fly
But Blue reached out and grabbed my belt
And set me on the sidewalk while
The rig reduced my ball to dust.
Blue took my hand and marched me home
10   Then disappeared without a word.
At times I think Blue's actually
Some gold-toothed angel, guarding me.

disguised
(dĭs gīzd')
adj. dressed up
to look like
another person

rig
(rĭg)
truck

REREAD
Why does
Damon think
Blue is a
guardian angel?

Damon & Blue

Damon & Blue
Just us two
Cruising up the avenue.

You strut, you glide
5   But mark our stride
Can't beat us when we're
      side by side.

THINK IT THROUGH

How do Damon and Blue get along now? Find the lines in the poems that tell you.

Read to find out what Damon does when he is kicked by a
bully.

Class Bully

A bully
kicks me in the knee.
That bully's name
is Tiffany.

5   I fume
but don't return the blow.
Guys don't hit girls
Blue says, and so
     I grab

10   her wrists 'til she
calms down, while
     Laughing
jeering kids stand 'round
and shout "You wimp!" But

15   they're all wrong.
     It's guys
who *don't* hit girls
     Who're strong.

fume
(fyo͞om)
get angry

jeering
(jîr′ ĭng)
adj. mocking or
shouting insults

THINK IT THROUGH

Damon explains how a strong guy acts. Do you agree with his
way of thinking? Why or why not?

FOCUS

What can you learn about Blue from his hands?

His Hands

His hands
are a rough sculpture
of thick fingers
& thumbs tipped
5   with work-proud
callouses, his badges
of tough, honest labor
down on the docks.
His hands
10 are strong stories.
He tells them
sometimes when
I let him hold mine.

callouses
(kăl′ ə sĭz)
n. small areas of
hard, thick skin

THINK IT THROUGH

List details about Blue's hands. What do they tell about him?

FOCUS —————————

Discover why Damon and Blue like to play one-on-one basketball.

One-on-One

The game is
Seventeen to four
But scoring
Isn't why we run
5 And dribble
And jump
While some
Aim guns.
We hit
10 The hoops
And shoot
For fun.

THINK IT THROUGH

What do Damon and Blue gain from playing basketball? Explain.

My Own Man

When Mom works late I wait with busy
hands, pry soup cans open, spread spicy

mustard on rye with lettuce and tomatoes
sliced so thin the cheese peeks through.

5   It's my Cheddar Deluxe, which Mom loves
better than anything I cook. The boys next

door say, "How's that look? You fixin' supper
like some girl." I shrug off their teasing

and go on pleasing *me*. I read my books,
10   choose Jazz *and* Rap, and quiet over

chatter. Blue says, "What's the matter
with that?" And, if I take care of my mom

so what? She takes care of me. "Don't be
no Mama's boy," kids say. Well, tough.
15   I'm made this way.

THINK IT THROUGH
| How does Damon show that he is someone who thinks for
| himself? What do his actions tell about his feelings for his
| mother?

FOCUS
Read to find out what Blue is training Damon to do.

Training Season

Blue and me
We spar every day.
Blue fakes a jab
To show me
5 How it's done.
I don't mind
Since he's the one
Throwing the punches.
He's just trying
10 To keep me fit
For this world.

spar
(spär)
practice boxing

THINK IT THROUGH
Blue is teaching Damon more than how to box. What is Blue teaching him about life?

FOCUS _____

Read to find out what Damon thinks about a shooting at his school.

The Plan

A boy got shot
At school last month.
My knees still knock
At the memory.
5   What makes somebody
Want to shoot, to kill?
"It's hate," says Blue.
"And fear. One
Holds the gun
10   While the other
Pulls the trigger.
When you're bigger,
You'll understand."
Well, I don't plan
15   On hating anyone.
But fear's already
Scratching at my door,
Which means
I got one down
20   And one to go.
So, Mister Fear,
If you're listening,
You best be leaving
Now.

REREAD

According to Blue, what makes people want to hurt each other?

THINK IT THROUGH

How does Damon plan to avoid hurting others? Do you think he will succeed?

Like Blue

One day
I'll be like Blue
Not fierce
In black leather
5 Or built like
A heavyweight
Boxing machine
But like that
Other Blue I've seen
10 The one who
Says he cares
And shows it.
The one who
Flashes gold
15 Every time he smiles.

THINK IT THROUGH

1. What does Damon think about Blue now?
2. What does Blue teach Damon?
3. Is Blue someone you would like to have as a friend? Why or why not?

LiTTLe THiNGS ARe BiG

ADAPTATiON OF AN eSSAY BY JeSUS COLON

A MAN JUST WANTS TO HELP. DISCOVER WHAT GETS IN HIS WAY.

Wow Car (1997), Colleen Browning. Oil on canvas.
Southern Alleghenies Museum of Art, Loretto,
Pennsylvania.

Connect to Your Life

Have you ever tried to help a total stranger? What did you do? How did the stranger react? Share your memories with a classmate.

Key to the Essay

A **personal essay** is nonfiction writing about one subject. The writer gives an opinion or makes a point. In this essay, Jesus Colon writes about a single event that touched him deeply.

The event took place on a subway train in New York City. Subway trains travel underground to different places in the city. Passengers must go down a flight of stairs to reach the platform where they get on the train. Once they get off the train, they must go up another flight of stairs to reach the street. As Colon discovers, subway travel can be hard on some people.

Vocabulary Preview

Words to Know
courtesy
prejudiced
misjudging

 Reading Coach CD-ROM selection

It was late on the night of May 31. She came into the subway at the 34th Street station. She had a baby on her right arm and a suitcase in her left hand. Two little children, about three and five years of age, were walking behind her. She was a pretty white lady in her twenties.

At N Street, I saw her preparing to get off at the next station. That was the place where I had to get off too. Just as it had been a problem for her to get on 10 the subway, it was going to be a problem for her to get off. She had two small children to take care of, a baby on her right arm, and a suitcase in her left hand.

There I was, also preparing to get off at the Atlantic Avenue station. I was not carrying anything.

As the train entered the Atlantic Avenue station, a white man stood up. He and the children exchanged smiles. Then he helped the white lady out of the car, lifting the children onto the long, empty platform. There were only 20 two adults on the long platform.

REREAD
How do you think the woman reacts to this help?

I could see the steep, long stairs leading up to the street. Should I offer my help as the white man had done? Should I take care of the girl and the boy? Should I take them by their hands until they reached the top of the stairs?

Courtesy is important to the Puerto Rican. And here I was—a Puerto Rican man. Hours past midnight. A suitcase. Three white children. And a white lady in 30 need of someone to help her.

courtesy
(kûr' tǐ sē)
n. polite behavior

But how could I, a black and a Puerto Rican, approach this white woman? I knew she might be

Libra (1977), Colleen Browning. Oil on canvas. Harmon-Meek Gallery, Naples, Florida. Collection of the Artist.

prejudiced against blacks and everybody who talked differently. And we were in a lonely subway station, very late at night.

prejudiced
(prĕj′ ə dĭst)
adj. judging unfairly usually based on outward appearance

THINK IT THROUGH
Why doesn't the narrator know what to do?

FOCUS
The narrator continues to think about his problem. Find out what he decides.

What would she say? What would be the first reaction of this white American woman? Would she say, "Yes, of course you may help me"? Would she think that I was trying to get too friendly? Or would she think worse than that? What would I do if she screamed as I went toward her to offer my help?

Was I misjudging her? I stopped for a long, long minute. The good manners that the Puerto Rican father passes on to his son were fighting inside me. I was face to face with a situation that I could not handle. I didn't know what to do.

> **misjudging**
> (mĭs jŭj′ ĭng)
> v. judging wrongly

50 It was a long minute. I passed her by as if I saw nothing. As if I did not care about her need. Like an animal walking on two legs, I ignored her. I ran down the long subway platform, leaving the children and the suitcase and her with the baby on her arm. I took the steps in twos until I reached the street. The cold air slapped my warm face.

> **REREAD**
> In your own words, describe what happens.

This is what prejudice can do to people and to a nation! Dear lady, if you were not prejudiced, I failed you. I know that there is one chance in a million that you will read these words. I 60 am willing to take that chance. If you were not prejudiced, I failed you, lady. I failed you, children. I failed myself.

I lost my courtesy on that night. But here is a promise that I make to myself here and now. If I am ever faced with a situation like that again, I am going to offer my help. No matter what happens.

Then I will have my courtesy with me again.

THINK IT THROUGH

1. What will the narrator do differently next time, and why?
2. Why is he so upset about his own behavior?
3. Do you think the narrator's problem is common? Would others share his feelings? Explain.

PUERTO RICANS IN NEW YORK

by Charles Reznikoff

She enters the bus demurely
with the delicate dark face
the Spaniards first saw
on an island in the Caribbean
5 and he follows—
a tall gentle lad.
He smiles pleasantly, shyly,
at her now and then,
but she does not look at him,
10 looking away demurely.
She holds a small package in her hand—
perhaps a nightgown—
and he a larger package:
a brand-new windowshade.

This family has eleven children. How would you feel in such a full house?

Never Home Alone!

from _The Families Book_ by Arlene Erlbach

Connect to Your Life

How many children are in your family? What is your place—oldest, youngest, only child?

Key to the Interview

In this interview, Erlbach wrote down what five children in the family said they liked or didn't like about having so many brothers and sisters. As you read, notice how each person's place in the family— oldest, middle, youngest—affects how he or she feels and thinks.

Vocabulary Preview

Words to Know

biological	mentor
adopted	identical
siblings	situations

Read to find out why Elizabeth has so many brothers and sisters.

Elizabeth, age 15: I'm part of a big family—eleven kids in all. It's fun. I'm never lonely, and I always have somebody around to talk to and be with. I don't have anything else to compare it to, but my dad does. He was an only child and didn't like it, so he wanted a big family.

Four of us are our parents' biological children and seven of us are adopted. Six of us are from Korea. But we were all very young when we were adopted, so none of us remembers living anywhere else. My mom has offered to take those of us born in Korea for a visit, but the only one interested so far is Kelly. To me, the United States is home, and I don't feel a connection with Korea. I'd rather go to Europe if I were going on a big trip.

I like having brothers and sisters both older and younger—and near my age. My sister Molly is eighteen. We share clothes and go shopping together. Molly tells me what's going to happen in the future at school—like which teachers are nice, which ones are mean, and which ones give lots of homework. Then I'll tell Jeff, who's a year younger than me, about my experiences. I'm glad we have each other to depend on for information. It's easier to deal with future changes at school if you're prepared for them.

Sometimes I have to baby-sit for my younger brothers and sisters—Sam, Kelly, Mike, and Anna. They can get pretty wild, especially Mike. He has the sort of personality that influences Anna to act wild, too. And sometimes when I'm in charge, Anna copies

> **biological**
> (bī′ ə lŏj′ ĭ kəl)
> *adj.* related by birth

> **adopted**
> (ə dŏp′ tĭd)
> *adj.* made part of a family by legal means

me. She'll say "Stop that!" to everyone after I say it. That's funny and pretty cool.

THINK IT THROUGH
What does Elizabeth like about having older and younger brothers and sisters?

FOCUS
What is good about being one of the oldest? Read to learn what Jeff thinks.

Jeff, age 14: One of the best things about being in a big family is that there's always something to do and somebody to do it with. I enjoy playing baseball with my brothers and sisters. Since I'm officially one of the oldest ones living at home permanently, my younger brothers and sisters listen to me. I feel like I have

40 power.

The older kids in my family do their own laundry. I like it that way—a lot! If my mom does it (and she has), my brothers grab all the clean clothes. Then one of them might take a shirt I like a lot. I'll have to let him wear it because my mom thinks we should all try to share.

There's lots of sharing things in a big family—toys,

50 clothes, and books. Sometimes my siblings take things without asking. I don't like that, but it's bound to happen—and I'm used to it.

> **siblings**
> (sĭb' lĭngz)
> *n.* brothers and sisters

One super thing about being in a big family is that my younger siblings look up to me. I'm Mike's mentor. He copies me and follows me around. My mentor is Matt. He's twenty-three and getting married

60 soon. Even though we're not blood related, we're a lot alike. My mom says, "You act exactly the way Matt acted when he was your age—all your mannerisms are almost identical." Nobody else in my family is that much like somebody else. I guess Matt kind of rubbed off on me because we've always been so close.

> **mentor**
> (mĕn' tôr')
> *n.* someone who teaches and guides another

> **identical**
> (ī dĕn' tĭ kəl)
> *adj.* exactly alike

THINK IT THROUGH

How does Jeff feel about the younger children in his family? Whom does Jeff admire?

FOCUS

Sam describes what he thinks about being "never home alone." What are his views?

Sam, age 12: One of the best things about being in a big family is there are lots of people to help you with

70 your homework. If I don't know something, I'll ask Elizabeth, Jeff, or Matt. They'll help me. Most other kids don't have that advantage.

Some of my brothers and sisters still live at home. Others are in college or are on their own, but everyone visits a lot. So we eat dinner with lots of people. I never know who might stop in. That's another thing about being in a big family that's lots of fun.

> **advantage**
> (ăd văn' tĭj)
> something that gives a person more than others have

At meals, we have two tables where we eat, the big

80 table and the little table. The big table is for the older

kids, and the little table is for the younger ones. We don't have any special age when we can sit at certain tables. It just depends on where there's room and who's at home.

We have seven bedrooms in our house. We use one as a den. Until we're in high school, we each have to share a room. I usually like the company, so getting my own room isn't a big deal. Right now I'm sharing a room with Jeff. He's nice to share with. He's neat
90 and quiet. I used to share with Mike, and he's kind of messy and noisy. But even though he bugged me a lot, he was pretty good company. I don't even know if I'd like sleeping in a room by myself all that much.

I never even think about being an only child. It's more fun having brothers and sisters—and company in my room.

THINK IT THROUGH
What does Sam like about having such a large family? Find the details that let you know.

FOCUS _____
Kelly is one of the younger kids. Read to see what she values in her family.

Kelly, age 11: I'm never bored or lonely. I always have somebody to talk to or play with.

Even though I have brothers and sisters of all ages,
100 there are some games we can all play together, like the card game Go Fish. A game like that bridges everyone's age, so it's something we can all share. Anna always tries to win, and if she doesn't she might get upset. Because she's the baby, sometimes we let her win. And if we're playing a game the younger kids don't know, they watch us. Then they'll

know how to play it when they're a little older.

Anna gets lots of help from
110 all of us, like with learning to ride her bike. My mom sometimes tells us, "Anna doesn't need so many helpers. She needs to learn to do things by herself."

But that's part of being in a big family. You live together and play together and help each other.

THINK IT THROUGH
What does Kelly think is the best thing about having a lot of brothers and sisters?

FOCUS
Does the second youngest have the easiest or hardest time? Mike explains what it's like.

Mike, age 10: Usually I like being in a big family. But I do get teased by Jeff, Sam, and Bill. They'll call me names like "wimp." This
120 probably happens because I'm the second youngest kid in the family. I ignore them, and since I know what it's like to get teased, I never tease anyone at school. So growing up in a big family lets me experience situations that have helped me learn how to treat other people.

> **situations**
> (sĭch′ o͞o ā′ shənz) *n.* events that happen at a certain time and place

REREAD
What has Mike learned?

Most of the things about being in a big family are good. I always have somebody to play with and help me with my homework. Whenever I'm
130 lonely or bored, I can count on Kelly to play with me. And I play a lot with Anna, too.

Playing with Anna makes me feel grown-up and responsible. Let's say we're playing and she leaves her toys on the floor. I'll pick up a toy and she'll copy me. That makes me feel like I'm very grown-up because I'm setting an example for somebody younger. My older brothers and sisters did that for me, and now I can set an example for Anna.

140   Besides being the second youngest, I have another very special place in the family. I was born on Thanksgiving. So we don't just have Thanksgiving at my house—we have my birthday celebration, too. That's pretty cool.

Holidays are a big deal at my house. My brothers and sisters who don't live at home anymore all visit. The minute they walk in, there's lots of hugging. That's really super. It's fun when all of us are together again.

THINK IT THROUGH

1. What does Mike think is special about being the second youngest?
2. What are some of the best things the kids like about being in a big family?
3. If you were in this family, would you like to be one of the younger kids or one of the older ones? Explain your answer.

A young man decides to raise a wild falcon as a pet. Will he be able to give the falcon what it needs most?

GOODBYE, FALCON

by Wenceslao Serra Deliz

Connect to Your Life

With a partner, discuss what you like and do not like about raising pets. What would it be like raising a wild bird, such as a falcon or an eagle?

Key to the Story

The falcon is related to the hawk. As a boy, the writer of this story raised a wild falcon as a pet. *Goodbye, Falcon* is based on his experiences. As you read, watch for clues to how the narrator in the story feels about his pet falcon. Which of these feelings do you think reflect those of the writer?

Vocabulary Preview

Words to Know

transparent   deftly
captivity   abruptly
warily

 Reading Coach CD-ROM selection

Goodbye, Falcon **127**

Sometimes things happen in our lives that seem worthy of a story. Things that we remember as part of a real and living dream.

What I am going to tell you happened to me. It all began in Barranquitas, a lovely and handsome town nestled between green mountains in the center of Puerto Rico.

The town of Barranquitas, Puerto Rico

10   It was one o'clock in the afternoon, and cool, even though the month of July had already begun. I was riding in a friend's car. We were returning from our work in town. At the exit where the road begins to climb the green mountain, a boy signaled to us. When my friend stopped the car, the boy held out his hand and said, "Two falcon chicks! For a peso each!"

20 The two scared baby birds were in a straw nest, maybe the same one in which they were born. They didn't have feathers yet, and their skin was very fine, almost transparent. Their hearts beat with such force it seemed they would pop out from their chests.

> **transparent**
> (trăns pâr′ ənt)
> *adj.* so thin it can
> be seen through

I bought them both and gave one to my friend. I knew that even though they were frightened, the two birds wanted to grow, and one day, to soar through the sky. . . .

FOCUS

The falcon is growing. Read to find out how it changes.

30   For the rest of the trip I talked with my friend
about the birds. The falcon is related to
and looks very much like the *guaraguao*.
Falcons live in the countryside of Puerto
Rico and prefer the warmest mountains.
Their feathers are colored like the
mountain mud, speckled with black.
With strong claws they trap small lizards
and insects to eat. Falcons like to fly
together with their mates.

> *guaraguao*
> (gwä′ rə gwou′)
> red-tailed hawk

> **REREAD**
> What does this passage tell you about falcons?

40   When I arrived at my home in the housing
development of Las Lomas, in the town of Río
Piedras, I put the tiny, transparent bird in a little wire
cage. I left him in my room on top of my desk. As the
days passed I noticed large, whitish stains on the wall,
the chair, and part of the bed. The bird had begun to
grow and since the little cage was too small, he had
soiled everything around him. I had to make a bigger
cage and put him out on the patio, where he would
stay from then on.

50   The weeks dragged by. Already his mud-colored
feathers were appearing. His body grew slowly, as a
child grows. I noticed small differences from week to
week. It is moving to see a living thing grow: a rabbit,
a dog, a little bird, or a tree we have planted. . . . All
of us can sense this great joy if we learn to see and
feel the living things that surround us.

   Months passed and soon the cage on the patio held
a handsome adult falcon. But then I noticed
something strange. A tired look in his eyes clashed
60 with the wild beauty of the bird. His sharp cries were
soon an unending complaint. They seemed to say that

Goodbye, Falcon   **129**

the cage where he had grown was now much too small. The message was clear: he could no longer endure captivity; his eyes needed a world full of light, of green trees and blue breezes. . . .

captivity
(kăp tĭv′ ĭ tē)
n. state of being locked up

THINK IT THROUGH

Why isn't a cage the best place for the falcon now? What details help you know this?

FOCUS ——————————————————————

Read to find out what happens when the narrator gives the falcon its freedom.

That same afternoon I opened his cage, like someone putting out a hand to help a friend. The falcon, surprised, looked all around. He didn't know
70 what to do at that moment, so new for him. I had to take him out with my hand. His great claws grasped me, frightened and trembling. I threw him then into the air and he flew just a bit, enough to perch in the fork of a breadfruit tree on the neighbor's farm. He stayed there a long time, until the night shadows gathered.

The night was like a bird with great black wings full of small new lights. I thought about the young falcon who had flown toward a new world. For him,
80 at that moment, there began a new freedom lit up by the stars and the fireflies, and perfumed by the simple flowers of the *moriviví*. . . .

At dawn the next day the falcon's shriek and the racket of his wings in the trees woke me. He must have been hungry. He was a hunter who still didn't know how to hunt alone.

I got out of bed, went to the refrigerator, and took out a piece of meat. I walked out to the road leading to the farm and spied the falcon high up in a tree.

90 When he saw me, he started to move to the lower branches. Looking at me warily, he didn't seem to want to trade his liberty for the cage on the patio. I held out my hand softly, letting him know that his freedom was assured. He balanced deftly on the lowest branch, opening his great wings in the cold dawn. Swiftly, he grabbed the meat and flew toward one of the farm's tall pines. I watched him with joy and
100 sadness. Sadness, because I knew that soon I would no longer see him. With joy, because he was already very happy in his newly discovered, green world. . . .

> **warily**
> (wâr′ ĭ lē)
> *adv.* cautiously

> **deftly**
> (dĕft′ lē)
> *adv.* skillfully and effortlessly

> **REREAD**
> What are the narrator's feelings about freeing the falcon?

From that moment, my friend decided to eat three times a day, like all of us. And three times he would come down from the tallest pine: in the morning, at noon, and at dusk. Affectionately, I offered him a piece of meat from my hand. He saw it from up high and prepared himself for the attack,
110 darting down like an arrow.

Then he landed on my arm. He took care not to scratch me with his strong claws. Grabbing the meat with his beak, he flew back up. Every day this happened. Many people came to see him, as he had become famous. A friendship between a bird of prey and a man is something we see very few times.

THINK IT THROUGH
Why do you think the falcon returns to the narrator each day? Find the part in the story that tells you.

FOCUS ————————————————————————
Read to find out what happens during the falcon's last visits.
What change is taking place?

One afternoon something funny happened. At the
moment that I offered him his usual meal,
he descended so abruptly that he couldn't

120 land on my arm. He flapped his wings
frantically over my head and I felt his claws
sink into my hair in an effort to balance his
body. I wasn't afraid because I noticed that my friend
made a loving effort not to hurt me. In spite of
everything I was able to raise my arm and offer him
his meal. He took it and returned again to the
murmuring green trees that waited for him.

> **abruptly**
> (ə brŭpt′ lē)
> *adv.* suddenly

I was surprised one day when I noticed that he had
come to eat only twice. I was very worried. Later, I

130 realized what was happening when I saw him fly by
accompanied by a mate of his same color. He had
company and was learning to hunt with her.

Soon he began to come down only once a day. His
mate waited for him on one of the low branches of
the pine tree. There was no doubt: he already knew
how to work for his meals and he was truly free. I
thought that now he came to get something to eat
only to see me and say goodbye.

Afterwards, his visits lost regularity. The day he

140 stopped visiting me I realized that in the last few days
he had really been saying goodbye. My friend learned
to love the freedom that he won bit by
bit through daily effort. I don't imagine
that it was easy for him, but the final
outcome must have been much happier
than the walls of his metal cage. . . .

> **REREAD**
> Do you agree
> with the narrator
> that animals
> have thoughts
> and feelings?

Goodbye, falcon. Knowing you made me realize that it is possible to have a friend from the air, the trees, and the nests. I learned that animals, too, can

150 be afraid of the unknown and still work and learn to be free. In my memory you are always part of the mountains where I met you. Of the sky where you flew. Of the dawn, and of the dusk. . . .

THINK IT THROUGH

1. What lets you know that the falcon is ready to be on its own?
2. What does the narrator learn from his experience with the falcon?
3. How well does the narrator accept the falcon's leaving him? Would you feel the same way?

Joining Forces

Unit 5

Drama

Everyone needs a little help once in a while. Sometimes people need to join forces to do something that one person alone could never do. In this unit, you will read two plays about the awesome power of two together.

Dramas are plays. The best way to enjoy a play is to watch it acted on a stage. When you read the written form, or **script,** try to imagine that you are watching actors on a stage. See how the actors' words and actions tell the story.

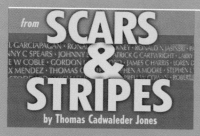

from

SCARS & STRIPES

by Thomas Cadwaleder Jones

A country boy and a city girl are both searching for something. Which one will find it?

What is it like to lose someone? A relative, a friend, a parent, a pet—these are difficult losses. What, if anything, helps people get over such a loss?

Key to the Drama

Dramas often have these special features to help you understand what's going on when you read a play.

- **cast of characters:** a list of the characters in the play
- **dialogue:** the words that characters say to each other
- **stage directions:** instructions (*in italics*) for the actors. They also describe the setting and tell much of the story.
- **scene:** a section of the play that happens in one time and place

Vocabulary Preview

Words to Know
directory
censored
resumes

In Washington, D.C., a monument honors the Americans who died in the Vietnam War. This monument was designed by a young art student named Maya Lin. She created two enormous walls. Each wall is about 245 feet long. On the walls, you can read the name of every American who died in the war. Over 58,000 names cover the walls.

The play *Scars & Stripes* takes place in front of the monument. Following is an excerpt from that play.

FOCUS

Read the cast of characters, setting, and stage directions. Then read on to find out how the boy goes about looking for his father's name on the wall.

Cast of Characters

Boy. P. T. Flagg, teenage boy

Girl. Jewel Robinson, teenage girl

Setting. In front of "the wall," the Vietnam Veterans Memorial in Washington, D.C.

(*The boy is reading names on the wall one at a time. The girl watches him for quite a while.*)

Boy. I'm just thinkin' 'bout how many names are up there, how long it's gonna take me to find his.

Girl. There's a directory.

Boy. I know that.

Girl. All you have to do is look up his name. It'll tell you where it's located.

10 **Boy.** Didn't you hear me, I know that—

Girl. Then, do it.

Boy. Told you this was special.

Girl. So?

> **directory**
> (dǐ rěk′ tə rē)
> *n.* book with names grouped in some way

Boy. So what's special about looking up his name in some directory and walking right up to it? No, I'm gonna start at one end an' read every one of those names till I find his.

Girl. That could take you a rather long time.

Boy. I got time.

THINK IT THROUGH
Why is the boy doing his search "the slow way"?

FOCUS

Read on to find out what the boy does for his father's buddy.

20 (*Silence. He moves closer to the wall, and begins to
read the names. He mouths them silently to himself.
She watches, finally speaks. She's been thinking this
for some time now.*)

Girl. When exactly did your father die?

Boy. Don't know.

Girl. Your grandpa didn't tell you?

Boy. Nobody ever told me anything.

Girl. Weren't there letters? Didn't your
father ever write?

30 **Boy.** If he did, Grandpa sorta censored the
mail.

Girl. Why would he do that?

Boy. Because he hated my dad for runnin'
off to that war and he hated me for
lookin' like him.

Girl. What about that other boy?

Boy. What other boy?

Girl. Your dad's friend. The one in the picture you
showed me. Didn't you ever ask him about your dad?

> **censored**
>
> (sĕn′ sərd)
> *v.* inspected and
> stopped; past
> tense of *censor*

> **REREAD**
>
> Why didn't his
> grandfather talk
> to the boy about
> his father?

40 **Boy.** They went over there together.

Girl. Oh.

Boy. I guess 'cause they were buddies, best friends, something like that. When Topper finally came back home, I was only a little kid. But I sure remember what he looked like when they took him off that bus. I was standing there, staring, thinking how he sure didn't look like Marlon Brando anymore. How he sure couldn't ride that motorcycle of his

50 ever again. People round town said his family just sorta parked his wheelchair in an upstairs corner room, and that's where he stayed till he died.

> **Marlon Brando**
> a handsome movie star in the 1950s

> **REREAD**
> Why and how did his father's friend change?

Girl. They abandoned him?

Boy. Something like that. I remember seeing something standing under a hickory tree, in the Williams' front yard, for years after that. It was all covered up with an old, green piece of canvas. One spring we had this big storm, and it blew the green canvas off.

60 There was this bright shiny black Harley-Davidson motorcycle standing there.

Girl. The one in the picture.

Boy. Funny thing was, nobody ever put the tarp back on it after that. Boy, I wanted that motorcycle bad. Another spring we had a big storm, and it blew the motorcycle over. One school morning, there it was, lying on its side. I kept wondering when somebody was gonna come out of that house and set that

70 motorcycle back up, but nobody ever did. So one morning I went by there

> **REREAD**
> Compare the way Topper's family treated the motorcycle with the way they treated Topper.

and jumped the fence and wrestled that motorcycle back up on its tires.

Girl. Good for you.

Boy (*shoots her a glance*). You liked that, huh?

Girl. Well, somebody should've done something.

Boy. After Topper died, they put a sign on that motorcycle. Hand lettered. Black paint on a white board. "For Sale—Cheap." C-H-E-E-P. Even I knew that's spelled wrong.

Girl. You should've bought it.

Boy. I did.

Girl. Good for you again.

Boy. Well, I had that picture of my dad and him and they were friends. I just bought it to keep somebody else from buying it. It wasn't worth anything, tires all rotted out . . .

Girl. But you bought it; that's what counts.

Boy. I musta pushed that motorcycle 'bout seven miles out of town. Took forever 'cause of those flat tires. Draped a worn-out American flag over it, I'd took off the pole at the high school. Made up a little prayer. Pushed it off an overhang out by the highway 40 bridge into the East Fork of the White River.

Girl. It was a good thing you did.

THINK IT THROUGH

Describe three things the boy does with the motorcycle. Why does he do these things?

FOCUS

Find out how the boy and girl want to stop wars.

Boy. When I was little, but I knew about that war, I asked Grandpa if they were gonna send me over there like my dad. He just laughed. "Not till you're eighteen, boy." He said, ". . . Not till you're eighteen . . ."

100

Girl. I asked my mother that, when I was little, if they sent girls to fight in wars.

Boy. What'd she tell you?

Girl. "Not if you're good and you eat your spinach." (*They both laugh at the* image.) She was always saying things like that when I was little. Things that didn't make a lot of sense. She laughed a lot, too. Then along came Mr. Best and everything changed . . .

110

> **image**
> (ĭm' ĭj)
> picture in your mind

(*Silence. They regard each other. He thinks she's told him something; he's not sure what. He* resumes *his search of the wall.*)

Boy. I never dreamed 58,000 was so many names . . . I wish . . .

> **resumes**
> (rĭ zo̅o̅mz')
> v. begins again

Girl (*She's watching him, still thinking about the loss of her father and his replacement, Mr. Best.*) Careful what you wish, it might come true.

REREAD
Who is Mr. Best?

120

Boy (*He shoots her a look.*) . . . If everybody who made the wars had to read all those names . . .

Girl. One by one . . . like you're doing . . .

Boy. Maybe there wouldn't be any more wars, huh? If they had to spend a minute with every name . . . all 58,000 . . . thinking about the one who died. . . . 'Bout how long you think that'd take anyway?

Girl (*She thinks, calculates in her head.*) . . . Forty days . . .

130 **Boy.** Forty . . . You do that in your head?

Girl. 58,000 minutes . . . divided by sixty is 966 hours . . . divided by twenty-four . . . that's forty days . . . If you spend a minute looking at each name, you're gonna be here a long, long time; I'll say that for you.

THINK IT THROUGH
What do the boy and girl think people who start wars should do? Why?

FOCUS
Will the boy find his father's name? Read on.

Boy. While back, I thought I'd lost my place. Got to thinking maybe I'd looked right past his name, missed seeing it, didn't even recognize it, when I came to it. All these names start runnin' together, if 140 you don't find one you know.

Girl. . . . Look, come over here for a minute . . . I want to show you something. (*She moves to a location beyond where he's been looking.*)

Boy. I'll lose my place.

Girl. No, you won't, I know which panel you stopped on. Come on over here.

Boy (*He goes to her.*) Okay, what?

Girl. Look right up there. (*She points to a special place on the wall.*)

150 **Boy.** Where?

Girl. Right there. There's *my* father's name. Julius A. Robinson. See?

Boy (*He spots it.*) Yeah.

Girl. Now that's a name for you to know. Because you kinda know me.

Boy (*Suddenly, his face changes.*) Oh, my . . .

Girl. What? (*She's staring at him, not looking at the wall.*)

Boy. Oh, my goodness . . .

160 **Girl.** What's wrong?

Boy (*He reaches towards the wall.*) Look . . . Oh, my goodness, look . . .

Girl (*Now she's staring at the wall, and she sees it.*) It's two lines down . . .

Boy. My father's name.

Girl. Phileas T. Flagg . . .

Boy. It's him . . .

Girl. I must have seen it a hundred times before . . . It just never meant anything to me until now.

170 **Boy.** That's him; it's gotta be . . .

Girl (*staring at him*). The boy in that picture . . .

Boy. Oh, goodness, that's him, that's my dad.

Girl (*staring at the wall*). He died in sixty-nine.

Boy. Yeah.

Girl. Same year my father was missing.

Boy. I found it. I found his name . . .

(*Blackout as both teenagers stare at the name.*)

THINK IT THROUGH

1. What did the two fathers have in common?
2. How did honoring his father's friend help the boy?
3. What feelings do the boy and the girl have at the end? Explain why you think so.

MAYA LIN:
Sculptor of Memories by Tamiko Sasaki

Since designing the Vietnam Veterans Memorial, Maya Lin has designed other important works. They help people remember key events in the nation's history.

In 1987, Lin designed a project for the civil rights movement. Dr. Martin Luther King, Jr., had talked about justice rolling down like water. Those words gave Lin
10 the idea to use moving water. She created a black granite disk and a nine-foot wall. On the disk are names and dates in civil rights history. On the wall are Dr. King's words. Water flows over them both. People can touch the water flowing over the names.

In the 1990s, Lin designed a project to honor women at Yale University. The work is a green granite table. Water
20 flows through a hole in the center. A circle of numbers shows how many women were at Yale each year. For the first 200 years, no women were allowed in the school. To show this, Lin filled the center of the circle with zeros.

Lin's works help people remember history. They also help heal the wounds that some events leave behind.

Westwoods

by Eleanor Farjeon   adapted by Aaron Shepard

John hates being

told what to do.

But when he does

the opposite, he

gets in trouble.

Connect to Your Life

Do you ever do the opposite of what people tell you to do? Why do you react this way? Discuss your feelings with a classmate.

Key to the Drama

This play has two narrators. In a drama, a narrator does not usually take part in the action. A **narrator** sets the scene and might comment on what happens.

The play also uses humor to describe the important events. **Humor** makes you laugh or smile. You will surely at least smile at the behavior of the young king in this play.

Vocabulary Preview

Words to Know
barrier
indignantly
decline

 Reading Coach CD-ROM selection

Cast of Characters

Narrator 1	**Princess of Eastmarshes**
Narrator 2	**Princess of Northmountains**
King John	**Princess of Southlands**
Selina	**King of Northmountains**
Minister 1	**King of Southlands**
Minister 2	
Minister 3	

John (*reading his poem, and writing the last few words*).

I know you are sweeter than grassfields in June,
And bright as the single star watching the moon.
I long for my grass, and I dream of
    my star,
Though I haven't the faintest idea . . .
who . . . you . . . are.

RERED

Read this poem aloud. Whom is the King seeking in this poem?

Narrator 1. As the young King of
Workaday finished writing his poem, Selina the
10 Housemaid knocked on the door.

John (*irritated*). What is it, Selina?

Selina (*steps in*). Your ministers want you.

ministers
(mĭn' ĭ stərz)
advisers

John. I'm busy!

Selina. "At once!" they said.

John. Well, go tell them—

Selina. *I've* got my *cleaning* to do.

Narrator 1. The King groaned and put down his pen.

Selina (*looking around*). While you're seeing the
ministers, I could do your room, I suppose.

20 **John.** Yes, but don't touch the desk, *please*. I always
have to *tell* you.

Selina (*putting up with him*). Oh, all right.

Narrator 1. The King gave her a cross look as he started for the Stateroom.

Narrator 2. The Kingdom of Workaday wanted a Queen, and his ministers had come to tell the young King so.

Minister 1. You've come of age, Your Majesty!

Minister 2. It's time for you to find a wife!

Minister 3. And of course, she must be a princess!

30 **John.** What princesses *are* there?

Narrator 2. . . . asked the young King, whose name was John because, as the old King his father had said, the name John had always worked well, and no nonsense about it.

Narrator 1. They did not believe in nonsense, there in the Kingdom of Workaday, and they kept their noses so close to their jobs that they couldn't see anything beyond them. But they did their jobs

40 thoroughly—and it was the ministers' job to see that their King married a princess, and the King's job to marry her. So John made no fuss.

> **REREAD**
> With a name like Workaday, what kind of place do you think this is?

Narrator 2. The ministers consulted their lists.

Minister 1. There is the Princess of Northmountains, the country to the top of Workaday on the map.

Minister 2. And there is the Princess of Southlands, which lies at the bottom.

Minister 3. And there is the Princess of Eastmarshes, which lies on the righthand side.

THINK IT THROUGH
What do the ministers want the King to do? Why?

| Will King John follow the ministers' wishes?

50 **John.** And what about Westwoods, that lies on the left?

Narrator 2. The ministers looked serious.

Minister 1. We do not *know* what lies in the West.

Minister 2. No one in living memory has gone there.

Minister 3. No one has passed the fence that stands between us and the country beyond!

John. Hmm. Tomorrow I will hunt Westwoods and find out.

Ministers 1, 2, & 3 (*terrified*). Sire, it is *forbidden!*

60 **John** (*thoughtfully to himself*). Forbidden!

Narrator 1. And then John remembered how in his childhood he had been warned by his parents never to go into Westwoods.

Narrator 2. The mothers of Workaday had *always* warned their children of the dangers that lay beyond the fence. And no Workaday children ever lost the wish to get *into* Westwoods—until they grew up and got married and had children of their own. Then they warned their *own* children of the 70 dangers they had never seen.

John. I will hunt Westwoods tomorrow! (*starts out*)

Ministers 1, 2, & 3 (*gasp*).

Narrator 1. He went to tell Selina to put out his things, and found her leaning on her broom over his desk, reading what he had been writing.

John. Don't *do* that!

Selina. Oh, *all* right.

Narrator 2. She began dusting the mantelpiece.
The King waited for her to say something
80 else, but as she didn't, he had to.

> **mantelpiece**
> (măn′ tl pēs′)
> shelf above a
> fireplace

John (*coldly*). I'm going hunting tomorrow. I
want you to put out my things.

Selina. Where are you hunting?

John. In Westwoods.

Selina (*in disbelief*). Never!

John (*exasperated*). I wish you would understand that
I mean what I say!

THINK IT THROUGH
Why does the King want to go to Westwoods?

FOCUS
What do you think the King will find in Westwoods?

Narrator 1. Selina began to dust the desk, and a flick
of her duster sent the King's writing to the floor.
90 The King picked it up angrily, hesitated, and got
rather pink.

John (*uncertainly*). So, you *read* this, did
you?

> **REREAD**
> Why is the King
> pink?

Selina (*still dusting*). Um-*hm*.

John (*waits for her to say something more*). Well?

Selina (*stops and looks at him*). It's a bit of poetry,
isn't it?

John (*testily*). Yes.

> **testily**
> (tĕs′ tĭ lē)
> in an irritated
> manner

Selina. I thought so. Well, I think your
100 room's about done, now.

Narrator 2. And she took herself out of it. The King felt so cross with her, he crumpled his poem into a ball, and threw it in the wastepaper basket.

REREAD
What do King John's actions show about him?

Narrator 1. The morrow came, and the King rode out on his white horse for Westwoods. Presently, the tall fence came in sight, and over it he jumped.

110 **Narrator 2.** His first feeling was of disappointment. In front of him was a barrier of brushwood. Caught in the barrier was all sorts of broken rubbish— torn pictures and broken dolls, rusty trumpets, chipped glass marbles, and useless books without covers.

barrier
(băr′ ē ər)
n. something that blocks the way

Narrator 1. He rode through the barricade of rubbish and found a waste of flat gray sand, flat as a plate, and like a desert in size. Flat as it was, he could not see the end of it.

barricade
(băr′ ĭ kād′)
barrier or blockade to keep people out

120 **Narrator 2.** The King turned his horse, rode through the barrier, and jumped to the Workaday side of the fence. Then he rode to the palace, where his ministers hailed him with joy.

Minister 1. Sire, you have returned!

Minister 2. Thank heaven you are safe!

Minister 3 (*anxiously*). What did you see?

John. Nothing and nobody! Tomorrow I will go to Northmountains, and begin my |wooing|.

> **wooing**
> (woo′ ĭng)
> urging someone to marry him

Narrator 1. And he went to his room.

130 **John** (*calling for her*). Selina! Pack my trunk!

Selina (*enters*). Where for?

John. Northmountains, to see the Princess.

Selina. You'll want your fur coat and your woolly gloves.

Narrator 2. And she went to see about them.

Narrator 1. The King thought his poem might come in useful too, but on looking in his wastepaper basket, he found that Selina had emptied it.

Narrator 2. This made him so cross that, when she brought him his glass of hot milk at bedtime, he

140 wouldn't say "good night."

Selina (*indignantly*). Hmph! (*leaves*)

> **indignantly**
> (ĭn dĭg′ nənt lē)
> *adv.* angrily

THINK IT THROUGH
Why is Westwoods a disappointment to John?

FOCUS
Read to discover what John finds in Northmountains.

Narrator 1. The next day, the King rode to Northmountains.

Narrator 2. It was more than cool there, it was freezing! Some people were in the streets, but nobody so much as glanced at him.

John (*to himself*). I've never seen such stiff, cold faces in my life.

Narrator 1. The King rushed on to the palace, which stood upon a glacier on a mountaintop.

glacier
(glā′ shər)
large, slow-moving mass of ice

Narrator 2. The Throne Room was hung in white, and felt like a refrigerator. At the far end, the King of Northmountains sat on his throne, and his courtiers stood in rows, as stiff as statues. At the King's feet sat the Princess of the North, completely covered with a snowy veil.

courtiers
(kôr′ tē ərz)
attendants;
servants

Narrator 1. Nobody stirred or spoke. John plucked up his courage and slid across the icy floor to the King's throne.

John (*to the King*). I have come to woo your daughter.

Narrator 2. The King gave the slightest nod towards the Princess at his feet. John couldn't think how to begin. If only he could remember his poem! He did his best, kneeling before the silent figure.

John (*reciting loudly with no thought of the meaning*).
You're whiter than snowflakes, you're colder than ice.
I can't see your face, and perhaps it's not nice.
I don't want to marry a lady of snow.
I've come to propose, but I hope you'll say no.

> **REREAD**
> Read this poem aloud. Does John mean to insult the princess? Then why does he do it?

Narrator 1. Such a complete silence followed his proposal, John began to think he must have gotten his poem wrong. He waited about five minutes, bowed, and slid backwards out of the

Throne Room. When he got outside, he jumped on
180   his horse and rode back to Workaday as fast as he
could.

Narrator 2. His ministers were waiting impatiently.

Minister 1. Did all go well?

Minister 2. Is everything settled?

John. *Quite* settled.

Minister 3 (*gleefully*). And when will the wedding take
place?!

John. Never!

Narrator 1. And he went to his room.

190   **John** (*shivering*). Selina! Light the fire!

Narrator 2. Selina was good with fires, and had a
splendid one burning in a jiffy. While she
was tidying the hearth, she asked,

Selina. How did you like the Princess of the
North?

John. Not at all.

Selina. Wouldn't *have* you, eh?

John (*glaring*). Learn to know your *place*,
Selina!

200   **Selina.** Oh, *all* right. Anything more?

John. Yes. Unpack my bag, and pack it up again.
Tomorrow, I'm going to see the Princess of
Southlands.

Selina. You'll want your straw hat and your linen
pajamas.

Narrator 1. And she started for the door.

hearth
(härth)
floor of a
fireplace

REREAD
What is unusual
about how
Selina treats the
King?

John. Uh . . . Selina . . . um . . . do you remember how that . . . uh . . . bit of poetry of mine went?

210 **Selina** (*huffily*). I've got too much to do to trouble myself to learn poetry!

REREAD
Why does the King keep asking Selina about his poem?

Narrator 2. She went out, and the King was so cross that, when she returned with a really hot hot-water bottle for his bed, he never said so much as "thank you."

Selina. Hmph! (*leaves*)

THINK IT THROUGH
In Northmountains, how successful was John in his mission?

FOCUS
Read more to find out how John does in Southlands.

Narrator 1. The next day, the young King set out for Southlands, and to begin with, he found the journey pleasant.

220 **Narrator 2.** But by the time he arrived, the sun burned so fiercely that the horse could scarcely move its limbs, and sweat poured down the King's forehead.

Narrator 1. The royal city was as silent as sleep, and nobody stirred in the streets. The King's horse dragged itself to the palace gates. It was as much as the King could do to stagger from his saddle and find his way to the Throne Room.

Narrator 2. There on a golden couch reclined the King of Southlands, with

230 the Princess lolling on a mass of golden pillows at his feet. All around

lolling
(lŏl' ĭng)
lying down lazily

the room lounged the
courtiers, on gilded
couches piled high
with cushions.

gilded
(gĭl' dĭd)
covered with
gold

Narrator 1. The Princess
was beautiful, thought John,
only very, very fat. Her father was still fatter.

John (*to* King). I have come to woo your daughter.

240 **Narrator 2.** The King's smile grew a little fatter and a
little drowsier. John thought he had better begin.
But words and energy failed him, and he decided to
recover, if he could, his lost poem. He sank on his
knees before the lady.

John.

You're fatter than butter, you'd melt by the fire.
You're very much fatter than I could
    desire.
When I see you, my courage
250   commences to ooze.
I've come to propose, but I hope
    you'll refuse.

REREAD
Read this poem
aloud. How is it
like what he said
in Northlands?
How is it
different?

commences
(kə mĕn' sĭz)
begins

Narrator 1. The Princess yawned in his
face. As nothing else happened, John
made his way out, clambered onto his
horse, and ambled back to Workaday.

John (*to himself*). I don't think that *could* have
been the poem.

Narrator 2. The ministers were awaiting him
260   with eagerness.

Minister 1. Is everything arranged?

Minister 2. Are you and the Princess of the South
of one mind?

John (*lazily*). Entirely.

Minister 3. And when does she become your bride?!

John. Never.

Narrator 1. And he went to his room.

John (*wiping sweat*). Selina! Bring me an iced orange squash!

270 **Narrator 2.** She made them very well, and soon had one ready for him. While he drank it, she asked,

Selina. How did you get on with the Princess of the South?

John. I didn't.

Selina. Didn't *take* to you, eh?

John. Mind your place, Selina!

Selina. Oh, *all* right. Is that all for now?

John. No. Tomorrow I am going to see the Princess of Eastmarshes.

280 **Selina.** You'll want your raincoat and boots.

Narrator 1. And she picked up his bag and started to leave with it.

John. Wait, Selina! Where do you put what you find in my wastepaper basket?

Selina. It goes in the dustbin.

John. Has the dustbin been emptied this week?

Selina. I sent for the dustman specially! It seemed *extra full* of rubbish.

Narrator 2. Her answer vexed the King so
290 much that, when she came in to tell him she had everything ready in the bathroom for a nice cold shower, he just

vexed
(vĕkst)
angered

drummed on the window with his back to her, as though she weren't there.

Selina. Hmph! (*leaves*)

THINK IT THROUGH
Why do you think King John isn't having any luck convincing a princess to marry him?

FOCUS
Read more to find out whether John has any luck in Eastmarshes.

Narrator 1. The next day, on the journey to Eastmarshes, the King was met by a harsh and noisy wind that nearly blew him from his saddle. The countryside was bleak and damp.

300 **Narrator 2.** The city was built of gray stone without any beauty. Everyone seemed to be rushing here and there, shouting at the tops of their voices as they stamped about their business.

Narrator 1. As John neared the palace, the doors flew open, and a crowd of people streamed toward him. They were led by a girl with a short skirt and flying hair, carrying two hockey sticks.

Princess. Can you play hockey? We're one man short! Come along!

310 **Narrator 2.** She thrust a stick into his hand, and he found himself dragged to a great open field behind the palace. For an hour, voices yelled in his ear, hands hurled him hither and thither, and mud spattered him from head to toe.

Narrator 1. At last the game ended, and the girl came over to thump him on the back.

320 **Princess.** Who *are* you?

John (*weakly*). I am the King of Workaday.

Princess. Oh, indeed! And what have you come for?

John. To woo the Princess.

Princess. You don't say! Well, go ahead!

John (*stares at her*). But . . . *you* . . . aren't. . . .

Princess. Yes, I am. Why not? Go to it!

Narrator 2. John made a wild effort to muster his thoughts and get hold of his lost poem.

John.

330   You're louder than thunder, you're harsher than
          salt.
      We're made as we're born, so it isn't
          your fault.

REREAD
Read this poem aloud. What do you think the princess will do?

      My tastes are not yours, and your
          manners not mine.
      I've come to propose, but I hope you'll
          decline.

decline
(dĭ klīn')
v. refuse; say no

Princess. Well, I never!

Narrator 1. And lifting her hockey stick
340   over her head, she made for him.

Narrator 2. John scrambled to his horse and put it to the gallop. At last the young King came, muddy, weary, and breathless, to his own door.

Minister 1. Greetings, sire!

Minister 2. Are you and the Princess of the East agreed?

John. Absolutely!

Minister 3. And when will she name the happy day?!

John. NEVER!

350 **Narrator 1.** And he rushed to his room.

THINK IT THROUGH
Tell in your own words what has been wrong with each of the princesses.

FOCUS
Read more to find out whom King John finally chooses.

John (*exhausted*). Selina! Come and turn down my bed!

Narrator 2. Selina was very quiet and deft about it, and soon had it looking invitingly restful and ready. As she put out his dressing gown and bedroom slippers, she asked,

> **deft**
> (dĕft)
> quick and skillful

Selina. What do you think of the Princess of the East?

360 **John.** I don't!

Selina. Hadn't any *use* for you, eh?

John. You forget your place, Selina!

REREAD
How is this conversation like others between the King and Selina?

Selina. Oh, *all* right. Will that do, then?

John (*turns on her*). No, it won't! *Nothing* will do until I FIND MY POEM!

Selina. Your poem? That bit of poetry, do you mean? Well, why couldn't you say so before?

Narrator 1. And she took it out of her pocket.

John (*exasperated*). You had it all the time!

370 **Selina.** Why *shouldn't* I? You threw it away! (*getting angry*) And a *nice* way to treat your work! A person that can't respect his work doesn't deserve to *do* any!

REREAD
How does this statement fit in with life in Workaday?

John (*backing down*). I . . . I *do* respect it, Selina. I was *sorry* I crumpled it up and threw it away. I only did . . . because *you* didn't like it.

Selina. I never said so.

John (*hopefully*). Well . . . *did* you?

Selina. It was all right.

380 **John** (*joyfully*). *Was* it, Selina? Oh, Selina, I've forgotten it! Read it to me!

Selina. That I shan't! Perhaps it'll teach you another time to *remember* what you write, before you throw it away!

John. Wait! I *do* remember! Listen! (*takes her hand*)

You're nicer than honey, you're kinder than doves.
You're the one sort of person that everyone loves.
I can't live without you, I cannot say less.
I've come to propose, and I hope you'll say *yes*.

390 **Selina.** (*looks uncomfortable, says nothing*)

John (*anxiously*). Wasn't that it?

Selina. More or less.

John (*softly*). Selina, say yes!

Selina. Ask me in Westwoods.

John. Westwoods?! Then do *you* go to Westwoods?

Selina. Yes, all the time! On my days off.

THINK IT THROUGH

How is King John's proposal different this time? Why?

FOCUS

What do you think will happen in Westwoods? Read on.

Narrator 1. The King and Selina set off for the fence that divided Workaday from Westwoods. They followed the slats of the fence, while Selina tapped each one and counted under her breath. When they came to the seven-hundred-and-seventy-seventh slat, Selina slipped her finger through a hole and tripped a little catch. The slat swung back like a narrow door, and Selina and the King squeezed through.

Narrator 2. The King could hardly believe his eyes. There, as before, was the barrier of branches. But the branches were living, and full of singing birds.

Narrator 1. It was easy to find a way through the flowers and leaves to what lay beyond, for Selina

400

410 led him by the hand. Instead of a gray stretch of desert sand, the greenest of plains stretched before them, filled with gay streams and waterfalls, and groves of flowering trees.

Narrator 2. Everything was bathed in radiant light, like mingled sun and moonshine.

John (*wonderingly, looking at everything but her*). Oh, Selina! Why did our parents forbid us to come here?

Selina (*in a different, lovely voice*). Because they'd forgotten, and only knew that in Westwoods there
420 is something that is dangerous to Workaday.

John. What is it?

Selina. Dreams!

John. But why did I not see all this when I came before?

Selina. Because you didn't bring anything or anyone *with* you.

> **REREAD**
> Why do Workaday citizens think dreams are dangerous?

John. And this time I've brought my poem.

Selina (*softly*). And me.

Narrator 1. The King looked at Selina for the first time
430 since they had entered Westwoods, and he saw that she was the most beautiful woman in the world.

John (*wonderingly*). Selina, are *you* a princess?

Selina. I am, always—in Westwoods.

John (*determined*). Where is my poem, Selina?

Narrator 2. She gave it to him, and he read aloud,

John.

I know you are sweeter than grassfields in June,
And bright as the single star watching the moon.
I long for my grass, and I dream of my star,
440 Though I haven't the faintest idea who you are.

Oh, Selina . . . will you marry me?

Selina. Yes—in Westwoods.

John (*exultantly*). And *out* of it, *too!*

Narrator 1. And seizing her hand, he pulled her after him, through the hedge of birds and flowers, to the other side of the fence.

John. *Now,* Selina! Will you?

Selina (*in her usual voice*). Will I *what?*

John. MARRY me, Selina!

450 **Selina.** Oh, *all* right. *(then smiles her princess smile at him)*

Narrator 2. And she did.

Narrator 1. And on the day of the wedding, the King removed for good the seven-hundred-and-seventy-seventh slat in the fence between Workaday and Westwoods,

Narrator 2. so that any child

Narrator 1. or *grownup*—

Narrator 2. could slip through,

460 **Ministers 1, 2, & 3** (*happily*). forever after!

THINK IT THROUGH

1. Why didn't Westwoods appear beautiful the first time King John went there?
2. Do you think that Selina knew all along that the King would ask her to marry him? Why?
3. Do you think Selina and John are right for each other? Why or why not?

Twists and Turns

Unit 6
Fiction

Do you like stories that surprise or shock you? The stories in Unit 6 all have an unusual twist or turn at the end that makes them hard to forget!

Fiction writing comes in many forms. In this unit, the writers use an **urban legend,** clever **short stories,** and a **horror story** to tell their tales. In each one, the story will keep you guessing. Read them all—if you dare!

The Stranger

by Sue Baugh

If you saw someone standing by
the road on a cold, rainy night,
would you stop to help?
One young man does—and gets a real surprise!

 Reading Coach CD-ROM selection

Connect to Your Life

Imagine being out alone somewhere at night. Would you be scared? Would you stop to help a stranger, or would you think only about getting home?

Key to the Urban Legend

A **legend** is a story told over and over until people believe it is true. An **urban legend** has a modern plot, characters, and setting.

Vocabulary Preview

Words to Know
clung
excuse
graveyard
headstone

A young man decides to help a stranger. Read to find out
what he learns about her.

Late one Saturday night, a young man was driving
home on a deserted stretch of road. He could hear the
rain beating against the roof of his car. His
headlights cut through a cold mist that
clung to the trees on either side of the road.
In the flashes of lightning, tree branches
seemed like ghostly hands grasping for his
car. He could feel the steady drumroll of
thunder. What a night to be out! He
10   shivered and wished he were safe at home.

clung
(klŭng)
v. held on

Suddenly, as he rounded a curve, his headlights lit up
a young woman standing by the side of the road. Her
hair and white dress were soaked from the rain. She
looked so alone. He couldn't just leave her there.

The young man skidded to a stop, then backed up
until he could see her face in the window. He leaned
over and opened the door.

"Would you like a ride?"

She nodded and he reached out his
20 hand to help her into the car. He shivered
at her touch—her hand was so cold!

REREAD
What does the
young man
notice?

She smiled at him and said, "Can you
take me home? I only live a mile away."

Now that she was sitting beside him, he could see
how beautiful she was. Dark hair framed her face, and
her eyes seemed unusually large and sad.

"Sure," he said. "You must be freezing." He
took off his letter jacket and gave it to her.

She draped the jacket around her shoulders.

30   "I'm always cold," she said, and held her
hands up to the heater.

letter jacket
jacket with a
letter for the
school name,
usually an award
for athletes

He drove ahead, and glanced at her.

"Why were you walking home?" he asked. "Did you have a fight with your boyfriend?"

She didn't answer. Instead she gazed out the window as they passed a school and a small church. He turned the corner onto a tree-lined street whose cheerful homes seemed warm and safe in the storm.

She sat up. "There's my house, the two-story one 40 on the corner."

He stopped the car next to the walk leading up to the house. He circled around to the passenger side and helped her out. Her hand still felt like ice. He walked her to the front door, wondering what it would be like to kiss her. They stood on the front porch for a moment, then suddenly she leaned over and kissed *him!* Before he could say anything, she stepped into the house and closed the door.

THINK IT THROUGH

What details about the stranger seem unusual? What one detail is mentioned several times?

FOCUS _____

Read to find out what the young man discovers the next morning.

He stood staring after her, too astonished to move. 50 Then he turned and walked slowly back to his car. It wasn't until he was behind the wheel that he remembered his letter jacket. She was still wearing it.

He looked back at the house, but it was dark, and her parents were probably asleep. He didn't want to wake them up and get her in trouble. Then he smiled. The jacket gave him the perfect excuse to see her again.

excuse

(ĭk skyoōs')
n. made-up reason

The next morning he drove back to the house and rang the bell. An older woman answered the door. She had the same dark hair and sad eyes as the girl.

"Excuse me, can I talk to your daughter?"

"My daughter?" The woman's eyes filled with tears. "Laura died a year ago last night, in a car accident. It happened about a mile from here."

The young man gasped in disbelief. "But . . . but I gave her a ride home last night! I walked her to the door, right here. I saw her go inside the house."

The woman shook her head. "That can't be. She died a year ago, young man. She's buried in the church graveyard around the corner. Go see for yourself—she's in the third row from the front."

graveyard
(grāv′ yärd′)
n. place where dead people are buried

The young man walked down the road to the church. He realized it was the same one they had driven past the night before. The small graveyard was behind the church. He found what he was looking for in the third row.

A white marble headstone was inscribed with the name *Laura.* The date of death was exactly one year and one day ago. Then he saw something that chilled his blood. There beside the headstone was his letter jacket, neatly folded on the wet grass.

headstone
(hĕd′ stōn′)
n. stone placed at the head of a grave

inscribed
(ĭn skrībd′)
carved

THINK IT THROUGH

1. What does the young man find out about the girl?
2. What detail at the end of the story is hard to explain?
3. What clues in the story hint at the surprise ending?

Cody is close to death. Even so, he knows what is going on around him. What gives him the will to live?

T O R

BY JAMES HOWE

Connect to Your Life

Think about a time when you or someone close to you was very sick. How did
the illness affect you? Did it change the
way you looked at life?

Key to the Story

The boy who tells this story is near
death. He cannot move or talk to others.
You will "see" the events in the story
through his point of view.

Vocabulary Preview

Words to Know

mysterious   concentrate
statement   exhausted

 Reading Coach CD-ROM selection

Cody is in the hospital. How sick is he? Read to find out.

I guess I do believe in miracles. I never did, but then one happened to me. See, I thought I was going to die. I don't mean to sound dramatic about it or anything, but that's the truth. Everybody else thought so, too. My mom was crying all the time, and my dad was all the time trying not to. I don't get that about guys. I mean, I was only twelve then, so I guess you could say I wasn't a man yet, but I'd learned a long time ago I shouldn't cry. Well, the way I feel about it

10 is this: If you found out your kid was going to die, it would be pretty stupid *not* to cry. Don't you think?

Anyway, I couldn't say to my dad, "Come on, let it all out, man," because I couldn't talk. Everybody else could. My relatives would come and hold my hand and say stuff like, "Lookin' good, Cody." Then they'd turn to my mom or dad, whichever one was on duty, and—keep in mind, they're still holding my hand here—they'd say, their voices all dry and cracked like old city

20 sidewalks, "I can't bear to see him lying here like this. It just breaks my heart." And then

REREAD

Do you think the visitors know that Cody hears them?

they'd put my hand back on the bed, soft as a peach they didn't want to bruise, and reach for my box of Kleenex and wipe their noses and hurry up their goodbyes, and they'd be out of there. Pretty soon, I'd be alone with my mom or dad and the sound of the IV dripping and the TV playing across the hall. And pretty soon after that, the room would start getting dark, and my mom or dad would bend over to me to

30 kiss my cheek and say, "Sweet dreams, Cody." And another day would come to an end.

When I was first in the hospital, everybody brought flowers or comic books or boxes of chocolates. But, seeing as how there was no way for me to enjoy any of these things and my mom was telling everybody she was getting fat eating all the chocolates, my visitors began showing up with nothing but sad faces. And then more time passed than anybody had figured on; it seemed I was going to keep on living, even if I wouldn't exactly have called it that, and they all remembered they had their own lives to live.

THINK IT THROUGH
What details tell you how sick Cody is?

FOCUS
What does Cody imagine as he lies in bed?

It started getting pretty lonely. A few of my friends still came around. Max. I could always count on him coming by at least a couple of times a week. And of course my mom and dad. They were there, one or both of them, every day. But there were long stretches of time when it was just me and the ceiling. Now here's the amazing thing about that ceiling—and this is important, even though I know it's going to sound crazy: I got to thinking that that ceiling was a place. You know, a real place you could go to. In your mind, anyway. It was made up of acoustical tiles; you know the kind, those squares with all the little holes and jig-jaggy lines in them. Well, if you've got nothing else to look at all day long, you'd be surprised

acoustical tiles
(ə koo′ stĭ kəl tīlz′)
tiles designed to deaden sound

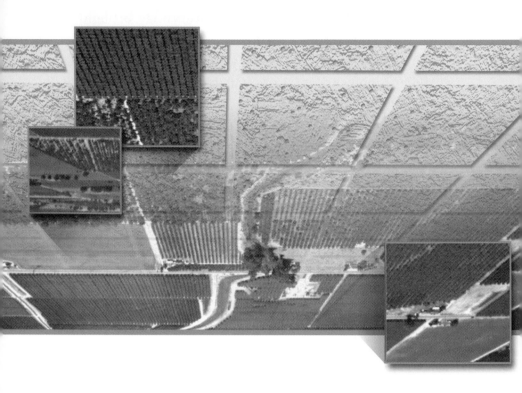

how much you can see in all those little holes and jigs
and jags. Rivers and lakes. Hills and valleys.
Highways. Back roads. After a while, I started
60 dividing up the whole ceiling (or the part of it I could
see, anyway; I couldn't move my head unless
somebody moved it for me) into villages and cities. I
called all of it the Land Above.

Pretty soon I was telling myself stories about the
people who lived in the Land Above. The funny thing
is, I never gave them names. I don't know why. I've
always liked to write stories, and one of my favorite
parts is coming up with the characters' names. But for
some reason I imagined these people right down to
70 their moles, but I never knew what to call them.

There was one person who lived in the Land Above I need to tell you about. He was old. And he was very strong—not strong like a weight lifter but solid strong, like an oak tree. And strong in his heart and mind. He was the one all the other people looked up to, the one they turned to when they were in trouble. He never spoke until he'd thought a long time, and then he always knew just the right words to say. His face was kind but as full of holes and jig-jaggy lines as that ceiling. Sometimes at the end of the day, before the nurses had gotten around to turning on the overheads and the light in the room was pale and sleepy, I could make out his face on the third tile down, two to the left. I decided that's where he lived. Third tile down, two to the left.

REREAD

What details help you picture the old man?

Nobody knew about the Land Above but me, of course. Nobody knew I had company even when I was alone. I guess to everyone else I was a sad case. Now that I think of it, I guess I was.

THINK IT THROUGH

What is the Land Above? Why do you suppose Cody made up this place?

FOCUS

Cody has a new visitor—Victor. Find out how Victor helps Cody.

Then one night long after my parents had kissed me and wished me sweet dreams, after their footsteps had carried them away from me and the elevator's *ting* had signaled that they were on their way back to what was left of the other parts of their lives, just as I was drifting near sleep, I heard a voice say, "Don't get many visitors anymore, do you?"

It was a man's voice, soft and deep as a forest, and as mysterious as one, too,
100 because I couldn't see him. He was somewhere to my right. I heard a chair scrape across the floor. He was sitting down, I figured.

mysterious
(mĭ stîr′ ē əs)
adj. unable to be explained

"The name's Victor," he told me. "Hope you don't mind if I keep you company."

He had no way of knowing if I minded or not. If I'd had the voice to say so I probably would have told him I wanted to be alone. But the truth was, I was glad he was there.

110 I don't know why Victor started coming to visit me. He never let me see his face, and sometimes he didn't even talk. But just knowing he was sitting there made me feel good, and when he did talk, his words were like warm bathwater to me. I'm sounding crazy again. But if you think about it, you'll get what I mean. My life was like one big ache, and the sound of Victor's voice was the only thing that made the ache go away.

ache
(āk)
steady pain

THINK IT THROUGH
What is one thing Victor does for Cody?

FOCUS
Victor helps Cody in another way too. What does Victor do?

It wasn't just the sound, though; it was the stories
120 he told me. They were all about me. Well, not about me really. They were stories he made up about

someone named Cody. In some of the stories Cody was thirteen, which was what I was going to be in a couple of months if I lived that long, and he'd be doing neat stuff like exploring caves or riding the waves on his surfboard or building his own camera.

In the other stories, Cody was older. He told me about the time Cody learned to drive a car and the time he scored the winning points for his varsity
130 basketball team and the first time he fell in love. I don't know if it showed on my face, but that last one had me blushing inside.

Victor told me stories about Cody and his kids and even his grandchildren. It was weird; when Victor wasn't around, I had trouble believing I'd make it to my thirteenth birthday, but listening to him talk, I could honestly picture myself as an eighty-year-old man.

> **REREAD**
> How is Cody's way of thinking about life changing?

My favorite story was the one about the time Cody
140 went mountain climbing. That's something I always wanted to do. Victor must have taken two hours to tell me that story. He made it so real, I felt the rope burning the palms of my hands and got dizzy imagining the sheer wall of rock above me. When Cody reached the top, I felt my own heart pounding inside my chest as if it was bursting to get out.

150 Victor didn't usually say anything after he'd finished telling a story, but that night he did. "Someday you'll climb a mountain like that," he told me, "and you'll be surprised how

much easier it's going to be than the mountain you're climbing right now."

I didn't understand what he meant then. It wasn't until after my thirteenth birthday that it made sense.

THINK IT THROUGH
How does Victor offer Cody hope?

FOCUS ———————
Read to find out about Cody's mysterious birthday gift.

160   I got a whole bunch of presents for my birthday. Max stayed late and opened all of them while my mother wrote down who they were from. Max kept saying things like, "Hey, cool tape," or "Cody'll really like this shirt." And my mom would comment on how nice it was of this person or that person to remember me. My dad didn't say a word until they were all through, and then he said what I'd been thinking all along, "How in the heck do people think Cody's going to use any of this stuff?" And then I could hear some sniffling, and my
170 dad's voice changed, and I heard him say, "I'm sorry, Max. People mean well, but it was crazy to give Cody all this. Why don't you take it home with you?" And that was when Max really let loose and my mom, too, and they had themselves a good cry. But not my dad. I could hear his silence loudest of all.

REREAD
How is Cody's dad dealing with his son's illness?

After a while the room got quiet again, and I heard my mom say, "Now where did that come from? I didn't see anyone bring that one in, did you, Brad?"
180 And my father said, "Sure is big." "And so beautifully wrapped," my mother added. "Someone

must have left it here before we arrived. Why, it's so light."

"Is there a card?" asked Max.

There was a moment's silence. My mom was looking, I guess. "No," she said. But I was sure I knew who it was from.

Then came the sound of paper being rustled and torn, and suddenly the air in the room changed. You know how it is when you've been having a good time with a bunch of your friends and everybody's laughing and all of a sudden somebody says something really mean and stupid and everybody stops talking and you can feel the air change. *Really* feel it. That's what I felt, but I didn't know why.

Until my father said, "Of all the cruel—"

"It's probably a mistake," said my mother.

My dad said, "The box is empty, Joan. This is no mistake. It's a trick, or maybe somebody's trying to make some kind of statement."

"Statement?" my mother asked. "I don't understand."

"Who knows?" My dad's voice was going up the scale. It rises when he gets angry, like mercury in a thermometer that's heating up and you wonder if it's going to blow out the top. "'Empty life.' 'Nothing to live for.' Who knows?"

"Well, we'll just ask at the desk if any of the nurses saw anyone leave this and if not, if not . . ." My mother's voice faded away, the way I'd heard it do so often in the past few months.

"I say we throw it out," my father snapped.

"Can't we just leave everything in the closet tonight?" Max asked. "Maybe there's a reason—"

> **statement**
> (stāt′ mənt)
> *n.* message presented through a sign or a symbol

190

200

210

"Yes, yes, all right." My father's voice was loud but as empty inside as the mysterious birthday present.

Why had Victor done it?

THINK IT THROUGH

How do Cody's family and Max react to the empty box? Why?

FOCUS

Read to discover why Victor gave Cody the box.

That's what I kept asking myself all night. When
220 he came and sat down next to me, he never said a
word about it. Never said, "Hope you liked my
present," or anything. But then if he'd meant to give
me an empty box what *would* he say? "Hope you
liked the big fat nothing I gave you for your
birthday"?

I don't remember anything Victor did say that
night. I'm pretty sure he told me a Cody
story, but who could concentrate? All I
could think about was the empty box.
230 And the more I thought about it, the
madder I got. My dad had been right, it
was cruel. The problem was, I just couldn't picture
Victor being cruel. He must have had a reason.

concentrate
(kŏn′ sən trāt′)
v. pay close attention

His voice went on and on, but it didn't soothe me
the way it usually did. It made me want to yell at
him instead, to tell him to shut up, or to say, "Stop
talking about things that don't matter!"

Finally, he stopped talking. And then, in a voice so
soft I might have been dreaming it, he said, "Happy
240 birthday, Cody."

All I could think about was the empty box. And the more I thought about it, the madder I got. My dad had been right, it was cruel.

It's hard to describe what happened next. You'd have to have been inside my life then—my life of faceless Victor and his nighttime visits, and a ceiling full of nameless companions, and a closet full of useless birthday presents, and an empty box—to understand what it was like to feel myself straining upward, using every muscle to climb up out of the darkness I'd been living in, up to the Land Above, up to the top of the mountain, up to Victor.

REREAD
Cody wants to live. What phrases tell you this?

250

I wasn't moving at all, of course—at least, not that anyone outside me could see. But inside me, well, inside me everything was in motion, everything was working to make one little word come out of my mouth.

"Why?"

It took a long time before Victor whispered, "Good for you, boy."

I forced the word out of me again: "Why?"

260   I felt his hand on mine, for the first—and, as it turned out, the last—time ever. "Well, the way I figure it," he said, "you'll be needing a box to take your things home in."

I don't remember what happened after that. I fell exhausted into a deep sleep. I dreamed that night about the Land Above. Everyone was packing as if they were going somewhere, but when I asked where, they didn't answer. They just kept saying, "It's 270 time to move on." Only the old man was staying, and he wouldn't speak at all. I tried to get him to talk, but it was no use. Just before I woke up, I looked into his kind, ragged old face and said, "Goodbye, Victor."

> **exhausted**
> (ĭg zôs′ tĭd)
> *adj.* extremely tired or without energy

THINK IT THROUGH

Why did Victor give Cody the gift of an empty box?

FOCUS

Read on to find out what happens the next day.

The next afternoon, both my parents came. They hardly talked. When they did, their voices were like autumn leaves, dry and dusty and old. Later, Max stopped by.

"Please," I heard my dad say to him, "take this stuff, Max. Cody would want you to have it."

280 "What about the box?" Max asked.

"Oh, that. We'll throw it away."

That's when the feeling came over me again. I began climbing, pulling myself up. It was a little easier this time, rising, reaching for a single word: "No."

I heard my mother gasp, and Max yelled, "Cody!" They all ran to me. I saw their faces. My father's tears fell on me, rain bringing me to life again.

> **REREAD**
> What changes are taking place in Cody and his father?

I never did find out for sure who Victor was. The nurses said there was an old man who walked the halls at night. His name wasn't Victor, though. And he died a couple of days after my thirteenth birthday. Whoever Victor was, he was good at miracles. And he sure knew a lot about me. He knew I'd explore caves and climb mountains. He knew I'd grow up and grow old. And he knew what I needed more than anything for my thirteenth birthday was an empty box to fill.

THINK IT THROUGH

1. What happened after Victor's last visit?
2. What "miracle" did Victor perform? How did he do it?
3. Who gave up on Cody? Who didn't?
4. Do you think Victor was a real person? Find proof to support your opinion.

A MAN, A CELL, AND ONLY ONE WAY OUT. THE CLOCK IS TICKING. IS THE MAN SMART ENOUGH TO ESCAPE BEFORE TIME RUNS OUT?

BY MARTIN RAIM

CAGE

Connect to Your Life

Think about how you judge people's mental powers. What kind of test might you create to measure how smart a person is? How would it work? Discuss your ideas with a partner.

Key to the Story

Every plot involves a problem, or **conflict**. In this story, the problem is stated in the first four paragraphs. Read to see if the man can solve the problem.

Vocabulary Preview

Words to Know

shield	riveted
cleverness	sidetrack

 Reading Coach CD-ROM selection

There was no way out.

The walls of his cell were built of thick cement blocks. The huge door was made of steel. The floor and ceiling were made of concrete, and there were no windows. The only light came from a light bulb that was covered by a metal shield.

There was no way out, or so it seemed to him.

He had volunteered to be part of a
10 scientific experiment and had been put in the cell to test the cleverness of the human mind. The cell was empty, and he was not allowed to take anything into it. But he had been told that there was *one* way to escape from the cell, and he had three hours to find it.

shield
(shēld) *n.* something that guards or protects

cleverness
(klĕv′ ər nĭs) *n.* brightness, smartness, or quick-wittedness

THINK IT THROUGH

Which sentence tells the purpose of the experiment? What does the man have to do?

FOCUS

Find out what steps the man takes to escape from the cell.

He began with the door. It stood before him, huge and gray. The three large hinges on the door were riveted into the wall and could
20 not be removed. The door itself seemed too big for the small cell, and for a minute he wondered if it had been put up first and the rest of the cell built around it.

riveted
(rĭv′ ĭ tĭd) *v.* fastened firmly; past tense of *rivet*

Finally he turned away from the door and looked around. He tried pushing against the cement blocks to see if any of them were loose. He searched the floor for a trap door. Then he glanced up at the ceiling. The shield! The shield around the light bulb! His mind raced. The metal shield could be used as a tool—the tool he needed! He had found the way to escape!

He moved under the shield and looked closely at it. One good strong pull would free it, he decided. He reached up, grabbed hold of it, and pulled. But the shield stayed attached to the ceiling. He grabbed the shield again, twisting it as he pulled. He felt it rip free, and he fell to the floor clutching his treasure.

The shield was shaped like a cone and had been fastened to the ceiling by three long metal prongs. These prongs were sharp. But they were not strong enough to cut through steel or concrete or cement.

prongs
(prôngz)
long, pointed metal clips that hold the shield to the ceiling

He felt a hopelessness creep over him. He could find no use for the shield as a tool. The shield was not what he needed to get out.

Then he had a brilliant idea. True, the metal prongs of the shield could not cut through the steel door or the concrete floor or the cement blocks in the wall. But the prongs might be strong enough to dig out the mortar that held the cement blocks in place. He pulled off one of the prongs and scraped hard at the mortar. The mortar crumbled into powder. His idea worked! If he removed enough mortar, he could loosen a couple of the cement blocks, then push them out, and escape!

REREAD
What did the man finally find to help him?

He selected two blocks near the door and set to work. The prong dug into the mortar and sent it flying out in a steady stream. The prong was just what he had needed. Now he was sure he would escape. But his hand made a sudden careless twist, 60 and the metal prong broke into two useless pieces.

THINK IT THROUGH
How good is the man's plan for escaping from the cell? Explain your answer.

FOCUS
What will happen next? Notice how the man's attitude changes as he tries to correct his mistakes.

At first a wave of anger stunned him. Then he remembered that the shield had two more prongs. He pulled off another prong and went back to work. He decided he must be more careful—nothing must go wrong. There was still plenty of time left.

Soon he had chipped out four inches of mortar. But the jagged edges of the cement blocks had torn the skin off his knuckles. His hands were bleeding from a dozen burning cuts. His back and shoulders hurt from 70 the strain of working in one position. The mortar dust blew into his eyes and down his throat. The work dragged on, slower and slower.

Suddenly the second prong broke.

For a minute he welcomed the excuse to stop working. But the thought of failure sent him back into action. He pulled off the third and last prong and went to work again. He was a man who did not like to lose—he had to win.

REREAD
What does this explain about the man's personality?

80 The work dragged on. He became numb to the pain in his hands, to the ache in his shoulders. His fingers

moved blindly, and his attack against the mortar grew weaker and weaker.

At last he broke through. He had dug out enough mortar so that now he could see light between the cement blocks.

With a spurt of new energy he chipped away at the rest of the mortar. Of course there was a way out. He had found it, hadn't he? He had proved that a clever mind could solve any problem. That's how he had done it—with his own cleverness.

90

THINK IT THROUGH

How did the man react each time a prong broke? Why does the man still think he will win?

FOCUS

Read to find out if the man succeeds in getting out in time.

At that instant the third prong snapped in his hand.

He stared at the useless pieces. Then in a blind rage he slammed his fist against the wall.

blind rage

(blīnd rāj)
anger so strong that it stops a person from thinking clearly

Behind him the door of the cell opened slowly. His time had run out. His part in the experiment was over.

He was not allowed to talk about the experiment or
100 about his plan of escape. However, he was sure that he could have escaped. He was convinced that he almost *had*.

Actually, he had not even come close.

The shield had been put around the light bulb only as a shade for the light. The metal prongs were not meant to be used as a tool.

The man had been clever, but he had let his cleverness sidetrack him. If he had not been so quick to use the shield as a tool, if he had not spent all his time chipping out the mortar, and if he had not stopped searching the cell, he might have found the real way out. He might have discovered that he could have left the cell as easily as he had entered.

For the huge door had never been locked.

sidetrack
(sīd′ trăk′)
v. turn away from the main goal

THINK IT THROUGH

1. How close did the man come to escaping in time? Find the details that tell you this.
2. Based on this experiment, how clever do you think the man was? Give evidence to support your answer.
3. Why do you think the man never tried to open the door? What is the writer saying about how people think?

The JIGSAW PUZZLE

by J. B. Stamper

What's so scary about a puzzle? Nothing, unless— like Lisa— you find the strangest jigsaw puzzle in the world.

Connect to Your Life

Have you ever had a game or puzzle that you couldn't stop playing—even when you wanted to? How did that make you feel?

Key to the Horror Story

In a **horror story,** the characters are put in danger by a person or an unknown power. The power can live in anything, even a simple game. Step by step, the characters become more trapped and afraid. Will they survive? Maybe . . . maybe not!

Vocabulary Preview

Words to Know

intrigued   resemblance
accumulated   unmistakable
coincidence

 Reading Coach CD-ROM selection

The Jigsaw Puzzle **197**

Read about what Lisa finds in an old junk shop.

It was on the top shelf of an old bookcase, covered with dust and barely visible. Lisa decided she had to find out what it was. Of all the things in the old junk shop, it aroused her curiosity most. She had looked through old books, prints, and postcards for hours. Nothing had caught her interest. Now the old box, high and out of reach, intrigued her.

intrigued
(ĭn trēgd′)
v. made curious; past tense of *intrigue*

She looked around for the old man who ran the store. But he had gone into the back
10 room. She saw a stepladder across the room and brought it over to the bookcase. It shook on the uneven floorboards as she climbed to the top step.

Lisa patted her hand along the surface of the top shelf, trying to find the box. The dirt was thick and gritty on the board. Then she touched the box. It was made of cardboard. The cardboard was cold and soft from being in the damp room for such a long time. She lifted the box down slowly, trying to steady her balance on the stepladder.
20 As the side of the box reached her eye level, she could read the words:

500 PIECES

She set the box down on top of the stepladder and climbed down a few steps. Then she blew away some of the dust that had accumulated on the lid. It billowed up around her with a musty, dead odor. But now she could make out a few more words on top of the box:

accumulated
(ə kyōōm′ yə lā′ tĭd)
v. piled up; past tense of *accumulate*

THE STRANGEST
JIGSAW PUZZLE
IN THE WORLD

30

There were other words underneath that, but they had been rubbed off the cardboard lid. The big picture on the cover had been curiously damaged. Lisa could make out areas of light and dark. It looked as though the scene might be in a room. But most of the picture had been scratched off the cardboard box, probably by a sharp instrument.

THINK IT THROUGH
What details show that the puzzle is strange or unusual?

FOCUS
Find out what Lisa discovers about the puzzle's pieces.

40   The mysterious nature of the jigsaw puzzle made it even more appealing to Lisa. She decided she would buy it. The lid was taped down securely; that probably meant that all the pieces would be there. As she carefully climbed down the stepladder, holding the box in both hands, Lisa smiled to herself. It was quite a find, just the sort of thing she had always hoped to discover while rummaging through secondhand stores.

> **rummaging**
> (rŭm′ ĭ jĭng)
> looking for something

Mr. Tuborg, the owner of the store, came
50 out of the back room as she was walking up to his sales desk. He looked curiously at the box when Lisa set it down.

"And where did you find that?" he asked her.

Lisa pointed to where she had set up the stepladder. "It was on top of that bookcase. You could barely see it from the floor."

"Well, I've never seen it before, that's for sure," Mr. Tuborg said. "Can't imagine how you found it."

Lisa was more pleased than ever about her find. She felt as though the puzzle had been hiding up there, waiting for her to discover it. She paid Mr. Tuborg the twenty-five cents he asked for the puzzle and then wrapped it carefully in the newspapers he gave her to take it home in.

> **REREAD**
> What is unusual about Lisa's find?

It was late on a Saturday afternoon. Lisa lived alone in a small room in an old apartment house. She had no plans for Saturday night. Now she decided to spend the whole evening working on the puzzle. She stopped at a delicatessen and bought some meat, bread, and cheese for sandwiches. She would eat while she put the puzzle together.

> **delicatessen**
> (dĕl' ĭ kə tĕs' ən)
> shop where sandwiches and other prepared foods are sold

As soon as she had climbed the flight of stairs to her room and put away the groceries, Lisa cleaned off the big table in the center of the room. She set the box down on it.

THE STRANGEST JIGSAW PUZZLE IN THE WORLD

Lisa read the words again. She wondered what they could mean. How strange could a jigsaw puzzle be?

The tape that held the lid down was still strong. Lisa got out a kitchen knife to slice through it. When she lifted the cover off the box, a musty smell came from inside. But the jigsaw pieces all looked in good condition. Lisa picked one up. The color was faded, but the picture was clear. She could see the shape of a finger in the piece. It looked like a woman's finger.

90 Lisa sat down and started to lay out the pieces, top side up, on the large table. As she took them from the box, she sorted out the flat-edged pieces from the inside pieces. Every so often, she would recognize something in one of the pieces. She saw some blonde hair, a window pane, and a small vase. There was a lot of wood texture in the pieces, plus what looked like wallpaper. Lisa noticed that the wallpaper in the puzzle looked a lot like the wallpaper in her own room. She wondered if her wallpaper was as old as the jigsaw puzzle.

100 It would be an incredible coincidence, but it could be the same.

coincidence
(cō ĭn′ sĭ dəns)
n. accidental happening where two events occur at the same time

THINK IT THROUGH
What strange details does Lisa see in the puzzle?

FOCUS
Find out what else the "strangest puzzle" shows.

By the time Lisa had all the pieces laid out on the table, it was 6:30. She got up and made herself a sandwich. Already, her back was beginning to hurt a little from leaning over the table. But she couldn't stay away from the puzzle. She went back to the table and set her sandwich down beside her. It was always like that when she did jigsaws. Once she started, she couldn't stop until

110 the puzzle was all put together.

REREAD
How does Lisa feel about jigsaw puzzles?

She began to sort out the edge pieces according to their coloring. There were dark brown pieces, whitish pieces, the wallpaper pieces, and some pieces that seemed to be like glass—perhaps a window. As she slowly ate her sandwich, Lisa pieced together the border. When she was finished, she knew she had been right about the setting of the picture when she had first

120 seen the puzzle. It was a room. One side of the border was wallpaper. Lisa decided to fill that in first. She was curious about its resemblance to her own wallpaper.

resemblance
(rĭ zĕm′ bləns)
n. likeness in appearance

She gathered all the pieces together that had the blue and lilac flowered design. As she fit the pieces together, it became clear that the wallpaper in the puzzle was identical to the wallpaper in her room. Lisa glanced back and forth between the puzzle and her wall. It was an exact match.

THINK IT THROUGH
What in the puzzle surprises Lisa?

FOCUS
Why does Lisa begin to feel uneasy?

130 By now it was 8:30. Lisa leaned back in her chair. Her back was stiff. She looked over at her window. The night was black outside. Lisa got up and walked over to the window. Suddenly, she felt uneasy, alone in the apartment. She pulled the white shade over the window.

She paced around the room once, trying to think of something else she might do than finish the puzzle. But nothing else interested her. She went back and sat down at the table.

140 Next she started to fill in the lower right-hand corner. There was a rug and then a chair. This part of the puzzle was very dark. Lisa noticed uneasily that the chair was the same shape as one sitting in the corner of her room. But the colors didn't seem exactly the same. Her chair was maroon. The one in the puzzle was in the shadows and seemed almost black.

maroon
(mə rōōn')
dark reddish brown

Lisa continued to fill in the border toward the middle. There was more wallpaper to
150 finish on top. The left-hand side did turn out to be a window. Through it, a half moon hung in a dark sky. But it was the bottom of the puzzle that began to bother Lisa. As the pieces fell into place, she saw a picture of a pair of legs, crossed underneath a table. They were the legs of a young woman. Lisa reached down and ran her hand along one of her legs. Suddenly, she had felt as though something was crawling up it, but it must have been her imagination.

REREAD
What happens when Lisa touches her own leg?

160 She stared down at the puzzle. It was almost three quarters done. Only the middle remained. Lisa glanced at the lid to the puzzle box:

THE STRANGEST JIGSAW . . .

She shuddered.

Lisa leaned back in her chair again. Her back
170 ached. Her neck muscles were tense and strained.
She thought about quitting the puzzle. It scared her
now.

THINK IT THROUGH
What about the puzzle bothers Lisa?

FOCUS
How do you think the final puzzle will look? Read to see if
you are right.

She stood up and stretched. Then she looked down
at the puzzle on the table. It looked different from the
higher angle. Lisa was shocked by what she saw. Her
body began to tremble all over.

It was unmistakable—the picture in the
puzzle was of her own room. The window
was placed correctly in relation to the
180 table. The bookcase stood in its exact spot against the
wall. Even the carved table legs were the same . . .

unmistakable
(ŭn′ mĭ stā′ kə bəl)
adj. very clear

Lisa raised her hand to knock the pieces of the
puzzle apart. She didn't want to finish the strangest
jigsaw puzzle in the world; she didn't want to find out
what the hole in the middle of the puzzle might turn
out to be.

But then she lowered her hand. Perhaps it was
worse not to know. Perhaps it was worse to wait
and wonder.

190 Lisa sank back down into the chair at the
table. She fought off the fear that crept into
the sore muscles of her back. Deliberately,

deliberately
(dĭ lĭb′ ər ĭt lē)
very carefully

piece by piece, she began to fill in the hole in the puzzle. She put together a picture of a table, on which lay a jigsaw puzzle. This puzzle inside the puzzle was finished. But Lisa couldn't make out what it showed. She pieced together the young woman who was sitting at the table—the young woman who was herself. As she filled in the picture, her own body slowly filled with horror and dread. It was all there in the picture . . . the vase filled with blue cornflowers, her red cardigan sweater, the wild look of fear in her own face.

The jigsaw puzzle lay before her—finished except for two adjoining pieces. They were dark pieces, ones she hadn't been able to fit into the area of the window. Lisa looked behind her. The white blind was drawn over her window. With relief, she realized that the puzzle picture was not exactly like her room. It showed the black night behind the window pane and a moon shining in the sky.

210

REREAD

Why does Lisa feel relief?

With trembling hands, Lisa reached for the second to last piece. She dropped it into one of the empty spaces. It seemed to be half a face, but not a human face. She reached for the last piece. She pressed it into the small hole left in the picture.

The face was complete—the face in the window. It was more horrible than anything she had ever seen, or dreamed. Lisa looked at the picture of herself in the puzzle and then back to that face.

220

Then she whirled around. The blind was no longer over her window. The night showed black through the window pane. A half moon hung low in the sky.

Lisa screamed . . . the face . . . it was there, too.

THINK IT THROUGH

1. What does the finished puzzle show?
2. Why does Lisa scream at the end?
3. What strange power does the puzzle seem to have?

HOUSE FEAR

by Robert Frost

Always—I tell you this they learned—
Always at night when they returned
To the lonely house from far away
To lamps unlighted and fire gone gray,
5 They learned to rattle the lock and key
To give whatever might chance to be
Warning and time to be off in flight:
And preferring the out- to the in-door night,
They learned to leave the house-door wide
10 Until they had lit the lamp inside.

Taking Chances

Nonfiction

Taking chances can change a person for good or bad. Why do people take chances? Reading nonfiction can help you find out.

In this unit, you will read biographies and biographical sketches. A **biography** is an account of a real person's life written by someone else. A **biographical sketch** is a kind of biography. It tells about one key event in a person's life. The real people in this unit all took chances. To achieve their dreams, they also took risks. For most, but not all, the gamble paid off.

RICHARD WRIGHT

and the

LIBRARY CARD

by William Miller

Some people will do almost anything for a good book! Richard Wright, a famous American writer, proved it.

Connect to Your Life

Do you believe that words have the power to change lives? Why or why not? What power do books have for you?

Key to the Biography

Richard Wright was a famous writer. He was born near Natchez, Mississippi, in 1908. His family was very poor. Life was hard. At this time in the United States, people of color were still not allowed many basic rights.

This biographical sketch is an example of **literary nonfiction.** It is based on facts, but the writer has made up some of the dialogue and scenes.

Vocabulary Preview

Words to Know
optician   suspicious   cautiously

 Reading Coach CD-ROM selection

Richard loved the sound of words. He loved the stories his mother told about the farm where she grew up.

"There was a willow tree by a bend in the river," she explained. "I dreamed all my girl dreams down there."

Richard loved to hear his grandfather tell about the war, how he ran away from his master and fought the rebel army.

"I was only a boy," his grandfather said proudly, "but I fought as well as any man. I
10 fought in the rain and the mud. I carried the flag at the head of the troops."

> **rebel**
> (rĕb′ əl)
> soldier of the South during the Civil War

Richard longed to read stories on his own, but his family was very poor. They moved often, looking for work in different towns and cities. His father cleaned office buildings; his mother cooked in the kitchens of wealthy white people.

Richard had little chance to go to school. His mother taught him when she could, reading the funny papers out loud, sounding each
20 word carefully.

> **funny papers**
> (fŭn′ ē pā′ pərz)
> comics section of a newspaper

When Richard finally learned to read, he couldn't buy or borrow the books he wanted so badly. Books were expensive; the doors of the library were shut against him because he was black.

So Richard read whatever he could find—old newspapers, books without covers pulled from ash cans. . . .

THINK IT THROUGH

How important are books to Richard? What details show he loves reading?

FOCUS

Read about Richard's new life in Memphis. What problems does he still face?

When Richard was seventeen, he caught a bus to
Memphis. He hoped to find work, earn enough
money to move to Chicago, where he would make a
new life for himself in the North.

Richard walked the hot streets looking for a job
that would be his ticket to freedom. He saw many
young men, like himself, searching for the same job,
the same way out.

He finally found a place in an optician's
office. He polished eyeglasses, swept the
floors, and ran errands for the white men.

As long as he kept his head down, as
long as he began every sentence with "sir,"
Richard was safe.

> **optician**
> (ŏp tǐsh' ən)
> *n.* person who makes and sells eyeglasses

At night, Richard returned to the boardinghouse
where he had rented a room. To save money, he ate
beans from the can, warmed by water from the tap.

Listening to the noise of the street below his
window, Richard felt a familiar hunger for words.
There were thousands of books in the public
library, but only white
people could get a card,
could take them out.

But Richard had an idea.
At work, he looked around
the office, trying to find one
man who might understand
his hunger for books.

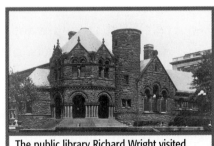

The public library Richard Wright visited

For the most part, they were like so many white
men he had known before. They would never
understand a black boy who wanted a library card, a

60 black boy who wanted to read books even they didn't read.

THINK IT THROUGH

Richard wants a library card. How do you think he might solve his problem? What details tell you this?

FOCUS _____

Read to find out how Richard solves his problem.

Only one man seemed different from the others. Jim Falk kept to himself, and the other men ignored him, as they ignored Richard. Several times, Richard had been sent to the library to check out books for him.

One day, when the other men were out to lunch, and Jim was eating alone at his desk, Richard approached him.

"I need your help," Richard said.

70 "Are you in some kind of trouble?" Jim asked with a suspicious look.

"I want to read books. I want to use the library, but I can't get a card," Richard said, hoping Jim would not laugh in his face.

> **suspicious**
> (sə spĭsh' əs)
> *adj.* distrusting or doubting

"What do you want to read?" Jim asked cautiously. "Novels, plays, history?"

Richard felt confused. His mind was racing so fast, he couldn't think of a single book.

80 Jim said nothing, but reached into his desk and brought up a worn, white card. He handed it to Richard.

> **cautiously**
> (kô' shəs lē)
> *adv.* carefully, in order to avoid danger

"How will you use it?" Jim asked.

"I'll write a note," Richard said, "like the ones you wrote when I got books for you."

"All right," Jim said nervously. "But don't tell anyone else. I don't want to get into trouble."

"No, sir," Richard promised. "I'll be careful."

After work, Richard walked through the crowded streets to the library. He felt as if he were on a train to Chicago, as if he were traveling North already.

But when Richard walked through the door, he felt the old fear again. Many heads were raised at the sight of a black boy in the library.

Richard kept his eyes down, not looking up until he stood before the check-out desk.

The librarian put on her glasses to make sure she wasn't seeing things. Richard handed her the note he had written and stepped back.

"Why can't Mr. Falk get his own books?" she asked sharply.

"He's very busy," Richard replied, his legs trembling.

"All right," the woman said. "But you tell Mr. Falk I'd rather see him in person next time."

Richard roamed the stacks, unable to believe there were this many books in the world. He touched the leather spines and fingered the pages he had dreamed about for such a long time.

"Are you sure these books aren't for you?" the librarian asked in a loud voice when he went to check them out.

Once again, heads turned and Richard felt the eyes of white people on him.

He thought he had been caught, that he would never be able to read the books he wanted so badly. But Richard told the lady what she wanted to hear, what she believed was true about all black boys like him.

> **REREAD**
> Why do you think the people in the library are acting like this?

"No ma'am," he said. "These books aren't for me.
120 Heck, I can't even read."

The librarian laughed out loud and stamped his books. Richard heard other people laugh as he walked out the door.

THINK IT THROUGH

How well did Richard's plan work? What did he have to go through to get the books?

FOCUS

How do library books change Richard's views on life?

That night, in his room, Richard read until the sun dimmed the electric light. He read the words of Dickens, Tolstoy, and Stephen Crane. He read about people who had suffered as he had, even though their skin was white. They longed for the same freedom Richard had spent his life trying to find.

130 With the light of the sun coming through the window, Richard put down the book. He felt sleepy, but the words he had read echoed in his ears, colored everything he saw. He wondered if he would act differently, if others would see how the books had changed him.

Richard knew he would never be the same again.

That morning, he carried his books to work in a newspaper. Whenever he had a chance, whenever the office was empty for a moment, he read.

Mr. Falk walked over, pretending that he was
140 asking Richard to go and pick up his laundry for him. "What'd you get?" he asked under his breath. Richard opened the newspaper and showed him.

Jim seemed shocked at first, but then a smile came over his face. "Those are powerful books, Richard,"

he said. "Those books will stay with you for the rest of your life. But for now," he said, looking around the office, "you should keep them to yourself."

Richard tried to do just that, but as the time for the journey North came closer, he didn't care who saw
150 him reading.

The men in the office either laughed at him or asked him if he was crazy: "What's a colored boy like you toting a bag full of books around for? Your head can't hold all them big words!" Every now and then, Jim smiled at him from across the room.

REREAD
What do the men's comments show about them?

The library books had changed some of Richard's feelings about white people. Richard still feared them, but he understood them better.

160 The day he left for Chicago, Richard stopped by Mr. Falk's desk.

"Thank you," Richard said. "Thank you for the books, thank you for everything. . . ." Jim didn't say a word, but he shook Richard's hand in front of everybody.

On the train going North, flying across the open fields, Richard remembered the books he had read.

The words came back to him, the stories more real than the train itself. Every page was a ticket to
170 freedom, to the place where he would always be free.

THINK IT THROUGH

1. How did the books Richard Wright read change his life?
2. How might helping Richard have changed Jim Falk? Explain.
3. Do you think reading books was worth the risk Richard Wright took? Why or why not?

El Chino

BY ALLEN SAY

How did a visit to Spain change Billy Wong into El Chino?

Connect to Your Life

Have you ever failed at something and then found something better to do? Tell a partner what happened.

Key to the Biography

Allen Say first read about Billy Wong in a newspaper article. Say thought Billy's story would make a good book. He wanted to talk with Billy, but the young man had died in a car accident. Instead, Say talked to his brothers and sisters. Then Say wrote the book *El Chino* using the first-person point of view. He uses "I" and "me" as if Billy were telling his own story.

Vocabulary Preview

Words to Know

spectacle	sensation
matadors	victorious
gore	

FOCUS _____

Read to learn what important advice Billy Wong's father gives his children.

My parents came from Canton, China, and had six children in Nogales, Arizona. I was the fourth child. They named me Bong Way Wong, but my brothers and sisters called me Billy.

Our home was a corner grocery store, and we were open for business every day
10 of the year.

The Wong children. Billy is the one holding the basketball.

"In America, you can be anything you want to be," Dad told us.

That was good news because none of us wanted to be a grocer when we grew up.

Lily, the eldest, was studying to be a librarian. Rose and Florence wanted to be teachers. My older brother, Jack, loved engineering. And Art, my baby brother, said he was going to be a doctor.

> **engineering**
> (ĕn′ jə nîr′ ĭng)
> the use of science and math to design or build useful products

20 All I wanted to do was play basketball.

"Who's ever heard of a Chinese athlete!" They laughed.

They didn't understand. I wanted to be a *great* athlete.

"Why don't you listen to Dad," I told them.

But Dad died suddenly when I was ten. Our days were dark after that, and we had to be a stronger family than we were before. We gathered around Mom and went on with our business.

THINK IT THROUGH

What does Billy learn from his father?

In high school I finally got to play serious
30 basketball. I was quick and fast, and I could shoot
from anywhere on the court. "My ace," the coach
used to call me.

But I never got to play in college. I was too short.

"Just think," I said to my brother, Jack. "Four
inches taller and I would've been famous!"

"Who's going to hire a Chinese ballplayer,
anyway?" he asked. "Learn a trade and earn a living
like everybody else."

So, like Jack, I studied engineering.

40 After college I got a job as a highway engineer. That
made everybody happy, especially Mom.

But I kept thinking about shooting the winning
basket with the clock running out.

"Give Billy the ball!" they used to yell.

And they always did. I'd spin and shoot all in
one motion, and the whole gym would explode with
my name.

"Billy! Billy! Billy!"

I never forgot that.

50 Give me the ball!

REREAD
How did Billy feel on the basketball court?

But by then I had a trade and earned a
living. For my first vacation I went to Europe. I liked
Spain best—it was hot there, like it was in
Arizona. I saw castles and museums,
cathedrals and Gypsy dancers.

Then I saw a bullfight.

cathedrals
(kə thē′ drəlz)
large churches

THINK IT THROUGH
Do you think Billy has given up his dream? Why or why not?

It's a sport where the bullfighter fools the bull with a cloth cape and kills it with a sword. Sometimes the bull kills the bullfighter. It wasn't anything like the
60 rodeo shows I'd seen back home.

The first time the bull charged the bullfighter, I closed my eyes.

"Olé!" The crowd screamed, and I paid attention.

Olé
(ō lā')
a Spanish cheer

It was a spectacle, all right, a very dangerous circus. And the bullfighter was some kind of an athlete. He was graceful, too, like a ballet dancer, and had the steadiest nerves I'd ever seen.

spectacle
(spĕk' tə kəl)
n. colorful public event

70 The bull kept missing him, and with each miss the audience yelled louder. I shouted with them, until my voice was gone.

When the fight was over, the bull was dead. And now it was the people who charged the bullfighter. Roaring at the top of their voices, they hoisted him onto their shoulders and
80 marched out of the arena. I rushed after them.

I didn't have to chase far. I even managed to stand right next to the amazing daredevil, and I got a shock. He was much shorter than me!

daredevil
(dâr' dĕv' əl)
someone who takes big chances

That night I didn't sleep. I couldn't get him to stop dancing inside my head, that short Spaniard in a fancy outfit.

REREAD
What amazes Billy about the bullfighter?

In the morning, I bought myself some Spanish
90 clothes. Then I got a room in a boarding house,
where I put away my old clothes and put on the new.
In the mirror, I looked like a fine Spanish gentleman.

Using my hands and arms, I asked the landlady,
"Where is the bullfighting school?"

"Ah, Señor." She gazed at me with great
pity in her eyes. "Only the Spaniards can
become true matadors."

She sounded like my mother. And that
reminded me to send Mom a telegram, and
100 also one to my boss. Very sorry and please
forgive, I am not coming home.

Señor
(sān yôr')
Spanish for "sir"

matadors
(măt' ə dôrz')
n. bullfighters

THINK IT THROUGH
| Why does Billy decide to stay in Spain?

FOCUS —————————————————————
| How can Billy become a matador? Read to find out what
| he does.

The school was just a clearing in a
wood outside the city, but the maestro
had been a famous matador when he was
young. We took turns playing the bull,
and the old master taught us to use the
cape and the sword.

maestro
(mīs' trō)
master of an art

"He is a good athlete," I heard one student say
about me.

110 "And he has courage and grace," said another. "But
he cannot be a matador. He is not Spanish."

My dad would've said a few things to them, but it
was no use. How could they understand? They hadn't
grown up in the United States.

Before I knew, it was springtime in Spain. That's when the bull ranchers hired student matadors to test their young cows for courage and spirit. And the students who fought well would go on to become real matadors. Like my classmates, I went looking for work.

120   Everywhere I went, though, the ranchers took one look at me and shook their heads. My family sent me love and money, and that kept me going, but after two years I still hadn't fought a single cow. Maybe it was time to give up, time to go home and be an engineer again.

But what would Dad have said to me now?

I'd tell him this wasn't Arizona, U.S.A. So I couldn't be a Spanish matador.

But *uno momento*, Señor. A Spanish
130 matador? What had I been thinking all this time?

uno momento Spanish expression meaning "wait a minute"

I'm Chinese!

I searched all over town, and finally found what I was looking for—a Chinese costume. I tried it on and hardly recognized myself in the mirror.

It was as if I were seeing myself for the first time. I looked like a *real* Chinese. And as I stared in the mirror, a strange feeling came over me. I felt
140 powerful. I felt that I could do anything I wished—even become a matador! Could it be that I was wearing a magical costume?

REREAD
Why do you think Billy feels powerful in his new clothes?

I went outside to see what would happen.

I was a spectacle.

Children followed me everywhere I went. Men greeted me from across the street. Women smiled.

"El Chino!" they shouted. The Chinese!

For the first time, people were taking notice of me,
150 and that was magic.
    It was time to go see a bull rancher.

THINK IT THROUGH
Billy almost gives up on his dream again. What changes the way he sees himself?

FOCUS
Read to learn what El Chino shows other people.

Sure enough, the first rancher I saw gave me the nod. Just like that, I was facing my first live bull.
    Actually, it was only a heifer, but it looked more like a black rhino, with horns that could gore right through me.

> **heifer**
> (hĕf′ ər)
> young cow

    "I will not back off," I said to myself, and waved the cape.
    The black hulk stood still, swishing a
160 tail like a lion's.

> **gore**
> (gôr)
> v. stab with a horn

    "*Ojo, toro-o-o!*" I called, giving the cape a good flap.
    The charge was sudden and fast.
    Like a tumbling boulder, the heifer came straight at me, and I swung the cape. At the last moment she swerved and went for the cape. *Swoosh!* With a hot wind she was past me. I spun around, flapped the cape, and she charged again. Then again.
    I didn't remember how many passes I'd
170 made before I heard the ranch hands shouting. They wanted to see how I would end the fight.

> **passes**
> (păs′ ĭz)
> uses of a cape to turn the charges of a bull

So I made her charge me one more time, and then I walked away without looking back, as I had seen real matadors do. I prayed the heifer wouldn't gore me in my back. She didn't move.

"Olé, olé!" The crowd applauded me. I'd passed the test.

The next morning a bald-headed man came
180 knocking on my door.

"I hear good things about you, Señor," he said. "I am a manager of bullfighters. Do you want me to help you become a matador?"

"Sí!" I almost shouted. "I would be honored!"

"*Bueno*. But you cannot fight in your strange costume. Come with me," he said, and took me to a tailor's shop.

There, I was fitted for the "suit of lights," which all matadors wear in
190 bullrings. I felt like a prince being groomed for an important ceremony.

> **groomed**
> (grōōmd)
> prepared

THINK IT THROUGH
Why do you think the manager wants to help El Chino?

FOCUS
How does Billy feel about his success? Read on.

And there *was* a ceremony. My manager had made an arrangement for me to fight a real bull in a month's time!

"You are a sensation," he told me. "The plaza is sold out, and it is El Chino everyone wants to see."

> **sensation**
> (sĕn sā′ shən)
> *n.* big success with the public

Finally it was my day.

In a short while my manager would be arriving
200 with a lot of reporters and photographers. I was big news. And my manager was supposed to help me get into the "suit of lights," but I couldn't wait any longer and got into it on my own.

In the mirror I looked splendid.

"Good thing you weren't four inches taller," I said to myself. "Show them you have grace and courage

like the best of them. Don't lose face , for your family's sake . . ."

As I stared in the mirror, I began to feel 210 victorious already. There had never been a Chinese matador before me. I could almost hear the sold-out plaza cheering me on. And if I fought well, maybe a crowd of Spaniards would carry me out of the arena on their shoulders, shouting my name the whole time.

And that's the way it happened. Just as I had dreamed it.

"Olé! El Chino, olé!"

Don't lose face
Chinese expression "Don't do anything to shame yourself or your family."

victorious
(vĭk tôr' ē əs)
adj. having won a game or struggle

THINK IT THROUGH

1. How did Billy feel about himself at the end?
2. Billy's brothers believed that no one wanted a short, Chinese athlete. Yet how did being short and Chinese help Billy become a matador?
3. What qualities do you think Billy had that helped him achieve his dream?

Let the Chips Fall

by Susan Pilár de la Hoz

When you go to a place to eat,
you don't expect the cook to serve food
that would make you want to leave.
One cook tried this on a
customer and got quite a surprise.

Connect to Your Life	Key to the Biography	Vocabulary Preview
Have you ever messed up something on purpose? Was the result good or bad?	Some great inventions we use every day were the result of mistakes. This biographical sketch is about a man who gets credit for an invention he wasn't trying to make.	**Words to Know** chef recipe resort restaurant

 Reading Coach CD-ROM selection

For a chef, the worst disaster is when a recipe fails. The second worst disaster is when a customer doesn't like the food. Yet thanks to a picky customer and a hot-tempered chef, we have the potato chip. The next time you bite into a chip, think about George Crum. He's the chef who invented that salty, tasty, little snack. Here's how it happened.

10   Back in 1853, Chef Crum worked at Moon Lake Lodge. This was a fancy resort in Saratoga County, New York. The resort served the richest people on the East Coast. They acted like kings and queens. They wanted things done their way and only their way.

Crum, who was part Native American and part African American, was proud of his cooking. He also had a temper like a volcano. If someone didn't like his
20   food, he didn't just give them something else. He would make something so awful that the person might even get up and leave the lodge.

Like many chefs, he offered French fries as part of the menu. People had loved French fries ever since Thomas Jefferson's day. Mr. Jefferson had brought the recipe back from France.

One day, an important customer came into Moon Lake Lodge to eat. Some people say it was Cornelius "Commodore"
30   Vanderbilt, a famous millionaire. He tasted Chef Crum's French fries and frowned. To

chef
(shĕf)
n. cook

recipe
(rĕs′ ə pē′)
n. directions for making a certain food

resort
(rĭ zôrt′)
n. place people go to have fun and relax

Chef George Crum

him the fries were like sponges—not crunchy enough.
He sent them back to the kitchen.

Chef Crum's temper was heating up. *Not crunchy
enough? We'll see about that.* The chef cooked another
batch of fries and sent them out to Vanderbilt.

The Commodore tasted one, and then shook his
head. The fries still weren't crunchy enough. Back
they went to the kitchen.

40   When Chef Crum saw the plate, he finally exploded.
I'll show that Vanderbilt a thing or two! He sliced
another batch of potatoes as thin as paper. You could
almost see through each slice. He fried the potatoes
until they were golden and crispy. You couldn't eat
these fries with a fork—they would break. Crum was
sure that Vanderbilt would hate them.

The Commodore loved the paper-thin chips. He ate
every one and asked for another batch, and then
another. Without meaning to, Chef Crum had
50 invented a new snack food—the potato chip.

THINK IT THROUGH
> What does Crum do to get back at Mr. Vanderbilt? What
> happens as a result of Crum's actions?

FOCUS ———————————————
> Read to find out how Crum's potato chips become so popular.

Soon everyone at the lodge began asking for these
new potato chips. At first, Chef Crum called them
"potato crunches." After a while, they showed up on
the menu as "Saratoga Chips."

The chef's "disaster" turned out to be one
of the best things that ever happened to him.
When Crum opened his own restaurant, he

> **restaurant**
> (rĕs' tər ənt)
> *n.* place people
> go to eat

placed baskets of chips on each table. He even sold the chips in 60 boxes for people to take home. (By the way, some people say that Vanderbilt helped Crum open his new restaurant!)

Soon potato chips were showing up in restaurants all over the country. Then someone decided to put them in bags and sell them to grocery stores. By 1929 a new 70 fryer was invented that could fry chips by the hundreds. Now people could ship thousands of bags of chips from coast to coast.

Today, potato chips are the most popular snack food in America. They come in many flavors—cheese, barbeque, hot pepper, onion, vinegar, and 80 more. We have Chef George Crum (and maybe Vanderbilt) to thank for this crunchy snack!

Who's Got the Best Chipping Potatoes?

Where do the best "chip" potatoes come from? Not from Idaho or Maine—the country's best potato states. Believe it or not, Pennsylvania grows the number one chipping potatoes in the nation. Over 70 percent of Pennsylvania's potato crop is turned into crispy chips. Other potatoes are too small, too tough, or too much in demand for other uses.

THINK IT THROUGH

1. How did Crum's potato chips become the most popular snack food in America?
2. Should Crum and Vanderbilt share the credit for inventing potato chips? Why or why not?
3. What does this biographical sketch explain? State the main point of the sketch.

Oakland
Miami
Atlantic Ocean
Puerto Rico
Senegal
Venezuela
Brazil
SOUTH AMERICA

A desire to fly—a tragic death. What made AMELIA EARHART try to set records for flying? Why did she take such chances?

AMELIA EARHART

AMERICAN PILOT

by CARLOTTA HACKER

Connect to Your Life

Does the thought of flying an airplane excite you or scare you? Would you ever want to be a pilot?

Key to the Biography

Although Amelia Earhart was not the first woman pilot, she is probably the most famous. This **biography** tells the story of her life and of the flight that ended it. The map shows the route she took on her last flight. Amelia was trying to be the first pilot to fly around the world.

Vocabulary Preview

Words to Know

solo	navigator
venture	destination

Read for clues that show Amelia Earhart might like flying.

Early Years

"Nothing scares Amelia," her sister, Muriel, used to say. She would watch in awe as Amelia galloped past her on horseback or shot down their homemade roller coaster. Amelia loved the feeling of speed. She and her sister often played outdoors.

The Earharts lived in Kansas City, Missouri, but they often visited Atchison, Kansas, where Amelia had been born. It was her grandmother's home. Later, the family lived in several different cities. Amelia's father,
10 Edwin, worked for the railroad, and he had to live where he could get work. Sometimes he had no job at all. This made things very tough for Amelia's family.

After finishing high school, Amelia enrolled in a school in Pennsylvania, and Muriel went to Canada. By this time, World War I was in full swing. When visiting Muriel in Canada in 1917, Amelia decided to help the war effort. She signed on as a volunteer at a military hospital. There she met men from the

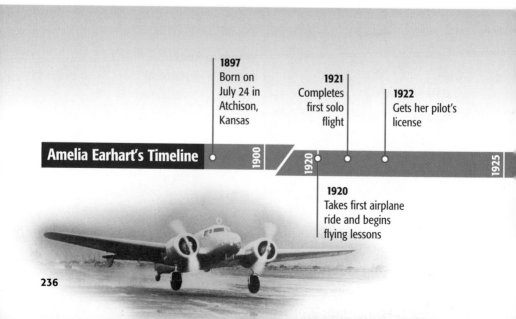

Amelia Earhart's Timeline

1897
Born on July 24 in Atchison, Kansas

1920
Takes first airplane ride and begins flying lessons

1921
Completes first solo flight

1922
Gets her pilot's license

1900   1920   1925

Royal Flying Corps . She was thrilled by
20 the stories they told. She asked if they
would take her up in a plane, but they were
not allowed.

Royal Flying Corps
Royal Canadian Air Force

THINK IT THROUGH
What facts about Amelia's early years hint that she would become a pilot?

FOCUS
Read to see what Amelia does early in her career.

Developing Skills

After the war, Amelia took a course in engine mechanics. That was an unusual subject for a woman to study in those days. However, it was a perfect course for anyone interested in airplanes. Amelia also took a medical course at Columbia University.

By this time, Amelia's parents were living in Los Angeles. She went to an air show there and had a ride

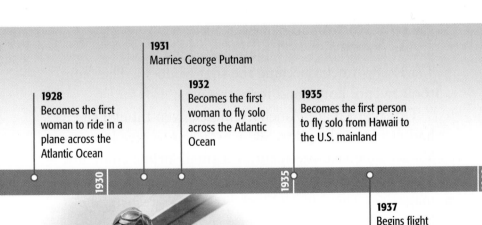

1931
Marries George Putnam

1932
Becomes the first woman to fly solo across the Atlantic Ocean

1928
Becomes the first woman to ride in a plane across the Atlantic Ocean

1935
Becomes the first person to fly solo from Hawaii to the U.S. mainland

1930   1935   1940

1937
Begins flight around the world; disappears over the Pacific Ocean

Amelia Earhart: American Pilot **237**

30 in a plane for $10. She was thrilled. It was the most exciting thing she had ever done. Amelia took a job driving a truck so that she could pay for flying lessons. Less than a year later, in June 1921, she made her first solo flight. She continued to work hard and save money. On her twenty-fifth birthday, she bought a small plane for $2,000.

solo
(sō' lō)
adj. alone

Soon after this, Amelia set her first record. She flew higher than any woman had done before—14,000
40 feet (over 4,000 meters). She also took to barnstorming at air shows, flying upside down and doing other stunts. But Amelia could not make a living this way. She had to have a job, so she became a social worker in Boston. She flew planes in her spare time and became well known as a skilled pilot.

A few years later, some people were looking for a woman to be part of the crew in a plane flying across the Atlantic Ocean. They
50 asked Amelia if she would go. "How could I refuse such a shining adventure?" she said. No woman had ever been across the Atlantic in a plane. On June 17, 1928, Amelia became the first to do so. The flight took twenty hours and forty minutes.

REREAD
What does this quote tell you about Amelia's character?

This flight made Amelia famous, even though she had not been the pilot. She was asked to give lectures. She became vice-president of a small airline company, and she wrote a column on flying for *Cosmopolitan*
60 magazine. Then, in 1932, she set a new record. She became the first woman to fly solo across the Atlantic. Amelia now felt she had earned the fame she

had gained four years earlier when she had just been a member of the crew.

THINK IT THROUGH
What did Amelia do to become famous? What records did she set?

FOCUS
Read to find out about Amelia's last flight.

Accomplishments

During the next few years, Amelia set several new records. In some cases, she was the first woman to do so. In other cases, she was the first person—man or woman. In 1935, Amelia was the first person to fly solo from Hawaii to the United States mainland.

70   Each time Amelia set a record, she was leading the way for others. She was showing how quick and convenient air travel could become. She wanted to show that it was possible to fly all the way around the world.

    Amelia could not do this long flight alone. She had three crew members with her in March 1937 when she took off from Oakland, California, heading west for Hawaii. That first leg of the journey went well, but the airplane

leg
(lĕg)
part of a journey

80 crashed when leaving Hawaii. No one was hurt, but the plane had to be sent back to the mainland for repairs.

    By the time the plane was mended, two of the crew had dropped out of the venture. As well, the winds and air currents had

venture
(vĕn' chər)
n. risky adventure

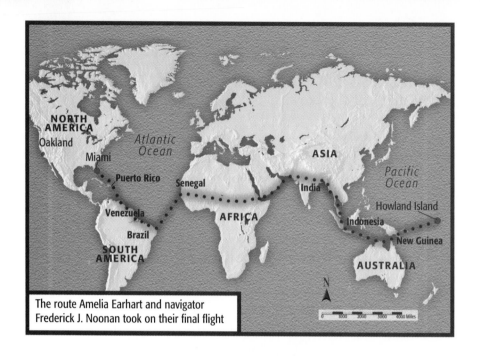

The route Amelia Earhart and navigator Frederick J. Noonan took on their final flight

changed. The best route was flying east. Thus, when Amelia finally began her world flight on June 1, 1937, she left from Miami, Florida. Her only crew member was the navigator,

90 Frederick Noonan.

> Their first stop was Puerto Rico. From there, they flew to Venezuela and Brazil before crossing the Atlantic to Africa. All went well as Amelia and Frederick made their way east, through Asia and Indonesia to Australia. By the beginning of July, they were in New Guinea, the huge island north of Australia. They had flown 22,000 miles (35,200 kilometers), about three-quarters of the way around the world.

100 Both Amelia and Frederick knew that the next leg of the journey would be the most difficult. Their destination was Howland Island, 2,500 miles (4,000 kilometers) away. Only 2 miles (3.5 kilometers) long, it is a tiny speck in the middle of the Pacific. They

navigator
(năv′ ĭ gā′ tər)
n. person who directs the course of an airplane

destination
(dĕs′ tə nā′ shən)
n. place to which one is going

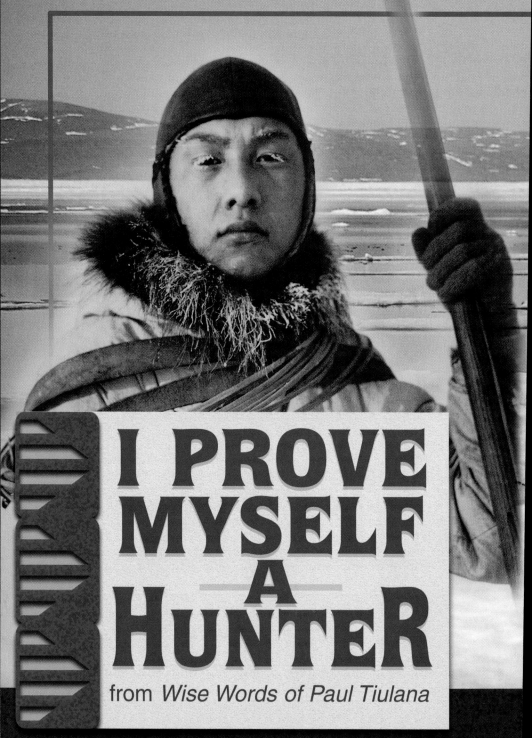

I PROVE MYSELF A HUNTER

from *Wise Words of Paul Tiulana*

as told to Vivian Senungetuk

A one-legged hunter in the Arctic? Impossible, you might say. But you don't know Paul Tiulana.

Connect to Your Life

What happens when you can't get what you really want? Do you give up or find another way to achieve your goal?

Key to the Autobiography

An **autobiography** is the story of a person's life as told by that person. It can cover many years of that person's life or focus on one special time.

In the case of Paul Tiulana, he told his story to writer Vivian Senungetuk. She helped Paul create his autobiography. In this excerpt Paul talks about a time when he almost gave up on his dream.

Vocabulary Preview

Words to Know

fracture   kayak
infection   handicapped
current

Reading Coach CD-ROM selection

Paul Tiulana is an Inupiat native who grew up in a small village near Nome, Alaska. His father was a great hunter who died when Paul was young. Paul's relatives trained him to take his father's place as a hunter and leader. When he turned 21, Paul went into the U.S. Army, where his troubles began.

FOCUS

Read to find out what happens to Paul's goal of becoming a great hunter.

I had been in the army for only one month, training in Nome, when there was an accident and I broke my leg. I was helping to unload a transport ship, moving some lumber. The sling slipped out from under some timbers and the lumber fell on me. I was put into the hospital in Nome but the doctors did not set the fracture properly and infection set in. That month the Japanese invasion started in the Aleutian Islands and the
10 doctors were trying to make room in the hospital for wounded soldiers. So they transferred quite a few patients, including me, to Barnes General Hospital in Vancouver, Washington. By this time gangrene had set into my leg. The doctors at Barnes said that if I had been sent sooner, they could have tried to save my leg, but it was too late. So they had to do three operations to amputate my leg. It was very painful.
20 I was sent to Bushnell General Hospital in Brigham City, Utah, to be fitted with a wooden leg. I was there about five months. I felt that I wanted to die. All my preparation to be a good hunter was lost. I had lost everything. I could not go out hunting on the moving

> **fracture**
> (frăk′ chər)
> *n.* break in a bone

> **infection**
> (ĭn fĕk′ shən)
> *n.* germs invading a wound

> **gangrene**
> (găng′ grēn′)
> decay of the flesh

ice any more. The Bering Sea ice moves all the time—
north, south, east, and west—and it is very dangerous.
It is a very dangerous place to be even with two legs.

After I was discharged from the army and sent back
home, my cousin made me crutches. I was disappointed,
30 angry, and depressed. The people who had a close
relationship to me said that they had lost somebody
who would have been a successful hunter. They had
tried to prepare me especially to be a polar bear
hunter. That is partly what all the running had been
for, to build my muscles to run after polar bears. And
I had lost that. I was twenty-one years old and I had
lost everything.

THINK IT THROUGH
What makes Paul feel that he has lost everything?

FOCUS
Learn what happens when Paul tries to hunt.

I decided that I would hunt anyway. What else could
I do? I made heavier crutches so that I could walk on
40 the ice. Starting out, I tried to hunt mostly on the shore
ice, because that ice does not move. I carried my rifle
and my hunting bag over my shoulders and I moved
across the shore ice using my crutches.

One day the weather was nice, the
current was not fast, and the wind was
calm. When the wind is calm, the current
is slow. I went out hunting and I got
myself a seal. I felt pretty good about it. I
had gone out into the moving ice and I had been
50 successful hunting. I started to drag the seal toward

current
(kûr′ ənt)
n. steady flow of water

the shore ice. I took a line from my hunting bag, tied it around the seal and around my waist, and headed home. I did not get very far. A lead opened up in front of me, open water, and I fell in, inside the moving ice. I could not get out. Good thing there was somebody nearby. I hollered at him and he came running and pulled me out.

Another time I went out hunting on the moving ice and I lost my rifle. I was catching a seal and I had 60 some of my equipment out near its breathing hole. My hunting bag and my rifle were some distance away. The ice cracked between me and my rifle and I could not jump over the split. I could not get my rifle. The lead was only about two or three feet wide. Anybody else could have jumped it but I could not. So I made a really long walk around the lead to try to get my hunting bag, but the ice cracked again and the rifle sank. The hunting bag was floating 70 in the water but I could not get it. It would have been saved if I had two legs. So I said to myself finally, "If I try to go out hunting on crutches, one day I will not come back. It is too dangerous."

REREAD
Why couldn't Paul jump across the split?

THINK IT THROUGH
How does having only one leg put Paul's life in danger?

FOCUS
Read to discover how Paul reacts to his problems.

So I built myself a little skin boat, about sixteen feet long. My brother's son and my brother helped me

make the wooden frame. Some of the women of the village sewed the split walrus hides to cover the frame. I thought I could hunt
80 from a skin boat more safely than on crutches. Whenever the north wind blew, I hunted in the open water on the south side of the

Skin boats are light enough for one person to handle.

village. That way I started getting more seals. I had used a kayak to hunt seals before my accident, but I could not balance myself anymore in a kayak with my wooden leg. To balance my kayak I had to lean toward one side and it was very hard on my
90 back. So I never used the kayak anymore. I used the little skin boat.

kayak
(kī′ yăk)
n. small, one-person boat

The people at King Island tried to be helpful to me. One winter my nephew, my brother, and I went out hunting on the east side of the island. We went out until we could not go out any farther because the area was closed in with ice and the skin boat could not go through. We pulled our little skin boat on top of the ice. I looked north and saw some object above the pressure ridge of ice off in the
100 distance. And above the object were two ravens flying.

pressure ridge of ice
raised line or strip on floating ice

Now when I was young, my mother used to tell me that whenever my father saw two ravens playing with something on the ice, that meant that an animal was there, maybe a fox or maybe a polar bear! I saw those two ravens go down and go up and go down and go up. I kept looking where they went down in the distance and I saw that object, and I knew it was a polar bear. I told my brother and my

110 nephew, "There is a polar bear coming toward us. Maybe we should pull our skin boat up some more so that it will not be carried away by the ice." So we pulled it up a little way from the water.

We went behind the big pressure ridges and we hid. We saw that there were three polar bears, a mother and two cubs almost the same size as the mother. Every time we looked, they

120 had come closer. They could not see us, only our skin boat. They may have thought the boat was a seal or a walrus. Finally, as they started to move away from us, we each took aim at one polar bear and we shot all three.

THINK IT THROUGH

How does Paul become a hunter again after he returns home?

FOCUS

Read to learn how other people treat Paul when he comes back from the hunt.

My mother was still alive then and when we came home she asked me, "Did you kill that polar bear, son?" I said, "Yes," and she began crying for joy. She had thought I would not be able to kill a polar bear with my wooden leg, but I managed to get one. We

130 used the meat for food and we sold the fur.

We had a polar bear dance about a week later. We gave away some food, rawhide, and furs from the animals. I was manager of the co-op store in the village then and I ordered an ice-cream maker that year, to make ice cream the white people's way. That was the first time we served ice cream at a polar bear dance. And the next day one of my close relatives said, "Paul, you should get another polar bear so that we can have more ice cream."

140   I think I hunted every type of animal at King Island—seals, walrus, polar bears, birds. I did what I had prepared for before I became handicapped. My preparation to be a good hunter was not wasted. When I started to hunt from my little skin boat, I could keep up with the other hunters. I never tried to be a great hunter but only to keep up with the others. But I proved myself to be a hunter—not a handicapped person, but a hunter.

> **handicapped**
> (hăn' dē kăpt')
> *adj.* having a physical or mental problem

THINK IT THROUGH

1. How did other people treat Paul after the polar bear hunt? What did Paul think of himself as a hunter?
2. What problems did Paul have when he tried to hunt? How did he finally succeed?
3. Paul could do other things, such as run a store. Why do you think he still wanted to hunt? Use examples from the story to support your answer.

Gail Devers

by Zoë Kashner

What does it take to become a winning athlete? Sometimes it takes more than you'd expect.

Connect to Your Life

Make a list of the athletes you most admire. What problems did they have to overcome? What helped them to succeed? Compare your list with those of your classmates.

Key to the Readers Theater

Gail Devers is a world-class Olympic runner. The author wrote the story of Devers's career in the form of a readers theater. **Readers theater** is a story that is written in the form of a play. Unlike other forms of drama, it has no stage directions. It is meant to be read aloud by different voices.

This play begins in the present and goes back to key events in Gail Devers's life. Every scene shows a different time in her life.

Vocabulary Preview

Words to Know

symptoms	antibiotics
diagnosed	determined

 Reading Coach CD-ROM selection

The play begins in the year 2000. Read to find out who Gail Devers is and what almost ended her career.

Characters

Reporter

*Narrator 1

*Narrator 2

*Gail Devers, an Olympic athlete

Coach Bob Kersee, coach of the UCLA track team

Dr. Smith, a doctor at the 1988 Olympics

Dr. Bob Forster, the UCLA sports doctor

Kid 1

Kid 2

Jackie Joyner-Kersee, an Olympic athlete, Bob Kersee's wife

Dr. Roberts, a doctor in California

*Starred characters are major roles.

Scene 1

Narrator 1. It's February of 2000. Olympic runner Gail Devers is resting after a workout. A sports reporter interviews her.

Reporter. Ms. Devers, you'll be competing in the Olympics this summer in Australia. Do you remember this picture, from your first Olympic race in 1992?

10 **Narrator 2.** The reporter shows Gail a picture of herself from 1992. She is the first person crossing the finish line in the 100-meter sprint.

Gail Devers (right) wins the 1992 Olympic 100-meter sprint.

Gail. Of course I remember. At that moment, I was the fastest woman in the world. Did you know that just a year and a half before that picture was taken, I almost had my feet amputated ?

Reporter. Tell me about it.

20 **Gail.** Well, ever since I was a kid I've loved running . . .

amputated
(ăm' pyoŏ tā' tĭd)
cut off

THINK IT THROUGH

What two things does the reporter want to learn about Gail Devers?

FOCUS

Scene 2 goes back in time to 1984. What does track coach Bob Kersee think Gail can do?

Scene 2

Narrator 1. Flashback to 1984. Gail Devers is a high school senior in Los Angeles. She has just won the state championship in the 100-meter hurdles and 100-meter sprint.

Narrator 2. Bob Kersee, a famous track coach at UCLA, is waiting for her in the stands.

Bob. Let me introduce myself. I'm Bob Kersee, the UCLA track coach. I'd like you to run for me on the varsity track team.

varsity
(vâr' sĭ tē)
school's main team

30 **Gail.** I'm on the team—just like that?

Bob. That's right, Gail—just like that.

Gail. I can't believe it!

Bob. Believe it. You're going to be in the Olympics someday! I'm going to coach you at UCLA until you get there.

Gail. Do you really think I can be in the Olympics?

Bob. Gail, you are going to be the fastest woman runner in the world someday. I just know it!

THINK IT THROUGH
How will Kersee help Gail's career?

FOCUS ————
Find out what health problems stop Gail from doing her best.

Scene 3

Narrator 1. It's 1988. Gail has been training for the
40   last four years. She has just graduated from UCLA. Her dream has come true. She's in the semifinals at the Olympics in Seoul, South Korea.

Narrator 2. But Gail is not feeling well. She doesn't make the finals. Later, she goes to the doctor.

Gail. I don't know what's wrong with me. Starting last week, my muscles have been aching and I have horrible headaches. I feel like I can barely move. But I'm not doing anything different!

Dr. Smith. You're probably just stressed out. Athletes
50   can sometimes crack under pressure.

Gail. I'm not stressed out. I was ready to win that race.

Dr. Smith. Gail, go home. You weren't ready for the Olympics.

Narrator 1. Sad and confused, Gail goes back to Los Angeles and continues training with Bob.

Scene 4

Narrator 2. Gail keeps training, but she is feeling worse and worse. When she runs, she feels like her body is falling apart. Her stomach hurts. Her head aches.

Narrator 1. One day on the track, Bob notices that Gail is stumbling.

Bob. Gail, what's wrong?

Narrator 2. He sees red patches on the skin of her arms and face. Then, he notices that her hair is falling out.

Bob. You don't look well. Are you sick?

Gail. I'm always exhausted. And I've got this problem with my hands.

Narrator 1. Gail holds out her hands. They are shaking.

Bob. This is really bad, Gail. Have you seen a doctor?

Gail. They all say different things. One doctor told me it was all in my head. But I just know there's something wrong with my body.

Narrator 2. Later, Gail runs into Dr. Forster, her old doctor from the UCLA team.

In the spring of 1988, Coach Bob Kersee times Gail Devers during a practice at UCLA.

Dr. Forster. No offense, Gail, but you look horrible!

Gail. I feel horrible. No one can figure out what's wrong with me! I'm starting to think maybe it *is* in my head—maybe I'm going crazy.

Dr. Forster. You know, you look like you've
80   got the symptoms of Graves' disease. Have you already been tested for that?

> **symptoms**
> (sĭm' təmz)
> *n.* physical or mental signs of an illness

Gail. Graves' disease? What's that?

Dr. Forster. Graves' disease damages the thyroid, a gland in the front of the neck below the voice box. The thyroid has an important role in the chemical functions in your body. All of the problems you've been having might be caused by Graves' disease.

> **REREAD**
> In your own words, describe Graves' disease.

THINK IT THROUGH

What symptoms made Dr. Forster think that Gail has Graves' disease?

FOCUS ————

Read to find out whether Gail gets help.

Scene 5

Narrator 1. Gail is diagnosed with Graves'
90   disease. Now she can finally get the treatment she needs. She starts getting radiation therapy, to kill the disease and save her body.

> **diagnosed**
> (dī' əg nōst')
> *v.* identified as having a disease; past tense of *diagnose*

Narrator 2. But the radiation treatments give her new problems. The treatments burn her hands and feet, and every inch of her skin itches constantly. Still, she keeps running.

> **radiation**
> (rā' dē ā' shən)
> treatment that exposes a patient to waves of X-ray energy

Narrator 1. Gail trains in the early morning, before anyone else is on the track. She doesn't want anyone to see her. She is so ashamed of how she looks. One day, as she leaves the track, she bumps into a couple of kids who were watching her run.

Kid 1. What's wrong with you?

Gail. What do you mean?

Kid 2. Your eyes look like they're about to pop out of your head!

Kid 1. You've got sores on your face.

Gail. I have Graves' disease.

Kid 2. Wow. I hope that never happens to me. You look gross!

Gail. Thanks a lot.

Scene 6

Narrator 2. Gail stops looking in the mirror. She feels like a monster. At the track, her friend, the famous runner and wife of Bob Kersee, Jackie Joyner-Kersee, talks to her.

Jackie. Gail, have your feet grown? What size shoes are those?

Gail. They're a men's size 12. My feet have been really swollen lately.

Jackie. Why are you still running?

Gail. You know better than anyone, Jackie. I can't stop running. It's what I live for.

Jackie. Let me see your feet.

Narrator 1. Gail takes off her shoes. Her feet are bleeding and covered with sores. Gail's white socks are stained red, and pieces of skin stick to the cotton.

Jackie. Gail, tell me you'll go to a foot doctor. I know you're getting radiation for your disease, but someone needs to look at those feet.

130 **Narrator 2.** Gail does go to the doctor. He tells her it's athlete's foot, and she should put medication on her feet.

> **athlete's foot**
> an itchy infection of the feet

Narrator 1. Two weeks pass, and Gail can barely walk. One day, she's riding a stationary bike next to the track. She feels faint and weak. Everything starts to spin around her. All of a sudden, she falls off her bike and collapses to the ground. Bob runs over to help her.

Bob. Gail, what's wrong? What happened?

140 **Gail.** I feel horrible. My feet feel like they're on fire. That athlete's foot medication isn't doing anything.

Bob. Gail—we're going to the doctor. Right now.

Narrator 2. Gail goes to another doctor. He examines her feet.

Dr. Roberts. I can't believe you waited this long to see a doctor!

Gail. I just went to the doctor. He said I had athlete's foot.

Dr. Roberts. Athlete's foot? No, you've got something
150 very serious! It's a severe reaction to the radiation therapy.

Gail. What does that mean?

Dr. Roberts. It means that if you had waited two more days to see me, I would have had to amputate these feet of yours!

Gail. No! I can't lose my feet! I need to run!

Dr. Roberts. Well, it's good you came in time. Your feet can still be treated with antibiotics .

> **antibiotics**
> (ăn′ tĭ bī ŏt′ ĭks)
> *n.* medicines that kill infections

THINK IT THROUGH

What new problems did the radiation treatments cause? What would have happened if Gail had not gotten treatment when she did?

FOCUS

How did Gail's illness change her?

Scene 7

160 **Narrator 1.** A month later, in April 1991, Gail is feeling much better. She runs without pain.

Narrator 2. By 1992, Gail is ready for the Olympics. She qualifies for the 100-meter hurdles and the 100-meter sprint.

Narrator 1. On August 1, 1992, Gail warms up for the 100-meter sprint in the Barcelona, Spain, Olympics. She is about to compete against the fastest runners in the whole world.

Jackie. Gail, remember when you wore a men's

170 size 12 shoe?

Gail. Don't remind me.

Bob. Win or lose, you know we love you. It's amazing that you came this far in a year and a half.

Narrator 2. Jackie gives Gail a hug. They both have tears in their eyes.

Jackie. You are so brave, Gail. You worked hard for this.

Gail. I'm just happy to be running.

1992 Summer Olympic Games in Barcelona, Spain Gail Devers (far right) wins the women's 100-meter finals on August 1, 1992. She crosses the finish line 0.01 second ahead of Jamaican runner Juliet Cuthbert.

Narrator 1. Gail lines up with the other world-class runners. The gun goes off.

180 **Narrator 2.** 10.82 seconds later, Gail crosses the finish line. She wins first place and becomes the fastest woman in the world.

Scene 8

Narrator 1. Flash forward to the present—February 2000. Gail has finished telling the reporter her story.

Reporter. You've been through a lot, and you're still running. You won the gold in the 100-meter sprint in 1996, too. Do you think you'll win this year in the Sydney, Australia, Olympics?

Gail. Well, I can't say I won't try! I don't wish what
190 I've been through on anyone, but I am a stronger, more determined person because of it. After conquering Graves' disease, I know there's no hurdle I can't get over.

determined
(dĭ tûr′ mĭnd) *adj.* firm in pursuing a goal

THINK IT THROUGH

1. How would you describe Gail's attitude toward life and toward her disease? Give evidence to support your answer.
2. Jackie Joyner-Kersee called Gail Devers "so brave." Do you agree? Why or why not?
3. What message do you get from Gail's story?

Editor's Note: On September 27, 2000, Gail Devers ran the 100-meter hurdles in the semifinals of the 2000 Summer Olympics in Sydney, Australia. Devers tripped over the fifth hurdle and fell due to an injury to her hamstring. The hamstring is the tendon at the back of the knee. This accident kept her out of the finals. When asked if she would ever run in the Olympics again, Gail replied, "Just because I didn't get the Olympic gold in 2000 does not mean that the other goals I have set for myself in the 100-meter hurdles won't come true. I'll just have to wait a little longer."

The Swimmer's Chant

by Carol D. Spelius

Like all athletes, the speaker in this poem wants badly to win. The race will be close. How can he beat his opponents?

Connect to Your Life

Remember a race or other tough contest in which you competed. How did you keep yourself going? Share your thoughts with a classmate.

Key to the Poem

In this poem, the speaker is competing in a swim meet. The poem expresses the speaker's thoughts and emotions as he swims his race.

This poem is called a **chant,** which is a sing-song way of speaking. Read the poem aloud. Listen for the rhythm. Find out how the speaker finishes the race.

 Reading Coach CD-ROM selection

The Swimmer's Chant

by Carol D. Spelius

Stroke. Stroke.
Time that turn.
Stroke. Stroke.
Eyes burn.
5 Save strength
for last length.
Tired body
keep that beat.
Don't dare
10 think defeat.
Ace this race.
Win this meet.
Stroke. Stroke.
Arms are dead
15 but he's ahead.
Go, legs, go.
Fly, arms, fly.
Pull. Pull.
Try, don't die.
20 Let *him* cry.

Stroke. Stroke.
Burn that turn.
Lean. Clean.
Fast last lap.
25 Stroke. Stroke.
Swim to win.
Mean it. Breathe it.
GO FOR BROKE!
Stroke! Stroke!

30 The race is over. The race is done.
The team screams, "We've won! We've won!"
I'd like to shout and jump about
but I'm . . . . all . . . . . tuckered . . . out.

THINK IT THROUGH

1. Who won the race? What details help you
   know this?
2. How does the rhythm of the speaker's chant
   help him win?
3. How is this poem's form like the swimmer's
   actions or movements?

from
BRIAN'S
RETURN

BY GARY PAULSEN

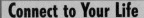

Connect to Your Life

Have you ever camped or hiked in the woods, in the mountains, or beside a lake? Does the outdoor life appeal to you? Share your thoughts with your classmates.

Key to the Novel Excerpt

A **novel** is a long work of fiction. *Brian's Return* is Gary Paulsen's fourth novel about Brian Robeson. Brian has survived a small plane crash and a freezing winter alone in the wilds of Canada.

    Brian's Return tells what happens after Brian goes home. He tries to fit in at home and at school, but he is very unhappy. In this part of the novel, Brian travels back to the woods, where he feels at peace. This is his second day in the Minnesota wilderness.

Vocabulary Preview

Words to Know

stable	collapsed
conscious	protruding
foresight	

 Reading Coach CD-ROM selection

BRIAN IS LOOKING FOR PEACE IN THE WILDERNESS, BUT HE ENDS UP IN A FIGHT FOR HIS LIFE.

Find out what steps Brian takes to make his trip safe and comfortable.

Brian awakened just after dawn, when the sun began to warm the tent. The sky was cloudless. He flipped the canoe, and when he went to lower his packs he saw the bear tracks.

One bear, medium size. It had come in the night so quietly that Brian hadn't heard it—though he had slept so soundly his first night back in the woods, the bear could have been tipping garbage cans.

10 It had done no damage. The tracks went by the fire, then moved to where he'd buried the fish leftovers. The bear had dug them up and eaten them. It had moved to the tent, apparently looked in on him, then gone to the packs. Brian could see that it had tried to stand and reach them. There were claw marks on the tree but the bear had never figured out the rope holding the packs and had gone off without doing anything destructive.

> **REREAD**
> How did Brian know what the bear had done?

"Company," Brian said. "And I didn't even wake up."

20 He slid the canoe into the water at the edge of the lake and loaded all his gear, tying everything in. He took time to gather some bits of wood and leaves to use as a smudge in a coffee can to fend off mosquitoes, then jumped in. It was still early but already warm, and he quickly stripped down to shorts.

He kept the map in its clear plastic bag jammed beneath a rope in front of him. He knelt to paddle instead of sitting on the small seat
30 because it felt more stable. He was not as confident in the canoe as he wished to be.

> **stable**
> (stā′ bəl)
> *adj.* steady

He'd taken it to a small lake near home to practice and rented canoes in other places, but he was very conscious of the fact that he had much to learn. By staying low and on his knees he had much more control.

conscious
(kŏn′ shəs)
adj. aware

He had only a mile to go in the present lake and then he would enter the river. He had the compass in one of the packs but didn't truly need it. The lakes were well drawn on the map and he could see where the river flowed out.

All that day he felt as if he were in a painting, a beautiful private diorama. He worked through a sheltered narrow lagoon and then out into the open to cross a small lake, then back under the canopy through the still water.

canopy
(kăn′ ə pē)
covering of tree leaves, like a roof

He had never had a day pass so quickly nor so beautifully and he nearly forgot that he had to find a camp and get some food before dark. He wasn't sick of boiled fish and rice yet, so in the late afternoon he took time to move back along the lily pads and drop the hook over. He caught a large sunfish immediately and took three more small ones, dropping them all over the side using a short piece of nylon rope as a stringer, running the nylon through their gills and out their mouths.

He took his time looking for a campsite and picked one on a flat area five or six feet above the surface of the lake. It was a clearing about 20 yards across. There were many such clearings, probably all made by beaver cutting down the small trees years before, allowing the grass to take over.

Brian pulled the canoe well up onto the grass and for no real reason tied a piece of line from the boat's bow to a tree.

Later he would wonder at this bit of foresight. He had not done it the night before, and since this site was higher he wouldn't have thought he'd need to secure 70 the canoe here.

foresight
(fôr′ sīt′)
n. ability to look or plan ahead

THINK IT THROUGH
What one safety step that Brian takes may be most important? Why?

FOCUS
Read to find out what happens when a storm hits. What damage will it cause?

The storm hit in the middle of the night.

It was not that there was so much wind—certainly not as much as he'd been through before with the tornado when he was first marooned in the wilderness—and not that there was so much rain, although there was a good amount of it.

It was a combination of the two.

He had cooked dinner and eaten, boiled water for the next day's canteen, pulled his packs up in a tree, 80 set up the tent and arranged his sleeping bag and weapons. Then he'd sat by the fire and written to his friend Caleb about the day in one of his journals, using tiny writing so he wouldn't waste the pages. He would have to give the letters to Caleb when he saw him again—there was no mailbox out here.

When he was done he put the book back in a plastic bag and crawled inside the tent to go to bed.

He was awakened by a new sound, a loud sound. Not thunder—it never did thunder or lightning—and 90 not the train-like roar of a tornado. This just started low, the hissing of rain driven against the tent. He snuggled back in his bag. He was in a good shelter, waterproof—let it rain.

Except that it kept coming and *kept* coming. It went from a moderate rain to a downpour and finally to an outright deluge. And with the rain came wind. Not violent, but enough to break off branches and push the rain still harder. Soon Brian found his bag wet as the
100 rain came in under the tent. He lifted the flap to look out but it was far too dark to see anything.

deluge
(dĕl′ yōōj)
flood-like storm

And it rained harder. And harder. The wind pushed stronger and still stronger and at last the tent seemed to sigh. It collapsed around him and he started rolling across the grass toward the edge of the clearing.

collapsed
(kə lăpst′)
v. fell down; past tense of *collapse*

Everything was upside down, crazy. He couldn't find the entrance and about the time he thought he had it, the tent dropped off the five-foot
110 embankment and he rolled down to the lakeshore.

He landed in a heap and felt an intense, hot pain in his left leg at the upper thigh and reached down to feel an arrow shaft protruding from his leg.

protruding
(prō trōō′ dĭng)
adj. sticking out

Great, he thought. *I've shot myself in the leg.* He hadn't, of course, but had rolled onto an arrow that had fallen out of the quiver just as the tent rolled off the embankment.

REREAD
How did Brian get an arrow in his leg?

120 He couldn't get his bearings, but he knew where his thigh was and grabbed the arrow and jerked the shaft out of his leg. There was an immediate surge of pain and he felt like passing out. He didn't, but then he

heard a strange *whump-thump* and something crashed down on his head. This time he did pass out.

He came to a few seconds later with a sore head, a sore leg, and absolutely no idea in the world what was happening to him. He was still wrapped in the tent and his bag was in his face and his bow and
130 arrows lay all around him and he seemed to be in water, almost swimming.

THINK IT THROUGH

In your own words, tell what happens to Brian after the storm wakes him up.

FOCUS

Brian is in trouble. Read to find out how he thinks through his problems.

All right, he thought, *take one thing at a time. Just one thing.*

I poked my leg with an arrow.

There. Good. I pulled the arrow out. My leg still works. It must not have been a broadhead because it didn't go in very deep. Good.

My tent collapsed. There. Another thing. I'm in a tent, and it collapsed. I just have to find the front zipper and
140 *get out and climb up the bank. Easy now, easy.*

Something hit me on the head. What? Something big that thunked. The canoe. The wind picked up the canoe, and it hit me.

There. I've poked my leg, rolled down a bank and been hit in the head with the canoe.

All simple things. All fixable things.

He fumbled around and at last found the zipper at the front of the tent, opened it and slithered out into
150 the mud on the lakeshore.

The rain was still coming down in sheets, the wind still hissing and slashing him with the water, but he had his bearings and it was not impossible to deal with things.

He dragged the tent back up the embankment onto the grass, limping as the pain in his leg hit him.

It was too dark to see much, but he could make out the shape of the canoe lying upside down. It had moved a good 10 feet from where he had left it, and 160 had he not tied it down loosely with the line it would have blown away across the lake.

He had forgotten the most important thing about living in the wilderness, the one thing he'd thought he would never forget—expect the unexpected. What you didn't think would get you, would get you. Plan on the worst and be happy when it didn't come.

REREAD
What had Brian forgotten about living in the wilderness?

But he had done one thing right: He had tied the 170 canoe to a tree. He dragged the tent to the canoe, crawled underneath and lay on the tent the rest of the night, listening to the rain, wincing with the pain in his leg and feeling stupid.

THINK IT THROUGH
How bad is Brian's situation? Why isn't it worse?

FOCUS
Finish reading the story to find out how Brian regains control of his situation. What does Brian learn from this experience?

It was a long night. The next day was a repair day both for the equipment and for himself.

Dawn was wet and dreary and it took him a full hour to find dry wood and leaves and get a decent fire going—all the time castigating himself. Had he forgotten *everything*? He hadn't made a secure camp, hadn't brought in wood so he'd have dry fire starter in the morning.

castigating
(kăs' tĭ gā' tĭng)
scolding

He limped through the woods around the campsite until he found a dead birch log with the bark still intact. Birch bark was nearly waterproof—it was what American Indians used for canoes—and beneath the bark he broke off slivers of dry wood. He took a double armful of bark and slivers back to the campsite and after three attempts—he should have needed only one match, he told himself—he at last got a sputtering flame going.

intact
(ĭn tăkt')
unhurt and in good condition

REREAD
What tips do you learn about starting a campfire?

Once the bark caught it went like paper dipped in kerosene. When the flames were going well he put on smaller pieces of the wet firewood. The flames dried the wood and started it burning, and in another half hour he had a good blaze going.

He took a moment then to examine his leg. There was a clean puncture wound not more than half an inch deep. He took some disinfectant from the first-aid kit and dabbed it on the hole, put a Band-Aid on it and then went back to work.

puncture
(pŭngk' chər)
hole made by a pointed tool

The wind had dropped and the rain had eased to a few sprinkles now and then. He saw clear holes in the clouds. He spread the gear to dry. His sleeping bag was soaked, and the tent was a sloppy mess.

He had to stay put, so he set the tent back up, this time pegging it down and using the small shovel to

210 dig a drainage ditch around the sides with a runoff ditch leading down to the lake.

The wind had tangled the packs in the tree limbs, but they were still intact. With effort, Brian lowered them to the ground.

Again he dried arrows and the quiver and checked his bow. Then he launched the canoe and took about 15 minutes to catch six good-size bluegills.

He cleaned the fish, put them on
220 to boil with a teaspoon of salt, put rice in the other pan and then suddenly found that all the work was done.

The sun was out—he could actually see steam coming up from his sleeping bag as it dried— and he lay back on the ground by the fire and went over what had happened. His leg throbbed in time with his thoughts as he learned yet
230 again: Never assume anything, expect the unexpected, be ready for everything all the time.

And finally, no matter what he *thought* would happen, nature would do what it wanted to do. He had to be part of it, part of what it was really like, not what he or some other person thought it should be like.

THINK IT THROUGH

1. Name four things Brian did to recover from his disaster.
2. What did Brian learn from this experience?
3. What qualities helped Brian survive the storm?

The Real Me

Unit 9

Poetry

In this unit about "the real me," all the poems have strong **themes,** or messages about life. The speakers are important in these poems as well. The **speaker** in a poem is the voice that talks to the reader.

Some of the poems use **rhythm,** or a regular beat, along with **rhyme**, or words that end in the same sound. Others use **free verse** to let ideas flow freely on the page. Some use **figurative language** to compare things and ideas. Poetry is all these things and more.

How can you feel happy and unhappy
at the same time?

I NEVER SAID I WASN'T DIFFICULT

by Sara Holbrook

Connect to Your Life

Have you ever felt lonely but didn't want to call a friend? What did you do? Discuss why it's sometimes hard to know what you want.

Key to the Poem

The **speaker** of a poem is the voice that talks to the reader. The speaker may be the poet, or it may be any character that the poet makes up. In this poem, look for **contrasts,** or opposites, in the speaker's feelings.

Vocabulary In line 9, **privacy** means "time alone."

 Reading Coach CD-ROM selection

I NEVER SAID I WASN'T DIFFICULT by Sara Holbrook

I never said I wasn't difficult,
I mostly want my way.
Sometimes I talk back or pout
and don't have much to say.

5 I've been known to yell, "So what,"
when I'm stepping out of bounds.
I want you there for me and yet,
I don't want you around.

I wish I had more privacy
10 and never had to be alone.
I want to run away.
I'm scared to leave my home.
I'm too tired to be responsible.
I wish that I were boss.
15 I want to blaze new trails.
I'm terrified that I'll get lost.

I wish an answer came
every time I asked you, "why?"
I wish you weren't a know-it-all.
20 Why do you question when I'm bored?
I won't be cross-examined.
I hate to be ignored.

I know,
I shuffle messages like cards,
25   some to show and some to hide.
But, if you think I'm hard to live with
you should try me on inside.

THINK IT THROUGH

1. Whom do you think the speaker of this poem is talking to? Which words or lines from the poem made you think so?
2. What does line 24 mean: "I shuffle messages like cards"? Find several examples in the poem.
3. Does the speaker know that his or her behavior upsets other people? How do you know?

PHIZZOG

by Carl Sandburg

Your phizzog is your face. Everyone has one.
Are you happy with yours?

Connect to Your Life

If you could change something about your face, would you? What would you change? Why?

Key to the Poem

 Reading Coach CD-ROM selection

A **theme** is a message that the poet wants to give you about life. This poet talks about your face, but maybe he means more than just the outside.

Vocabulary In line 2, **phizzog** comes from the word **physiognomy,** which means "your face and what it shows about your character."

PHIZZOG   by Carl Sandburg

This face you got,
This here phizzog you carry around,
You never picked it out for yourself,
    at all, at all—did you?
5 This here phizzog—somebody handed it
    to you—am I right?
Somebody said, "Here's yours, now go see
    what you can do with it."
Somebody slipped it to you and it was like
10   a package marked:
"No goods exchanged after being taken away"—
This face you got.

THINK IT THROUGH

1. In lines 3–4, what does the speaker seem to be saying about people's looks?
2. According to the poem, should anyone feel proud or ashamed of his or her looks? Why or why not?
3. Reread lines 7–8. Which does the poet think is more important: how you look or how you act? Explain.

Eastern Eskimo Song

Do most people like themselves?

 Reading Coach
CD-ROM selection

▌Connect to Your Life

Try an experiment. Ask two people to tell you what they like about their looks. How different were their answers? Did you expect those answers?

▌Key to the Poem

Sometimes a poet writes in **free verse**. Free verse does not have to rhyme. It's like conversation. When the words flow freely, so do the ideas. You will find some happy ideas flowing from this poem.

Eastern Eskimo Song

Ayii, Ayii, Ayii,
I am good looking.
My face is beautiful.
I have long shining hair.
5 My lips and cheeks are red.
And my nose between the eyes
is flat and well formed.
Ayii, Ayii.

THINK IT THROUGH

1. What is the first idea expressed in this poem?
2. What details do the other sentences use to build on that idea?
3. What does the writer of this poem think of himself or herself?
4. How does this message compare with the message in the poem "Phizzog"?

Old Snake

by Pat Mora

Even a snake knows about life. Here's a snake that gives good advice.

Connect to Your Life

Think about a time when you tried to change something about yourself. How hard was it to change? Are you glad you made the change? Why or why not?

Key to the Poem

 Reading Coach CD-ROM selection

In **figurative language,** words and phrases describe things in unusual ways. For example, you can use a **simile** to compare two things using the word *like:* "His eyes were like coals." You can also use **personification:** giving human traits to objects, animals, or ideas—like a talking snake.

Vocabulary In line 5, *Víbora* means "snake."

Old Snake   by Pat Mora

Old Snake knows.
Sometimes you feel
you just can't breathe
in your own tight skin.
5 Old *Víbora* says, "Leave
those doubts and hurts
buzzing like flies in your ears.
When you feel your frowns,
like me wriggle free
10 from *I can't, I can't.*
Leave those gray words
to dry in the sand
and dare to show
your brave self,
15 your bright true colors."

THINK IT THROUGH

1. Look at the simile in lines 6–7. How are doubts and hurts like flies?
2. What does the snake tell you to do with doubts and hurts? Why do you think the snake says "wriggle free" in line 9?
3. What advice does the snake give in lines 11–15?

APRENDER EL INGLÉS

LEARNING ENGLISH

by Luis Alberto Ambroggio

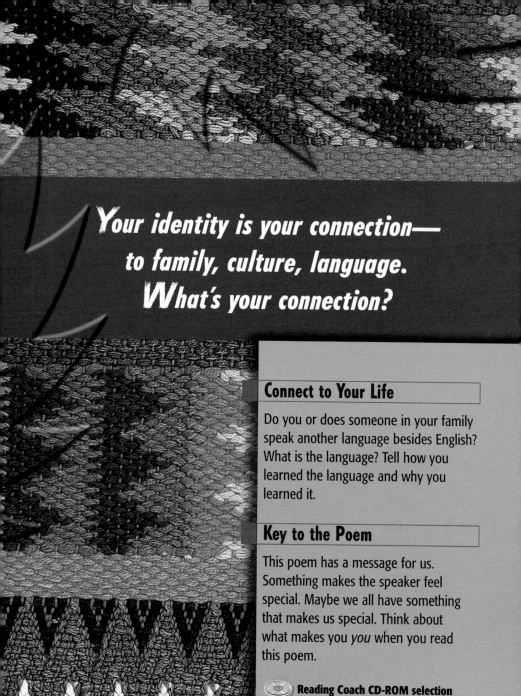

Your identity is your connection—
to family, culture, language.
What's your connection?

Connect to Your Life

Do you or does someone in your family speak another language besides English? What is the language? Tell how you learned the language and why you learned it.

Key to the Poem

This poem has a message for us. Something makes the speaker feel special. Maybe we all have something that makes us special. Think about what makes you *you* when you read this poem.

Reading Coach CD-ROM selection

APRENDER EL INGLÉS   Luis Alberto Ambroggio

Vida
para entenderme
tienes que saber español
sentirlo en la sangre de tu alma.

5   Si hablo otro lenguaje
y uso palabras distintas
para expresar sentimientos que nunca cambiarán
no sé
si seguiré siendo
10   la misma persona.

LEARNING ENGLISH   by Luis Alberto Ambroggio

Life
to understand me
you must know Spanish
feel it in the blood of your soul.

5   If I speak another language
and use different words
for feelings that will always stay the same
I don't know
if I'll continue being
10   the same person.

THINK IT THROUGH

1. What is the poet's main language? What does he fear would happen if he spoke another language?
2. What message might the poet be sending about language and heritage?
3. The poet wrote this poem in both English and Spanish. How does that fact go along with his message?

by Naomi Long Madgett

MIDWAY

When you've gone halfway, is it better to go back or to keep going forward? It depends on what's ahead.

 Reading Coach CD-ROM selection

Connect to Your Life

Have you ever tried to do something that was so hard you wanted to stop? Did you stop or keep going? Why? Were you glad you did what you did?

Key to the Poem

The **rhythm** of a poem is its beat, or its pattern of strong and weak syllables. This poet has made the rhythm stronger by repeating similar words. Read the poem aloud and listen for the beat.

Vocabulary In line 12, **destination** means "goal." In line 13, **abhor** means "dislike greatly." In line 14, **deride** means "make fun of."

MIDWAY by Naomi Long Madgett

I've come this far to freedom and I won't turn back.
I'm climbing to the highway from my old dirt track.
    I'm coming and I'm going
    And I'm stretching and I'm growing
5 And I'll reap what I've been sowing or my skin's not black.

I've prayed and slaved and waited and I've sung my song.
You've bled me and you've starved me but I've still
       grown strong.
    You've lashed me and you've treed me
    And you've everything but freed me
10 But in time you'll know you need me and it won't be long.

I've seen the daylight breaking high above the bough.
I've found my destination and I've made my vow;
    So whether you abhor me
    Or deride me or ignore me,
15 Mighty mountains loom before me and I won't stop now.

THINK IT THROUGH

1. What group of people do you think the speaker represents? What clues tell you this?
2. What is the speaker's message?
3. Reread lines 1–5 aloud. Clap your hands to the rhythm. Which words or syllables are spoken with more force?
4. What does the strong rhythm show about the speaker's feelings?

Uncommon Heroes

Nonfiction

Who is a hero to you? Is it someone who shows unusual courage? Is it a person at all? Maybe an animal is a hero to you.

In this nonfiction unit, all the heroes are real. The first and last articles are **biographies** about two heroic people. You can find more information about these people in the library or on the Internet. The second story is a **true account** of an animal's unusual bravery.

Read to find out what makes all three heroes so uncommon.

How did one man's desire for excellence help others find success?

DETERMINATION + HARD WORK = THE WAY TO

JAIME ESCALANTE:
MATH TEACHER

by Nancy Lobb

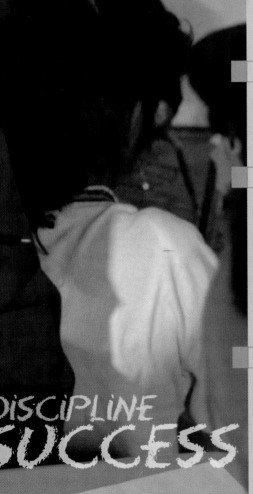

Connect to Your Life

Who was the best teacher you ever had?
What made that teacher so good? Discuss
your choice with your classmates.

Key to the Biography

Jaime Escalante (hī′ māy ĕs′ kə lăn′ tāy)
became famous for teaching hard math
courses to poor students. Escalante and
his students were written about in books,
and their story was made into the movie
Stand and Deliver. This biography tells
the story of Jaime Escalante's life.

Vocabulary Preview

Words to Know

physics	scholarship
mediocre	calculus

Escalante comes from a family of teachers. Read to discover what kind of teacher he becomes.

Jaime Escalante was born in 1930 in Bolivia. His parents were both teachers. They taught in a small Indian village.

Family life for Escalante was not happy. His father drank too much and beat his wife. When Escalante was nine years old, his mother left his father. She moved her five children to La Paz, Bolivia.

When Escalante was fourteen, his mother sent him to a private high school. In school Escalante was
10 known for his jokes. He was also a good fighter. He usually tried to get out of doing his homework. But he couldn't get enough of math and science.

Escalante finished high school. He decided to train to become a teacher.

When Escalante was in his second year of college, a local high school physics teacher died. Escalante was asked to take his place. At the same time, he kept studying to complete his teaching degree.

> **physics**
> (fĭz′ ĭks)
> *n.* science of matter and energy

20 In 1954 Escalante got a job teaching physics at his old high school. At the same time, he taught part-time at two other schools.

Escalante was a tough teacher. He assigned his students fifty to a hundred problems a night. A student who broke the rules might get another two hundred problems. He pushed all his students to their limit. His motto was, "What is mediocre is useless."

> **mediocre**
> (mē′ dē ō′ kər)
> *adj.* ordinary

> **REREAD**
> Why is Escalante so hard on his students?

30 Escalante soon became known as a great teacher. His students won many awards. But

Los Angeles, California

teachers were not well paid. Escalante had to work at three or four jobs. He decided to move his family to Los Angeles.

But Escalante was in for a shock. To teach in the United States, he would have to repeat college. California would not accept his Bolivian teaching degree. That meant four years of college and one year of graduate study before he could teach.

THINK IT THROUGH

Escalante was known as a great teacher. What shocked him when he came to Los Angeles?

FOCUS

Look for clues that tell you what kind of person Escalante is.

40   He began taking night courses at Pasadena City College. To support his family, he took a job washing floors in a restaurant. Soon, he became its chief cook.

Escalante was a good student. But it was slow going to school part-time. Then Escalante won a scholarship. Now he could go to school full-time. He got his teaching degree at the age of forty-three.

> **scholarship**
> (skŏl′ ər shĭp′)
> *n.* money awarded to a student to use for going to school

Escalante in his classroom

Escalante started to teach math at Garfield High School. This school was in the barrio of East Los Angeles. Its students came from poor families. The school was overrun with gangs. Graffiti covered the walls. Trash was all over the school grounds. Most of the students did not finish high school.

REREAD

What problems did Escalante face as a teacher in the barrio?

Escalante went to work. On Saturdays he came to school and cleaned up his room. He and some students painted. He put up posters of the L.A. Lakers.

And he set to work on his students. He pushed them hard. He decided that the math book was far too easy. He asked the principal for new books. He was told there was no money. After he threatened to quit, money was found.

Escalante looked past the background of his students. He saw many of them had a lot of ability.

He began teaching harder math courses.
Finally, he added a course in calculus .

calculus
(kăl′ kyə ləs)
n. branch of
mathematics
beyond algebra

In his first year of teaching calculus, only
five students passed the course. Everyone
70 else dropped out.

THINK IT THROUGH
What qualities do you think Escalante shows as a teacher?

FOCUS
Read to find out how good test scores become a problem for
Escalante and his students.

The story that made Escalante famous involved
the Advanced Placement exam for calculus. The
Advanced Placement exam is a national test given at
the end of the school year. Students across the
country who pass the test are given college credit for
the course. The test is hard. Very few
students in the country pass. But the
first year Escalante taught calculus, two
of his five students passed.

REREAD
Why is the
Advanced
Placement exam
so important?

80 That was good. But Escalante knew
he could do better. He scouted the lower grades
for good students. Each year his calculus courses
were a little larger. And more of his students
passed the Advanced Placement exam for
calculus.

In 1982 eighteen Garfield High students took the
AP Calculus exam. *All* of the students passed. This
kind of success was unheard of.

But then the test correctors noted a problem.
Twelve of the students had solved one of
the problems in the same way. They
accused the students of cheating on the
exam. The scores were thrown out.

REREAD
Why were some of the students' test answers a problem?

Escalante and his principal complained. Some of the students' parents complained too.

Finally the testers agreed that the students could retake the test. So in August all the students took the test again. But it had been months since the last test. Would they remember their calculus well enough to pass?

They did! Again all the students passed. All won college credit for calculus. They had not cheated. They had solved the problems in the same way because that was how they had been taught.

The story hit the newspapers across the country. No one could believe that a school like Garfield could have so many students pass the AP test. Most schools, even in wealthy areas, only had a few pass each year. Yet Garfield, in the barrio of East Los Angeles, had eighteen.

The reason was Jaime Escalante. He believed in his students. He kindly yet firmly insisted that they do the tough work he assigned. Anyone who did not work hard could expect a call to their parents. And extra work before school, after school and/or on weekends.

THINK IT THROUGH
Why was the students' success such a huge victory?

Read to learn how the students' test scores made Escalante famous.

Escalante's classroom became a showcase. Visiting teachers and principals
120 studied his teaching methods.

Actor Edward James Olmos (left) with Jaime Escalante on the set of the movie *Stand and Deliver*

The story of Escalante's life was shown in the hit movie *Stand and Deliver.* Escalante was played by Edward James Olmos. The movie made Escalante the most famous math teacher in America.

Escalante himself starred in a PBS series called *Futures.* The series shows how math is important for
130 success on the job. He has also done a PBS show with Bill Cosby called *Math . . . Who Needs It?*

Today, Escalante's new students know what to expect. One thing is for sure: They will work hard, and they will succeed. And they will always remember Escalante's rule:

"Determination + Hard Work + Discipline = The Way to Success."

THINK IT THROUGH

1. Outside his own classroom, how did Escalante use his success to inspire more students?
2. Reread Escalante's rule for success. How does his teaching style reflect this rule? Give details to support your opinion.
3. Which events might have made Escalante angry enough to give up? How did he solve his problems?

by Jeannette Sanderson

PATCHES

A stormy night and an icy lake mean trouble for a man and his dog.

Connect to Your Life

What dog heroes do you know about from the news, books, or movies? Do you think the special relationship between dogs and people makes the animals more willing to risk their lives? Why or why not?

Key to the Article

Many magazines and newspapers carry **true accounts** about heroic rescues. These articles are written like stories and bring the action vividly to life. In this article, a man and his dog must fight for their lives. Their exciting story will keep you in suspense until the end.

Vocabulary Preview

Words to Know

raw	ancestors	pneumonia
braced	momentum	

Reading Coach CD-ROM selection

Marvin Scott was exhausted. He had worked late at his furniture store. Now all he wanted was to be home relaxing in his warm house.

It was nearly ten o'clock by the time Mr. Scott pulled into his driveway. As he stepped out of his car, the wind slapped him in the face. The thermometer hovered around zero. It was a bitter-cold night, especially on the shores of Washington's Lake Spanaway, where Mr.

10 Scott and his wife lived.

> **hovered**
> (hŭv′ ərd)
> stayed in the same place

Mr. Scott bent his head and hurried up the walk. His ears were filled with the howling of the wind. But then he heard something else. It was a banging sound. And it was coming from down by the dock. Mr. Scott thought he knew what it was. He sighed and opened the door to the house.

When Mrs. Scott met her husband at the door, she could see he wasn't happy.

"Is something the matter?"

20 she asked.

"I'm afraid we've got ice on the lake," he said. "With this wind, if it gets too thick it will punch a hole right through the patrol boat."

Mr. Scott knew he had to do something about that ice. He went to the closet to get his heaviest coat.

30 "Can't it wait until morning?" Mrs. Scott asked.

"I don't think so."

The tired man was about to head back out when his dog, Patches, came running to the door. He wanted to tag along. Mr. Scott was glad for the company in the raw night.

> **raw**
> (rô)
> *adj.* cold and damp

THINK IT THROUGH

Why is Scott going down to the lake?

FOCUS ———————————————

Find out what happens when Scott tries to free his boat from the ice.

Patches trotted beside his master down the icy 300-foot slope that led to the dock. His master braced himself against the cold, but
40 Patches didn't seem to mind it at all. The black-and-white dog was part collie and part Alaskan malamute. His ancestors had been Alaskan sled dogs.

> **braced**
> (brāst)
> *v.* got ready for danger or pain; past tense of *brace*

> **ancestors**
> (ăn′ sĕs′ tərz)
> *n.* family members from long ago

When Mr. Scott reached the dock, he saw that a film of ice had formed around the boat. It was too dark for him to notice that the spray from the lake had frozen on the dock. There was a thin sheet of ice under his feet.

Mr. Scott picked up a piece of wood and began
50 pushing at the boat's stern line. The ice was thicker than he realized. He pushed harder. As he did so, his feet gave way from under him. He tumbled forward and slipped off the icy pier. With a powerful thud he hit a floating dock and tore almost all of the muscles and tendons in both of his legs. Then the momentum of the fall carried him into the icy 15-foot-deep water. With his

> **momentum**
> (mō mĕn′ təm)
> *n.* force and speed

legs utterly useless to keep him afloat, and his heavy coat weighing him down, Mr. Scott began to sink.

THINK IT THROUGH

What trouble is Scott facing? Give three details that tell you this.

FOCUS ——————

Scott is badly hurt. How can Patches help him?

60   The seriously injured man was sinking deeper and deeper, with no hope for survival. Then, suddenly, he felt his head jerk. Something had grabbed him by the hair. It was Patches. The dog had watched his master disappear into the icy, black waters, and quickly dove in after him.

   Patches weighed 85 pounds. Mr. Scott weighed close to 200 pounds. But the dog, clenching a clump of his master's hair, paddled up with all his might. Finally, Patches and his injured master

70 broke the surface. Now the dog had to pull the dazed, shivering man to the dock, which was 20 feet away.

REREAD

Why is saving Scott such a challenge for Patches?

   The wind whipped the water around them. It forced water into Patches' nose and mouth as the dog struggled to reach safety. Patches was cold and choking. But he was his master's only hope. So he pushed on until they reached the dock and Mr. Scott was able to grab onto the edge of it.

   Now Patches was in trouble. The brave dog

80 couldn't get out of the water alone. And he was so exhausted from his rescue efforts that he wouldn't be

able to fight this rough water much longer. If he didn't get out soon, he would drown.

Mr. Scott was so badly injured that he was only half aware of what was happening. But he sensed Patches was in trouble. And, somehow, he managed to muster the strength to push his rescuer up onto the dock.

muster
(mŭs′ tər)
bring forth

THINK IT THROUGH

What problems does Patches have while trying to rescue Scott?

FOCUS

Read to find out why Patches and Scott are still in trouble.

Then Mr. Scott tried to pull himself up onto the
90 dock. He could only use his arms, as his legs were totally useless. He pulled and pulled, but his body had been through too much. His terrible injuries, the freezing cold, and the water that he had swallowed caused him to black out. He lost his grip on the dock, slid back into the water, and went under again.

black out
faint

Patches jumped right back in after him. The dog grabbed his master's hair again. Then he pulled Mr. Scott to the surface and towed him about four feet to
100 the dock.

Mr. Scott grasped the icy wood and tried to recover enough of his senses to figure out what to do next. Patches swam in circles around him, fighting the wind and cold that were beginning to get the better of him. Again, Mr. Scott saw the dog was in trouble. With the last of his strength, he pushed Patches up onto the dock.

Then Mr. Scott began screaming for help. But it was no use. The cries could barely be heard over the noise of the choppy water. And then they were stolen by the wind.

A shivering Patches paced the dock and watched his master. He stopped to lick Mr. Scott's icy hands. He whined and whimpered. But no one was coming to help. And, since Mr. Scott couldn't help himself, it was all up to Patches.

REREAD
What words let you know that Patches is worried about Scott?

THINK IT THROUGH
What problems do Scott and Patches still face?

FOCUS
Will Patches and Scott survive? Read to see what Patches does.

The dog firmly planted his four feet on the dock boards. He grasped the collar of Mr. Scott's coat with his teeth. Then he pulled with all his might. When Mr. Scott realized what Patches was doing, he began to feel some hope. This feeling allowed him to tap every last ounce of energy he had in his body. He pulled as Patches tugged. With Mr. Scott's help, Patches was finally able to pull him up onto the dock.

Once there, Patches still held on to Mr. Scott's collar. He waited until the gasping man regained his breath. Then the dog and his master—both soaked and shivering—began the 300-foot climb up the hill. Mr. Scott crawled while Patches pulled.

The climb was like torture. Both Mr. Scott and Patches were freezing and exhausted almost to the point of collapse. Patches' muscles were cramping.

And Mr. Scott's already agonizing pain became even more unbearable on the icy, rock-studded incline.

The real Patches–Dog Hero of the Year

140 Finally, the two were within a stone's throw of the back door of their house. Mr. Scott picked up a stone and threw it at the door. Mrs. Scott appeared at the door moments later. When she saw who it was, she ran outside.

Mr. Scott was rushed to Tacoma General Hospital. He was near death for 25 critical days. Pneumonia was a constant threat. And the massive operations Mr. Scott needed to
150 repair his seriously injured legs posed many dangers.

pneumonia
(noo mōn′ yə) *n.* serious disease in which the lungs become inflamed and sore

But Patches' rescue efforts were not in vain. Mr. Scott's recovery was slow, but he did recover. Six months after the accident he returned to work, walking with the aid of canes.

For his amazing rescue, Ken-L Ration named Patches Dog Hero of the Year for 1965.

THINK IT THROUGH

1. How did Patches and Scott finally get to safety?
2. In what ways did the friendship between Patches and Scott help them rescue each other?
3. How well does Patches fit *your* definition of a hero? Do you think he deserved the award?

CHIEF JOSEPH

OF THE NEZ PERCE

by Matthew G. Grant

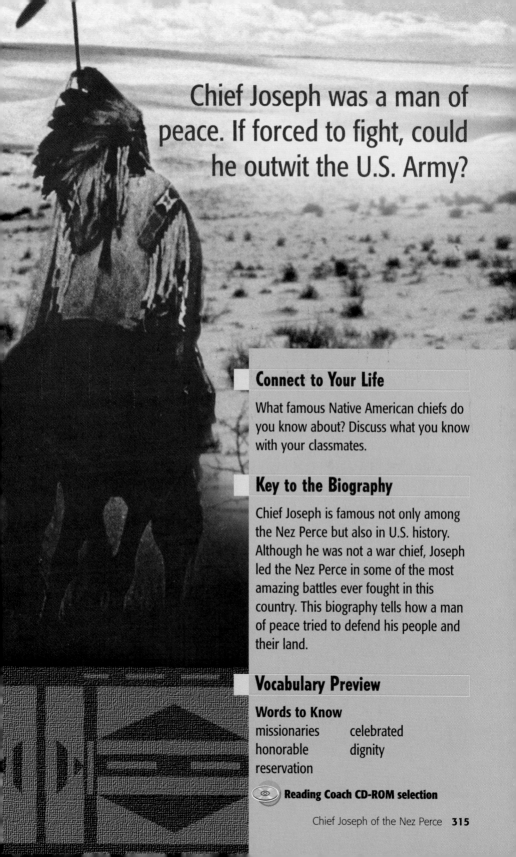

Chief Joseph was a man of peace. If forced to fight, could he outwit the U.S. Army?

Connect to Your Life

What famous Native American chiefs do you know about? Discuss what you know with your classmates.

Key to the Biography

Chief Joseph is famous not only among the Nez Perce but also in U.S. history. Although he was not a war chief, Joseph led the Nez Perce in some of the most amazing battles ever fought in this country. This biography tells how a man of peace tried to defend his people and their land.

Vocabulary Preview

Words to Know

missionaries   celebrated
honorable   dignity
reservation

Reading Coach CD-ROM selection

The Nez Perce Tribe

Beyond the Rocky Mountains, in lands that are now part of Oregon, Idaho, and Washington, lived a strong Indian tribe. The people called themselves Nimipau. But white explorers who found them gave them the name Nez Perce Indians.

Nimipau
(nē mē pōō)
the People

The tribe lived along the great rivers of that country. They caught salmon. The women dug roots and made good

10 food from them. And from time to time the men went east over the mountains to hunt buffalo.

Nez Perce
(nĕz' pûrs')
French for
"pierced nose."
The French
thought the
Nimipau were
part of another
tribe who pierced
their noses.

The Nez Perce people had beautiful spotted horses that we now call Appaloosas. The tribe was proud and well-to-do. When white men came into their country, the Indians treated them well. White men had power—and the Nez Perce admired it.

The chiefs wanted their people to be as clever and

20 rich as the white traders. They asked for white

Wallowa Valley—once home to the Nez Perce in Oregon.

teachers, and so missionaries and their families went to the Nez Perce.

> **missionaries**
> (mĭsh′ ə nĕr′ ēz)
> *n.* people who are sent to teach religion to others

Many of the Indians became Christians. They thought that if they did this, they would gain some of the white man's power. One of the most important Christian chiefs was Old Joseph, who lived in the Wallowa Valley. About 1840, a son was born to the chief.

30   The missionaries called the boy "Young Joseph." When he was five or six years old, he went to the mission school.

In 1847, trouble came to the white missionaries. Deadly sickness infected the Cayuse tribe, neighbors to the Nez Perce. The Cayuse blamed the white people, and killed 12 of them. The U.S. Army was sent to punish the Cayuse.

> **Cayuse**
> (kī yōōs′)

Old Joseph watched the missionaries flee. He thought: "Perhaps the white religion is not so strong after all."

40   Several years went by. The chief and his family were no longer Christians. They had returned to the old religion of their people. They called the Earth their mother and loved the land. When he was ten years old, Young Joseph went off alone to pray to the Great Spirit, the Maker-of-All, just as all young men of his tribe did. As he prayed, he was given a vision. He heard a voice give him a name: Thunder-Rolling-in-the-Mountains. It was a name of

50 great power.

> **REREAD**
> Why do you think Old Joseph went back to his old religion?

THINK IT THROUGH
How do the feelings of Old Joseph and his son change toward the whites? Find one or two details in the text that tell you why.

Broken Promises

The chief's son grew older. He became a hunter and a warrior. But more than this, he was wise and honorable. He worried, as his father did, when more and more white people poured into the Indian lands. Trouble lay ahead.

honorable
(ŏn′ ər ə bəl)
adj. worthy of trust and respect

60   In 1855, the U.S. government made a treaty with the Nez Perce. The tribe promised to live only on a reservation in the Wallowa Valley. In return, the government would pay money, food, and supplies. Even though the government did not keep its promises, the Nez Perce kept theirs. They stayed at peace with the whites for more than 15 years.

reservation
(rĕz′ ər vā′ shən)
n. land set aside by the U.S. government where Native Americans have to live

But now gold miners and settlers invaded the reservation. And Old Joseph, the chief, was dying.

The old man called his son. He said:

"My son, now you will be the chief of these people.
70   They look to you to guide them. You must stop your ears if white men ask you to sign a treaty and sell your home. A few more years and the white men will be all around you. They have their eyes on this land. But never forget my dying words! This country holds your father's body. Never sell the bones of your father and your mother."

THINK IT THROUGH
Why is Old Joseph worried about what would happen to Nez Perce land? Give examples from the text to support your answer.

The Young Chief

In 1871, Thunder-Rolling-in-the-Mountains became chief of his people. The white leaders called him Chief Joseph, and this is the name that has gone down in
80   history. From the first, he set out to fulfill the promise made to his father.

Many white ranchers came to live in the Wallowa Valley Reservation. The government tried to make a new treaty with the tribe. Chief Joseph's people were told to move north, to another reservation.

But they refused. The chief remembered the old promises that had been broken. Why should he believe new promises?

"You *must* move," the government agents said.
90   Joseph replied: "This land is our mother. We will not go."

Finally, in May of 1877, the U.S. Army was sent to the valley to force the Nez Perce onto the new reservation.

Chief Joseph saw that many warriors were ready to fight. He tried to prevent bloodshed by urging the people to pack up and leave. Sad and angry, they left their home forever.

REREAD
Why did Chief Joseph tell the people to leave their land?

100   Burdened by children, old people, cattle, ponies, and goods, they could only travel very slowly. They met Chief White Bird's band at Rocky Canyon and made camp.

Hot-headed young men called for white blood. Joseph could not stop them from riding out. The

young warriors murdered four white men, then came back to say:

"Now you will have to fight with us. Soon the soldiers will be here.
110 Prepare for war! Prepare for war!"

For years, Joseph had worked for peace. But now the people rose up in fury. All of the other chiefs wanted war. Joseph, their leader, could only follow.

Bands of warriors attacked white settlements. Army troops sent after the Nez Perce rode into an ambush at White Bird Canyon. The army forces were crushed by the red men. It was
120 the worst white defeat since the Battle of the Little Big Horn the year before.

The happy Indians celebrated their victory. But Joseph knew that a black future lay ahead. More soldiers would be coming. What would happen to the people then?

celebrated
(sĕl′ ə brā′ tĭd)
v. marked an event with special food, games, and music; past tense of *celebrate*

REREAD
Why wasn't Joseph happy about the great victory?

Now Chief Joseph took command once more. He proved to be the military equal of General O. O. Howard, who was sent
130 out to capture him. Howard had about 600 soldiers. Joseph had perhaps 200 warriors, with 400 more women, children, and old people. It should have been easy for the white army to subdue the refugee band.

General O. O. Howard
a famous general who fought for the North in the Civil War

But Chief Joseph seemed to outwit the white general at every turn. The Indians won fight after fight.

THINK IT THROUGH
What causes Chief Joseph to fight the Army? What are the effects of that fight?

The Long Retreat

Chief Joseph planned to lead his people to Canada, as Sitting Bull had done after the Battle of Little Big Horn. But the border

140 was more than 1,000 miles away. Many people were sick or wounded. Nevertheless, they started northward.

Again and again the white army tried to trap the Nez Perce. But the warriors fought the troops and won, while the people escaped. All over the United States, people read about the war and marveled at the skill of the red men, led by Chief Joseph. He took them over high mountains, through trackless wilderness.

150 For four months they traveled, until winter was upon them. Then, 30 miles from the Canadian border, Chief Joseph and his people were surrounded. It was the end.

retreat
(rē trēt′)
moving to a place of safety

marveled
(mär′ vəld)
admired greatly

trackless wilderness
wild areas with no trails or paths

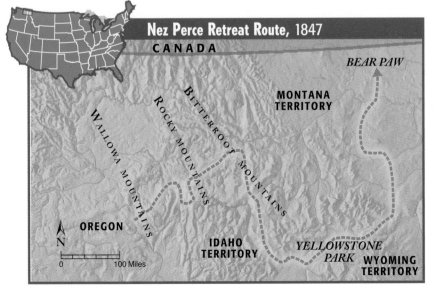

Nez Perce Retreat Route, 1847

CANADA

BEAR PAW

MONTANA TERRITORY

BITTERROOT MOUNTAINS

ROCKY MOUNTAINS

WALLOWA MOUNTAINS

N

OREGON

0   100 Miles

IDAHO TERRITORY

YELLOWSTONE PARK

WYOMING TERRITORY

Chief Joseph rode forward alone toward General Howard and General Nelson A. Miles. With dignity , he gave them his rifle. Then he said:

> **dignity**
> (dĭg′ nĭ tē)
> *n.* self-respect and pride

160 "Tell General Howard I know his heart. . . . I am tired of fighting. Our chiefs are killed. . . . It is cold and we have no blankets. The little children are freezing. We have no food. Hear me, my chiefs. I am tired. My heart is sick and sad. From where the sun now stands, I will fight no more forever."

> **REREAD**
> Read this passage aloud. Try to show how Chief Joseph feels.

White men had promised Chief Joseph that his people would be returned to their own country. But once again, the white promise was broken. The Nez Perce were sent to Kansas, then to the Indian
170 Territory (now Oklahoma). Many died there.

Finally, in 1885, Joseph and his band went to a reservation in the state of Washington. The chief spent the rest of his life trying to make the government fulfill its promises. He died September 21, 1904, still waiting.

THINK IT THROUGH

1. What reasons did Chief Joseph give for wanting to end the war?
2. What did the government promise the Nez Perce before and after the long retreat? How many of its promises did the government keep?
3. What qualities should a good leader have? How many of these qualities do you think Chief Joseph had? Give examples from the text.

THE SPIRIT OF THE HORSE

Today, the Nez Perce in Idaho and the U.S. government are working together. The government is helping the Nez Perce raise a new kind of horse. The Nez Perce are mixing their Appaloosas with a rare Central Asian horse. The new breed will be called the "Nez Perce horse."

This program is also helping Nez Perce children learn about their proud history. The Nez Perce have started two groups: the Young Horseman Project and the Mounted Scholars. These groups help young people
10 aged 14 to 21. Each child is given one of the new horses. By learning to care for the animal, the young people are learning to care about themselves. As Rosa Yearout, a project member, says, "The outside of a horse helps the inside of a kid."

The Nez Perce hope that many people will
20 buy the new horses. This will create new business and new pride for the people. The spirit of the horse is helping the Nez Perce build for the future.

Bridges to History

Mixed Genres

How do people learn about life in the past? Clues come from different sources—from old bones to legends and folk tales. We learn the history of the world piece by piece.

In this unit you'll join an explorer as he investigates a legend about Mayan ruins. You'll read about life in castles during Europe's Middle Ages. You'll learn about culture and values in Japan and West Africa through folk tales. These pieces give you a taste of cultures from different parts of the world.

from
ARCHAEOLOGY
by Dennis B. Fradin

What can you learn from old objects found deep in the earth?

Perhaps more than you might think!

Connect to Your Life

Archaeology (är′ kē ŏl′ ə jē) is the study of very old objects. The goal is to learn how people lived in the past. Create a concept web like the one below to show what you know about archaeology.

Purpose — ARCHAEOLOGY — Tools
Methods — ARCHAEOLOGY — Jobs

Key to the Article

This excerpt from *Archaeology* tells how the science got started. It also explains what **archaeologists** (är′ kē ŏl′ ə jĭsts), the people who study old objects, do in their jobs.

To get the most from your reading, pay attention to the headings in darker type. They are clues to the main idea of that part. Look for details that tell about each heading. Also, be sure to read the captions and time line.

Vocabulary Preview

Words to Know

ancient	relics	site
artifacts	excavate	

 Reading Coach CD-ROM selection

What is Archaeology?

Did you ever see an Egyptian mummy in a museum? Or statues dug from ancient cities? If so you already have been introduced to archaeology.

> **ancient**
> (ān' shənt)
> *adj.* from a time long past

Archaeology is a science. It is the study of very old objects such as buildings, bones, and tools.

The scientists who find and study old objects are called archaeologists. They look for objects that are many hundreds or thousands of years old. They study
10 old objects to learn how people lived in ancient times.

THINK IT THROUGH
How would you define *archaeology?* What is the job of an archaeologist?

A Short History of Archaeology

Up until the 1700s, people had little interest in studying things from the past. When they found ancient objects (called artifacts), they kept the ones made of gold. Less valuable ones were often thrown away!

> **artifacts**
> (är' tə făkts')
> *n.* objects created by humans, such as tools, weapons, or jewelry

In 1748 a farmer digging in a field in Italy struck an underground wall. A digging crew then unearthed an ancient city. It was Pompeii, which had been destroyed by a
20 volcano nearly 1,700 years earlier. The excavation (digging) at Pompeii was one of the first done in an organized way.

> **Pompeii**
> (pŏm pā')
> city in Italy that was buried by a volcano in A.D. 79

But archaeologists of the 1700s still mainly sought treasure. They tossed aside many other artifacts in search of it.

Sir Flinders Petrie (1853-1942) was one of the first archaeologists to study everything he found.

30 Petrie worked in Egypt during the late 1800s. When Petrie dug, he searched the earth "inch by inch," as he described it. Petrie found pottery, tools, and other items used by Egyptians in their daily life. Because he worked so carefully, Petrie is called the "Father of Modern Archaeology."

Flinders Petrie and his sister-in-law at an Egyptian excavation site in 1900

Today's archaeologists use the "inch by inch" method. They keep detailed records of everything they find. They know that the smallest artifact can help us understand 40 how ancient people lived.

THINK IT THROUGH

How did Petrie's work differ from that of earlier archaeologists?

FOCUS

Read to find out how archaeologists decide where to look for artifacts.

Knowing Where to Look

The world is a big place. How do archaeologists know where to look for ancient relics? They don't just guess. Like detectives, they search for clues.

Old books often provide good clues. The Bible, the works of Homer, and other old

relics
(rĕl' ĭks)
n. objects that are important for their age and historic interest

Homer
(hō' mər)
famous Greek poet who lived around 750 B.C.

manuscripts	describe ancient towns. Some of those towns are still there—buried under layers of dirt. Archaeologists study the

manuscripts
(măn′ yə
skrĭpts′)
books or other
documents
written by hand

50 books to determine where the ancient sites may be located.

People often tell stories about past events. For example, people may tell of a sunken ship. Archaeologists listen to such stories for clues about the ship's location.

Archaeologists often use photographs taken from airplanes. They show things that can't be seen from the ground.

fertile
(fûr′ tl)
good for growing
things

An aerial photo may show a piece of land

60 to be more fertile than nearby land. This may be because ancient people worked the soil there.

Cameras are also used to spot undersea wrecks.

Archaeologists have many other tools to help them decide where to work. These include magnets, metal detectors, soil studies, and electrical tests of the ground.

THINK IT THROUGH

Describe three ways archaeologists find places to search for artifacts.

FOCUS

How do archaeologists find artifacts and decide how old they are?

excavate
(ĕk′ skə vāt′)
v. uncover by
digging

Digging

It can take many lifetimes to excavate a site. Archaeologists have been digging at Pompeii since 1748. There's still much to do there. Because digging takes so long,

70 archaeologists hate to waste time.

site
(sīt)
n. place where
something, such
as a building, was
once located

When they've found a likely site, they sink trial shafts. These are holes that show how far down the site goes. They also dig trial trenches. These show how long and wide the site is. Once they know the size of the site, archaeologists hire a crew and organize the digging.

sink trial shafts
dig sample holes

Pictures are taken of any object the crew finds. Then an archaeologist carefully removes the artifact from the ground with a little knife or brush.

How Old Is It?

80 Once archaeologists have found an artifact, they have several questions. A main one is: How old is it? Knowing the ages of artifacts helps chart the growth of civilization.

Machu Picchu In Peru, archaeologists make discoveries about the ancient Inca.

(Top) Preserving fabric from an Incan burial site

(Bottom) Mummy of a young girl believed to be an Incan human sacrifice

The archaeologist Christian Thomsen (1788-1865) worked out the Three Age System. The three are the Stone Age, Bronze Age, and Iron Age.

90 The Stone Age was when people used stone tools. It began over a million years ago and ended about five thousand years ago. During the Bronze Age people made tools out of the metal bronze. It extended from about five thousand years ago to around three thousand years ago. The Iron Age 100 began about three thousand years ago. We are still in the Iron Age.

REREAD

Read the boxed text. Then look at the time line on the right. What do the terms *stone, bronze,* and *iron* refer to? Which age lasted the longest?

By learning what an artifact is made of, scientists obtain a very rough idea of its age. They also have ways to learn its 110 age more exactly.

One important method is called carbon-14 dating. When living things die, they give off a substance called carbon 14. The longer an object has been dead, the less carbon 14 it has. By measuring the amount of carbon 14 in a piece of wood or other object that once was alive, scientists can tell its age.

The Three Age System

about 3 million B.C.–3000 B.C.

STONE AGE
• This is the earliest known period of human culture.
• Stone tools are first used.

3000 B.C.–1000 B.C.

BRONZE AGE
• Weapons and tools are now made from bronze or copper.

1000 B.C.–present

IRON AGE
• People discover how to get iron from ores.
• Iron is used for weapons, tools, and decorations.
• In Europe, the Iron Age began later than in other parts of the world.

Carbon-14 dating only works for objects that lived within the past forty thousand years. Scientists have other methods to date objects older than that.

THINK IT THROUGH

How do archaeologists figure out the age of an artifact? Why is the age important?

FOCUS —————————————————————————

Find out about the other jobs archaeologists do.

All Kinds of Archaeologists

120 There are other kinds of archaeologists besides those who dig for artifacts. Some translate old writing. Others work in museums. Government archaeologists make sure that old sites aren't destroyed.

Many archaeologists teach. One good teacher can train hundreds of future archaeologists.

Many finds are yet to be made in archaeology. Sunken ships still lie underwater. Lost cities lie beneath the ground. Statues, caves, and mummies wait to be found. Writing tablets need to be translated.

130 Perhaps you will become an archaeologist. Then you will help our human race learn more about its past.

THINK IT THROUGH

1. Besides digging for artifacts, what other types of work do archaeologists do?
2. How does studying artifacts teach us about history? Give examples to support your opinion.
3. Based on your reading, what skills does an archaeologist need to succeed? What details helped you know this?

The Sacred Well

by Judy Donnelly

What dark secrets lie at the bottom of this ancient well? One man risks his life to find out.

Connect to Your Life

Where has your curiosity taken you? Have you ever explored a place that seemed dangerous? What were the risks involved? What did you find?

Key to the Article

Edward Thompson (1856-1935) was not a trained archaeologist. But he had a burning desire to learn more about the ancient **Mayans** (mä′ yənz). They were the rulers of Mexico and Central America from about A.D. 800 to the mid-1500s.

Thompson moved to Mexico in 1885. He lived close to the modern Mayan Indians, learned their language, and even followed their way of life. The Indians helped him find ancient Mayan ruins, including the Sacred Well. This true account tells the exciting story of what Thompson found hidden in the well.

Vocabulary Preview

Words to Know

empire   skeletons
dredge

 Reading Coach CD-ROM selection

What is the Sacred Well, and why does Edward Thompson want to explore this site?

Deep in the jungles of Mexico stands an empty city. It is called Chichén Itzá. It was built more than a thousand years ago by the Mayan Indians. The Mayan empire spread over parts of Mexico and Central America. The Mayans built many beautiful cities. But they deserted them. No one is sure why.

> **Chichén Itzá**
> (chē chĕn′ ē tsäh′)
> an ancient city where many religious ceremonies were held

> **empire**
> (ĕm′ pīr′)
> *n.* large area ruled by a king or emperor

In 1904 a man named Edward
10 Thompson was walking in the empty city of Chichén Itzá. He had come to learn about the Mayan people.

He followed a path that led to a mysterious pool of water. It was called the Sacred Well. It was as big as a small lake—almost 200 feet wide. Its water was strange and dark and still. It was very, very deep.

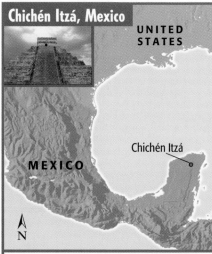

Chichén Itzá, Mexico

UNITED STATES

MEXICO

Chichén Itzá

N

Location of Chichén Itzá and the Sacred Well. Small photo shows El Castillo, the main temple in Chichén Itzá.

20 The Indians who lived in the jungle were afraid of the well. They said giant snakes and monsters lived at the bottom. They said sometimes the water turned to blood. And indeed Edward noticed that the water often did change to a dark reddish color.

Once Edward had read a strange old story. It said
30 the Mayans believed a rain god lived in the bottom of the well. Sometimes rain didn't fall. Sometimes crops

didn't grow. The Mayans thought the rain god was angry then. So they would march slowly to the well. They would throw rich treasure and beautiful young girls into the dark water. The Mayans hoped their actions would please the rain god.

Edward could not forget this story. He wanted to explore the mysterious well.

THINK IT THROUGH
What makes the Sacred Well so mysterious to Edward?

FOCUS
Read to learn what he uses to uncover some of the well's secrets.

His family and friends thought he was crazy. They
40 tried to make him change his mind. But Edward went ahead anyway. He took deep-sea diving lessons. Then he bought a machine called a dredge . The machine had a bucket that hung from a long steel rope. Edward could lower the bucket into the well. It could scoop up whatever was at the bottom and bring it up.

> **dredge**
> (drĕj)
> *n.* machine used to bring up objects from the bottom of rivers and lakes

But where should he dig? The well was so big. Then he remembered the story about treasure
50 and girls thrown into the well. He found logs the size and shape of a human being. One by one he threw them into the dark water. They all fell in at about the same spot. That was where the young girls must have fallen, too. That was the place to lower the dredge.

> **REREAD**
> How did Edward solve the problem of where to dig?

Day after day Edward and his Indian helpers worked at the well. But the dredge brought up only sticks and mud.

Weeks passed. One day, just as usual, the dredge
60 came up with sticks and mud. But hidden in the mud was treasure! Each day there was more. A golden bowl and cups. A bell. Beautiful necklaces. Rings that had been worn a thousand years before.

Treasure *had* been thrown into the Sacred Well! But was the rest of the story true? Edward soon knew the answer.

The dredge found human skeletons.

But Edward wasn't satisfied. The dredge was coming up empty again. It had hit
70 bottom. He decided to dive into the well and explore its hidden places.

skeletons
(skĕl′ ĭ tnz) *n.* bones that support the human body

Again his friends tried to get Edward to change his mind. They said, "No one can go down into the well and come out alive!"

THINK IT THROUGH

In your own words, tell how Edward proves that the story about the Sacred Well is true.

FOCUS

Does Edward live through the dive and satisfy his curiosity? Read to find out.

But Edward did not listen. He climbed into his diving suit. It had a big helmet, a long air hose, and iron shoes. The heavy shoes would drag him down to the bottom of the well. His Indian helpers would pump down air for him to breathe. They had to do
80 their job carefully. Edward's life depended on them.

Edward with diving suit, air hose, air pump, and recovery basket. Small photo shows jade carving—2¼″ high—found in the well.

One by one his helpers shook his hand. Their faces were sad. They thought they would never see him again.

When Edward jumped into the well, he sank down, down, down. He felt pain in his ears. The water was so dark, he couldn't see at all.

90 At last his iron shoes touched bottom. He felt a strange thrill. So many people had died in this place. But *he* was going to come out alive!

He turned on his flashlight. It didn't help. Here the water was like thick mud soup. He had to feel his way. But Edward got used to the strange darkness. And he went down into the well again and again. In the deepest part he came upon the skeletons of three women. They

REREAD
What made Edward a good explorer?

looked as though they were
100 reaching out for help. One still
wore a necklace.

Skull of a young man. It
was found on one of
Edward's dives into the
Sacred Well.

Edward found many skeletons in
the well. Skeletons of women,
men, and children, too. Some were
probably slaves. Some may have
been prisoners of the Mayans.
Edward was sure they had died
because the Mayans were trying to
please the rain god.

110 Edward found much more treasure too. Weapons
and jewelry. Strange carvings. Even scraps of clothing.
He hoped these things would help scientists learn
more about the ancient Mayans.

Edward kept working at the well. Finally he went
home to the United States. He was a hero. He had
risked his life. And he had solved a mystery—the
mystery of the Sacred Well.

THINK IT THROUGH

1. What else does Edward find to show how the
   ancient Mayans used the Sacred Well?
2. What steps does Edward take to solve the mystery
   of the well?
3. Why do you think he risks his life so many times to
   explore this site?

Power of the Sacred Well

In the 1960s, a team of scientists explored the Sacred Well again. They had much better equipment than the simple dredge Edward Thompson had used. They found that the ancient Mayans had kept using the well long after leaving Chichén Itzá.

The team recovered hundreds of religious bells, jars, gold ornaments, and other items. They also found many more skeletons of men, women, and children. Perhaps the ancient Mayans believed that the Sacred

10 Well was the only true home of the powerful rain god. The Mayans stopped using the well in the 1500s. This was when the Spanish took over Mexico and Central America.

Photo of Chichén Itzá. El Castillo is in the distance. A path leads to the dark waters of the Sacred Well.

from Castles

by Jenny Vaughan

It is said that "a man's home is his castle." What might it be like to call a castle home?

Connect to Your Life

Castles were more than homes to the people who lived in them. With a partner, fill in a chart like the one below to show what you know about castles.

What I know about castles	What I want to find out	What I learned

Key to the Article

In Europe during the Middle Ages, A.D. 1000 to 1500, kings and noblemen had strong castles built. The first castles were built around A.D. 1000 in what is now France and Germany.

Over time, castles appeared across Europe and the Middle East. Castles were also built in parts of Asia, including Japan. The age of castles ended around the 1400s, when guns came into use.

Vocabulary Preview

Words to Know

fortress   concentric   rebellions
siege   hostile

 Reading Coach CD-ROM selection

What Is a Castle?

A castle was a home that was also a
fortress. Castles were built hundreds of
years ago by kings and noblemen.

When a king conquered a new land, he
had to stop his enemies winning it back. So
he gave parts of it to his noblemen. In
return, they kept their area safe for the king.

Each nobleman had knights to help him. He had to
protect his knights and their horses from attack. To
10 do this, the nobleman built a castle.

Because the land was full of enemies, the nobleman
had to build his castle quickly. So he built it of wood,
for wood was easy to get and cheap, and building
with wood was quick.

> **fortress**
> (fôr′ trĭs)
> *n.* large place
> that is strong and
> secure

Stone Castles

Wood is not the best material to use for
building because it rots. A wooden castle
could also be burned down. Where stone
was easily available, it was used instead of
wood. In other areas, the wooden castles
20 were strengthened with stone.

> **bailey**
> (bā′ lē)
> yard inside a
> castle wall

A stone wall, or curtain wall, was built
around the bailey. Like the palisade, this
had a walkway inside and was crenellated.
A crenellated wall had regular gaps,
called *crenels,* at the top. Guards standing
on the walkway could look out through
them. The stones between the gaps, called
merlons, often contained loopholes
through which arrows could be fired.

> **palisade**
> (păl′ ĭ sād′)
> pointed wooden
> fence that
> surrounds the
> bailey of a
> wooden castle

> **REREAD**
> Look again at
> this passage and
> the diagram on
> page 345. What
> helped protect
> the castle from
> enemies?

30   Within the curtain wall there was a
strong stone tower, called a *keep*. This was
so heavy that it was usually built on hard
ground rather than on a motte . Keeps
were often very high and some had walls as
thick as 20 feet (6 meters).

> **motte**
> (mŏt)
> mound of earth
> on which the first
> wooden castles
> were built

THINK IT THROUGH

> Why did people build castles? In what ways is a stone castle
> an improvement over a wooden one?

Stone Castle

merlon

crenel

moat

keep

bailey

curtain wall

gatehouse

drawbridge

The ruins of Bodiam Castle in Sussex, England, as they look today.
A deep ditch filled with water, called a *moat,* surrounds the castle.

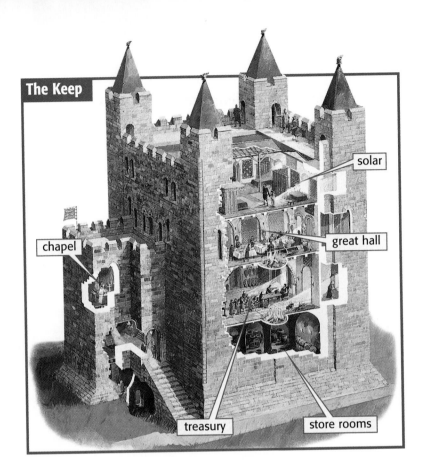

The Keep

solar

chapel

great hall

treasury

store rooms

FOCUS
Read to learn about the importance of the keep.

Inside a Castle

The keep was the safest place in the castle. It was also the home of the nobleman and his family.

This keep had four stories. A staircase led up to the well-guarded entrance in the middle stories. Here
40 there was a large hall where the lord received visitors and, occasionally, held banquets. Many of his visitors were the people who farmed his lands. He sorted out their problems and settled disputes among them.

The keep also had a room called the *solar.* This was the family's bedroom and sitting room, and the place where they usually ate their meals. The solar was the most comfortable room in the castle, and the walls were often plastered and decorated. But it was drafty, because the windows had no glass in them.

50   The keep often contained a chapel, another bedroom, and an office as well. . . .

The king and many of his noblemen owned more than one castle. These were often great distances apart, and the lord would spend part of the year in each one. A chief guard, known as the *constable,* was in charge of the castle while the lord was away.

Each castle also had a steward. He was usually informed in advance when the lord planned to visit the castle. The steward made sure that there was

60   enough to eat, and that everyone had a place to sleep.

THINK IT THROUGH
In what ways is a keep like a modern home? In what ways is it different?

FOCUS
Find out what castle life was like.

Life in a Castle

The castle buildings and weapons had to be kept in good repair in case of attack. The nobleman, his family, priests, knights, and often his guests, had to be fed and clothed. So, many servants were needed, including stablehands, cooks, tailors and launderers. One of the most important was the keeper of the wardrobe. He looked after the lord's clothes and other goods.

The lady of the castle ensured that the household was well run. Her daughters were taught at home, but

70   her sons were often sent to another castle. They learned good manners, how to shoot with a bow and

arrow, and how to fight with a sword. They also had to be able to read and write, and understand Latin.

Castle Amusements

Life in a castle was not all hard work. The lord and his family also had time to enjoy themselves. They played chess, checkers and dice, and read or sang.

Sometimes tournaments were held, in which groups of knights fought mock battles. This was good practice for warfare, as well as being fun.

80 People often went hunting with hounds for stag or boar. Another popular sport was falconry, in which birds of prey were trained to catch small animals.

THINK IT THROUGH
Describe the life of a nobleman living in a castle.

FOCUS
Read to find out what happens when a castle is attacked.

Attacking a Castle

Although a castle could be a comfortable home, no one inside it could forget that it was also a fortress and might one day be attacked. Everyone hoped that the walls and gates were strong enough to keep the enemy out.

90 In those days there were no powerful explosives or guns. The attackers had to climb over the walls or try to knock them down. They could also prevent supplies from reaching the castle.

REREAD
What are three ways an enemy might take over a castle?

Soldiers used ladders and scaling towers to help them get over the walls and into the castle.

A Castle Under Siege

Siege Weapons

1. **Scaling Tower** had a platform on top that lowered like a draw-bridge.

2. **Battering Ram** swung like a pendulum to crack castle walls or knock down drawbridges.

3. **Trebuchet and Mangonel** worked like giant slingshots.

4. **Mantlet** shielded soldiers.

5. **Tortoise** moved slowly on wheels and sheltered soldiers from falling arrows.

Several machines could be used to damage a castle. One was a battering ram, which was a strong tree trunk with an iron tip. Other machines, such as mangonels and trebuchets, could hurl heavy rocks at the walls or knock the corners off the towers. They
100 were also used to throw missiles over the walls, smashing the buildings inside.

Under Siege

An attack or siege on a castle could last for weeks or months. During this time, no

> **siege**
> (sēj)
> *n.* military blockade meant to cut off supplies and aid

fresh food or water could reach the castle. When all the supplies had been used up, the castle had to surrender. So the people inside the castle fought back as hard as they could, hoping to drive the enemy away quickly or to be rescued.

110 They built wooden platforms, called hourds, out from the walls. These had slatted floors so that missiles could be dropped, and arrows fired down, on to the enemy.

THINK IT THROUGH
How might the enemy get people inside the castle to surrender?

FOCUS
Find out how castles change during the late 1200s.

The Keep Gatehouse

The design of castles continued to change. By the late 1200s, some castles were so strong that it was almost impossible for enemies to break in.

The weakest part of any castle was usually the gate. So its defenses were much improved. Visitors first had to pass through a strongly guarded outer gate, the barbican. The drawbridge had to be lowered before

120 they could cross over the moat to the gatehouse. Here, the entrance was blocked by a huge iron-covered gate, called a portcullis, set in grooves in the wall.

REREAD
Draw a picture of a castle entrance as you imagine it to look.

The gatehouse was as strong as a keep in an older castle. So, it is called a keep gatehouse. Soldiers could continue to defend it, even when the rest of the castle was overrun. Like a keep, the keep gatehouse was also a home—the home of the constable. The lord lived in a more comfortable building within the castle.

The Concentric Castle

130 A keep gatehouse guarded the entrance to a concentric castle. A concentric castle had two sets of walls, one inside the other.

A wide moat surrounded the castle. The lower, outer wall was sometimes strengthened with towers. Barbicans and gatehouses guarded the entrances. If enemy soldiers broke through this wall into the outer bailey, they were surrounded by archers . For within the outer bailey was a stronger, taller wall
140 containing massive gatehouses and towers.

> **concentric**
> (kən sĕn′ trĭk)
> *adj.* having a common center, such as one circle inside another circle

> **archers**
> (är′ chərz)
> soldiers who shoot arrows

Concentric Castle

Le Krak des Chevaliers, the Castle of the Knights, is the finest example of a concentric castle. It was built by European crusaders in Syria over 800 years ago.

It was very difficult for an enemy army to break into and capture a concentric castle. But the people in the castle could still be forced to surrender through hunger. Also, many of the defenders fought for the lord only because they were paid to. If the enemy paid them more, they sometimes let them in.

THINK IT THROUGH
What are the advantages of living in a concentric castle? How can it be captured?

FOCUS
Read to learn how castles were built and how they changed.

Building a Castle

The big stone castles, particularly the huge concentric ones, often took more than ten years to complete. As many as 3,000 workers at a time might be employed
150 on them.

First the site was chosen and the plans of the castle were drawn up. If there was no suitable stone in the area it had to be brought, sometimes over many miles. Carpenters, masons and other craftsmen, and laborers were hired and supervised by the master mason. They sometimes traveled great distances, too, and needed a guard through hostile country.

masons
(mā′ sənz)
people who work with stone or brick

hostile
(hŏs′ təl)
adj. unfriendly or belonging to an enemy

The Castle Becomes a Home

160 Gradually, times changed. The kings and lords who owned the castles no longer fought among themselves. There were fewer rebellions, and the owners of castles

rebellions
(rĭ bĕl′ yənz)
n. internal wars meant to overthrow a ruler

were no longer in danger from the people living around them. Wars were now fought by full-time soldiers in the king's army, not by knights and followers of the king's noblemen.

170 For all these reasons, castles no longer had to be fortresses. They could be made more comfortable, by removing some of their defenses and putting in wide glass windows to let the light in. Or their owners could move out into large country houses.

People's lives began to change, too. Most of their time used to be spent preparing for battle. Now they were free to enjoy poetry, music, dance and other pleasures.

THINK IT THROUGH

1. It took from six months to more than ten years to build a castle. Why did it take so long?
2. What caused people to stop building castles?
3. Would you have liked to live in a castle during the Middle Ages? Give details to support your answer.

Matajuro's Training

Connect to Your Life

Did you ever make a big mistake and wish for a second chance? Did you get it? If so, share your story with a partner.

Key to the Folk Tale

From the 1100s to the mid-1800s, samurai (săm′ ə rī) warriors fought under rival lords in Japan. **Samurai** means "one who serves."

These highly trained fighters followed strict rules of behavior. They were expected to have undying loyalty for their lord. They also showed courage, fairness, respect for the gods, and kindness. According to samurai rules, dying an honorable death was more important than enjoying a long life.

The samurai tradition was the source of a family's honor and pride. Boys, and even some girls, were trained from an early age. To fail in samurai training brought shame, as Matajuro finds out.

Matajuro learns too late that a warrior has to train hard. Will anyone give him a second chance?

Vocabulary Preview

Words to Know

humiliation	wielding
tolerate	reflexes
opportunity	

 Reading Coach CD-ROM selection

Matajuro is not like his brothers. Read to find out what his father is forced to do.

Yagyu Matajuro, the son of a samurai family, showed skill with the sword at an early age. However, he was lazy. He refused to practice or exercise. While his brothers trained hard with their *sensei*, Matajuro would sneak out of the dojo to go fishing. Threats and punishment did no good. Matajuro's father scolded him before the entire clan—a terrible

10 humiliation. Matajuro didn't care. The day arrived when he refused to do anything. He insulted his *sensei* and fought with his brothers when they tried to make him behave.

His father, extremely angry, told Matajuro to gather his belongings. "You come from a samurai family, but you have shown yourself unworthy. I will not tolerate your laziness and disrespect. You are my son no

20 more. Get out!"

sensei
(sĕn' sā)
Japanese for "teacher of fighting arts"

dojo
(dō' jō)
Japanese for "fighting-arts school"

humiliation
(hyōō mĭl' ē ā' shən)
n. loss of self-respect and dignity

tolerate
(tŏl' ə rāt')
v. put up with

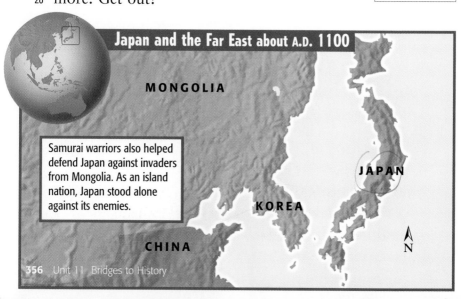

Japan and the Far East about A.D. 1100

MONGOLIA

Samurai warriors also helped defend Japan against invaders from Mongolia. As an island nation, Japan stood alone against its enemies.

JAPAN

KOREA

CHINA

N

Matajuro had to leave home. He was cold and hungry. Sometimes a kind farmer would give him a bit of rice and allow him to sleep in his barn. But most often the country people, who once had bowed to him with respect, chased him away.

"Begone, you lazy boy! You were a samurai's son once, but no longer. You didn't want to work or study. How does it feel now, having to beg for food?"

30 Matajuro soon realized what a terrible mistake he had made. He vowed to change his ways. He went to his father and begged to be taken back.

"I have learned my lesson," he pleaded. "I promise to work hard from now on. I will be lazy and disrespectful no longer."

His father refused to listen. "You had your opportunity to make something of yourself. I warned you many times not to waste it. You ignored me; now I ignore you. Maybe you can find someone to

40 teach you the way of the samurai, but it will not be me."

opportunity
(ŏp' ər tōō' nĭ tē)
n. chance to do or have something

THINK IT THROUGH
Why doesn't Matajuro's father take him back?

FOCUS
Read to learn if Matajuro finds someone willing to teach him.

Matajuro had to leave home again, this time for good. He became a vagabond, wandering around the countryside, hoping one day to find a *sensei* who would accept him as a pupil. Unfortunately, every *sensei*

vagabond
(văg' ə bŏnd')
person who travels from place to place

Dojos often had quiet rock gardens, like this one, outside their training areas.

"I want to be a swordsman, Master. Please accept me as your pupil...."

he spoke to already knew his story.

"I want students who work hard and show respect," each said. "Your own father threw you out.
50 Why should I take you in?"

One day Matajuro learned of a *sensei* named Banzo, a monk who lived in a hut near the Kumano Machi Shrine. He was known to be kind and patient with his students. Matajuro went to see him. He kneeled at the *sensei's* door and begged to be accepted as his pupil.

> **Kumano Machi Shrine**
> famous Japanese religious site

Banzo stepped over the boy as if he wasn't there, but Matajuro was not ready to give up. He knew this
60 was his last chance. He lay in the doorway for a month, hoping that the *sensei* would notice him.

Banzo paid no attention at all. He stepped over Matajuro as he went in and out of his hut.

> **REREAD**
> Should Banzo accept Matajuro? Why or why not?

But one day Banzo asked, "What are you doing here, boy? Why are you lying in my doorway?"

"I want to be a swordsman, Master. Please accept me as your pupil. I promise to work hard, day and
70 night. Don't turn me away. Teach me how to be a samurai."

Banzo sighed. "All right. Come in."

Matajuro lived with Banzo for the next three years. He cooked the rice, washed the clothes, swept the floor, gathered the firewood. The *sensei* did not talk to him at all, except to tell him what to do. As for learning swordsmanship, Matajuro never even saw a sword.

Matajuro began to grow impatient. *I am not learning to be a samurai,* he thought. *I am only a servant. All I*
80 *do is cook and clean. If the sensei is not going to teach me anything, perhaps I should move on.*

THINK IT THROUGH
What is Banzo's attitude toward Matajuro? Why do you think he feels that way?

FOCUS
Read to discover how Banzo begins training Matajuro.

He spoke to Banzo the next day. "Master, I have been here three years. When are you going to teach me something about swordsmanship?"

"Oh," said Banzo. "So you want to learn swordsmanship? Very well." He opened a chest and tossed Matajuro a wooden sword. "Practice with this."

Matajuro felt better, but not for long. Though in his spare moments he practiced the few exercises he
90 remembered from his father's house, his *sensei* did not criticize or correct him. Banzo did not attempt to

teach him anything. He ignored Matajuro, just as before.

One night, while Matajuro lay asleep, a heavy object whacked him across the shoulders. He cried out in pain. Opening his eyes, he saw Banzo standing over him, wielding a wooden sword. *Whack!* The sword came down again.

wielding
(wēl' dǐng)
adj. waving

100 "Master! Why are you hitting me?" Matajuro cried.

"If you don't like being hit, defend yourself!" Banzo struck him again.

"I can't! My sword is hanging on the wall."

"Why is it there?" Banzo beat Matajuro mercilessly with the wooden sword. Every time the boy

110 tried to get up, the *sensei* knocked him down.

After that, Matajuro made sure to sleep with his sword at his side. He carried it with him during the day, because he never knew when Banzo might attack him. When he least expected it—*whack!*—there came a

120 blow across his head, legs, or shoulders.

Slowly, Matajuro learned to defend himself. He practiced harder and harder,

Sculpture of a samurai wielding a bamboo staff

developing lightning reflexes and split-second timing. After a while he could sense when an attack was about to come. Banzo seldom caught him off guard. This was
130 vital, because they practiced with real swords now.

reflexes
(rē' flĕk' sĭz)
n. reactions

THINK IT THROUGH
What methods does Banzo use to teach Matajuro the sword?

FOCUS
Read to find out what Matajuro learns from Banzo.

One day Matajuro was cooking rice when Banzo attacked without warning. Matajuro was ready. He didn't bother to draw his sword. Holding the pot's iron lid in his left hand, he parried his *sensei's* thrusts while continuing to stir the rice with his right. When the rice was done, he filled a bowl and offered it to Banzo with a bow.

parried
(păr' ēd)
turned aside

thrusts
(thrŭsts)
sword strikes

"Master, here is your dinner."
140 Banzo threw down his sword and embraced him. "You are ready, Matajuro. You have mastered the swordsman's art completely. There is nothing left for you to learn."

"Thank you for teaching me," Matajuro said.
Banzo shrugged. "You are mistaken. I did not teach you anything. The skills you possess were always yours. They were inside you from the beginning. I merely showed you how to let them out."

REREAD
Why doesn't Banzo take credit for Matajuro's success?

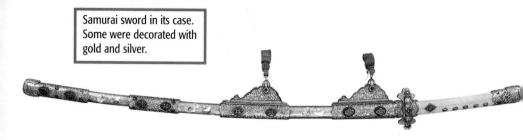

Samurai sword in its case. Some were decorated with gold and silver.

150   Banzo presented Matajuro with a fine sword on the day the boy left the Kumano Machi Shrine to return to his family. Matajuro became a famous samurai. His family was proud of him.

    Matajuro never saw his *sensei* again, but he never forgot the lesson Banzo had taught him: Before one can master any art, one must first learn to master oneself.

THINK IT THROUGH

1. How does Matajuro show Banzo that he has mastered the sword?
2. "Before one can master any art, one must first learn to master oneself." What do you think this means? What shows that Matajuro mastered himself?
3. Based on the story, what qualities do you think a samurai in training should have? Give examples to support your answer.
4. Do you think Matajuro deserved a second chance? Why or why not?

Samurai Arms and Armor

by Tamiko Sasaki

Samurai warriors carried several deadly weapons into battle. Their short sword *(wakizashi)*, worn around their waists, was for hand-to-hand fighting. A longer sword *(katana)*, thrust through their belts, could be wielded from horseback. Many used long poles with curved blades
10 *(naginata)* that could break the enemy's arrows fired at the samurai.

   Their armor was made from separate plates of metal or wood, held together with leather or silk. Their metal helmets usually had flaps to shield their necks. Warriors often
20 wore fierce-looking face masks to frighten their enemies. With this armor, a samurai was always ready for battle!

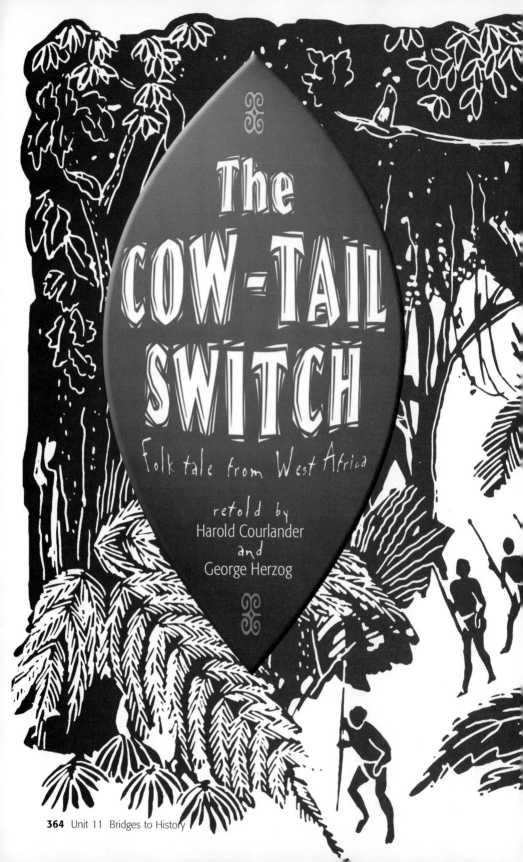

The

COW-TAIL SWITCH

Folk tale from West Africa

retold by
Harold Courlander
and
George Herzog

How can a simple question bring a man back to life?

Connect to Your Life

Talk with a partner about how your family passes on family history. Do they rely on pictures or stories, or both? What is one of your favorite family stories?

Key to the Folk Tale

From A.D. 800s to 1100s, West African kingdoms grew in wealth and power. But people still used folk tales, legends, and myths to pass on their history and values.

"The Cow-Tail Switch" is based on a folk tale from the West African nation of Liberia. These stories often are about a problem or puzzle that listeners try to solve. The decorated cow-tail switch in the story is a symbol of power in many West African nations. In this tale, the switch is also a symbol of a father's love.

Vocabulary Preview

Words to Know

hover   sinews
scattered   clamor

 Reading Coach CD-ROM selection

Read to find out what happens to Ogaloussa and his family.

Near the edge of the Liberian rain forest was the village of Kundi. Its rice and cassava fields spread in all directions. Cattle grazed in the grassland near the river. Smoke from the fires in the round clay houses seeped through the palmleaf roofs, and from a

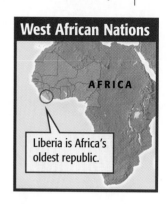

West African Nations

AFRICA

Liberia is Africa's oldest republic.

10 distance these faint columns of smoke seemed to hover over the village. Men and boys fished in the river with nets, and women pounded grain in wooden mortars before the houses.

hover
(hŭv' ər)
v. hang above something

mortars
(môr' tərz)
bowls in which grain is pounded into flour

In this village, with his wife and many children, lived a hunter by the name of Ogaloussa.

One morning Ogaloussa took his weapons down from the wall of his house and went

20 into the forest to hunt. His wife and his children went to tend their fields, and drove their cattle out to graze. The day passed, and they ate their evening meal of manioc and fish. Darkness came, but Ogaloussa didn't return.

Another day went by, and still Ogaloussa didn't come back. They talked about it and wondered what could have detained him. A week passed, then a month. Sometimes Ogaloussa's sons mentioned that he hadn't come home. The family cared

30 for the crops, and the sons hunted for game, but after a while they no longer talked about Ogaloussa's disappearance.

REREAD
What has happened to Ogaloussa?

Then one day, a few months later, another son was born to Ogaloussa's wife. His name was Puli. Puli grew older. He began to sit up and crawl. The time came when Puli began to talk, and the first thing he said was, "Where is my father?"

THINK IT THROUGH

How do family members act when Ogaloussa fails to return?

FOCUS

Read to discover how Puli's question affects his brothers.

The other sons looked across the rice fields.

"Yes," one of them said. "Where is Father?"

40   "He should have returned long ago," another one said.

"Something must have happened. We ought to look for him," a third son said.

"He went into the forest, but where will we find him?" another one asked.

"I saw him go," one of them said. "He went that way, across the river. Let us follow the trail and search for him."

REREAD

Why do you think the brothers decide to look for their father?

So the sons took their weapons and started out to

50 look for Ogaloussa. When they were deep among the great trees and vines of the forest they lost the trail. They searched in the forest until one of them found the trail again. They followed it until they lost the way once more, and then another son found the trail. It was dark in the forest, and many times they became lost. Each time another son found the way. At last they came to a clearing among the trees, and there on the ground scattered about lay Ogaloussa's bones and

scattered

(skăt′ ərd)

adj. thrown about

60 his rusted weapons. They knew then that Ogaloussa had been killed in the hunt.

One of the sons stepped forward and said, "I know how to put a dead person's bones together." He gathered all of Ogaloussa's bones and put them together, each in its right place.

Another son said, "I have knowledge too. I know how to cover the skeleton with sinews and flesh." He went to work, and he covered Ogaloussa's bones with sinews and flesh.

sinews
(sĭn′ yōoz)
n. muscles and tendons

70 A third son said, "I have the power to put blood into a body." He went forward and put blood into Ogaloussa's veins, and then he stepped aside.

Another of the sons said, "I can put breath into a body." He did his work, and when he was through they saw Ogaloussa's chest rise and fall.

"I can give the power of movement to a body," another of them said. He put the power of movement into his father's body, and Ogaloussa sat up and opened his eyes.

80 "I can give him the power of speech," another son said. He gave the body the power of speech, and then he stepped back.

Ogaloussa looked around him. He stood up.

"Where are my weapons?" he asked.

They picked up his rusted weapons from the grass where they lay and gave them to him. They then returned the way they had come, through the forest and the rice fields, until they had arrived once more in the village.

THINK IT THROUGH
What does each son do to help his father?

FOCUS

What do you think Ogaloussa will do when he returns home?

90 Ogaloussa went into his house. His wife prepared a bath for him and he bathed. She prepared food for him and he ate. Four days he remained in the house, and on the fifth day he came out and shaved his head, because this is what people did when they came back from the land of the dead.

Afterwards he killed a cow for a great feast. He took the cow's tail and braided it. He decorated it with beads and cowry shells and bits of shiny metal. It was a beautiful thing. Ogaloussa carried it with him to 100 important affairs. When there was a dance or an important ceremony he always had it with him. The people of the village thought it was the most beautiful cow-tail switch they had ever seen.

REREAD
Try to picture in your mind what the cow-tail switch looks like.

Soon there was a celebration in the village because Ogaloussa had returned from the dead. The people dressed in their best clothes, the musicians brought out their instruments, and a big dance began. The drummers beat their drums and the women sang. 110 Everyone was happy.

Ogaloussa carried his cow-tail switch, and everyone admired it. Some of the men grew bold and came forward to Ogaloussa and asked for the cow-tail switch, but Ogaloussa kept it in his hand. Now and then there was a clamor and much confusion as many people asked for it at once. The women and children begged for it too, but Ogaloussa refused them all.

clamor
(klăm′ ər)
n. noise made by many people

Finally he stood up to talk. The dancing stopped and 120 people came close to hear what Ogaloussa had to say.

"A long time ago I went into the forest," Ogaloussa said. "While I was hunting I was killed by a leopard. Then my sons came for me. They brought me back from the land of the dead to my village. I will give this cow-tail switch to one of my sons. All of them have done something to bring me back from the dead, but I have only one cow tail to give. I shall give it to the one who did the most to bring me home."

So an argument started.

THINK IT THROUGH
What does Ogaloussa decide to do?

FOCUS
Read to find out which son Ogaloussa chooses.

"He will give it to me!" one of the sons said. "It was I who did the most, for I found the trail in the forest when it was lost!"

"No, he will give it to me!" another son said. "It was I who put his bones together!"

"It was I who covered his bones with sinews and flesh!" another said. "He will give it to me!"

"It was I who gave him the power of movement!" another son said. "I deserve it most!"

Another son said it was he who should have the switch, because he had put blood in Ogaloussa's veins. Another claimed it because he had put breath in the body. Each of the sons argued his right to possess the wonderful cow-tail switch.

Before long not only the sons but the other people
of the village were talking. Some of them argued that
the son who had put blood in Ogaloussa's veins
150 should get the switch, others that the one who had
given Ogaloussa's breath should get it. Some of them
believed that all of the sons had done equal things,
and that they should share it. They argued back and
forth this way until Ogaloussa asked them to be quiet.

"To this son I will give the cow-tail switch, for I
owe most to him," Ogaloussa said.

> He came forward and bent low and
> handed it to Puli, the little boy who had
> been born while Ogaloussa was in the
> 160 forest.

REREAD

Is this the son you thought would get the cow-tail switch? Why or why not?

The people of the village remembered then that the
child's first words had been, "Where is my father?"
They knew that Ogaloussa was right.

For it was a saying among them that a man is not
really dead until he is forgotten.

THINK IT THROUGH

1. Each of the sons helps bring his father to life. How
   does Puli's question help his father the most?
2. What do you think this saying means: "a man is
   not really dead until he is forgotten"? How is
   Ogaloussa almost forgotten?
3. If you were Ogaloussa, to which son would you
   give the cow-tail switch? Explain your answer.

Reader's Choice

Longer Selections for Independent Reading

Unit 12
Fiction

What kind of challenge do you like to read about? Someone fighting for survival? Someone going against the crowd? How about someone surviving a really, *really* bad day?

You've read short pieces—now try biting into a longer story. What's better about longer? The writers can put more twists and turns in their plots. They can vary their settings and give their characters more to say and do.

Which story do you want to read first? The choice is yours!

from

The Call of the Wild

by Jack London
retold by Teresa Langness

Buck is thrown into a world where only the strong survive. Will he kill or be killed?

Connect to Your Life

Have you ever visited a place totally different from your neighborhood or hometown? What was it like? How did people treat you there?

Key to the Novel Excerpt

Jack London sailed to the Klondike, in Canada, to write about the gold rush of 1897. In that frozen country, people traveled mostly by dogsled. This created a huge demand for dogs. London watched as dogs from warmer climates struggled to live in the harsh land. Nature was a stern teacher. Those who couldn't learn, died. These chapters from *The Call of the Wild* tell the beginning of this exciting story from a dog's point of view.

Vocabulary Preview

Words to Know

realm	dominance	eerie
primitive	edible	

 Reading Coach CD-ROM selection

from The Call of the Wild   **375**

| What kind of life does Buck have in his home in California?

Chapter I: **Into the Primitive**

Buck did not read the newspapers, or he would have known that trouble was coming. Trouble was in store for every strong dog with warm, long hair, from Canada to California. Because men had found a yellow metal, ships and trains were rushing men to the Northland. These men wanted dogs. They wanted heavy dogs with strong muscles and furry coats to keep off the frost.

10   Buck lived at a big house in the sun-kissed Santa Clara Valley. Judge Miller's place, it was called. It stood among trees and wide lawns. In back there were horse stables, servants' cabins, orchards, and berry patches. There was a water tank where Judge Miller's boys swam. And Buck ruled over all this land. Here he had lived for all the four years of his life. It was true, there were other dogs, but they didn't count. They lived in the kennels or in the house. But Buck was neither house-dog nor kennel-dog. The

20 whole realm was his.

kennels
(kĕn′ əlz)
shelters for dogs

realm
(rĕlm)
n. kingdom

    He jumped into the swimming tank or went hunting with the Judge's sons. He took long walks with the Judge's daughters. At night he lay at the Judge's feet before the roaring fire. He guarded the Judge's grandsons on their trips to the berry patches. He was king over all the creeping, crawling, flying things of Judge Miller's place, humans included.

REREAD
What details show that Buck is a leader?

30   Buck's father, Elmo, a huge St. Bernard, had been
the Judge's best friend. Buck had now taken his
father's place. He was not as large as his father—he
weighed only one hundred and forty pounds, for his
mother had been a Scotch shepherd dog.

Buck had grown up with pride, like a country
gentleman, but he was not lazy. He hunted outdoors
and loved to swim. This was the kind of dog Buck
was in the fall of 1897, when the Klondike gold strike
dragged men from all over the world into the frozen
40   North.

THINK IT THROUGH

How would you describe Buck's life? Find three or four details
in the story to support your answer.

FOCUS

Read about the changes that begin to happen in Buck's life.

Manuel was one of the gardener's helpers at
Judge Miller's place. Buck did not know that
Manuel was not to be trusted. He had lost money
gambling, and he needed some cash to feed his
family. One night when the Judge was not home,
Manuel took Buck on a long walk. He walked Buck
all the way to a park and stopped to talk to a man.
The man handed Manuel money and asked him to
put a rope around Buck's neck. Manuel wrapped a
50   rope around Buck's neck and said,
"Twist it if you need to choke him."

REREAD

What has
Manuel done
with Buck?

Buck stood quietly. He trusted people
he knew, but when the stranger took the
rope, he began to growl. To his surprise,
the rope tightened around his neck. He sprang at the

man, who grabbed him by the throat and threw him on his back. The rope tightened again. Buck struggled, more angry than he had ever been—he had never been treated this way. The man threw him onto the baggage car of a train, and away they went.

Buck's tongue hurt, and he felt like a kidnapped king. The man saw his angry eyes and tried to grab his throat again. Buck bit the man's hand, so he was choked again, until his senses left him. The next day, they got off in San Francisco. The man took Buck, who was still dazed and in pain, to a little shed behind a saloon on the waterfront. The man grumbled that he only got fifty dollars for delivering the dog and hurt his hand doing it. The saloonkeeper helped him take the collar off Buck's neck and put him in a cagelike crate.

What did they want with him, these strange men? Why were they keeping him in this crate?

There Buck lay for the rest of the night. He could not understand what it all meant. What did they want with him, these strange men? Why were they keeping him in this crate? Several times during the night he heard a noise and jumped up, hoping to see the Judge. Each time it was only the saloonkeeper. When Buck saw him, his joyful bark would become a growl. But the saloonkeeper left him alone.

THINK IT THROUGH
What is happening to Buck for the first time in his life?

Read to find out what Buck learns from his first trainer.

80   In the morning, four men came and picked up the crate. Buck barked at them through the bars. They laughed and poked sticks at him. After that, the crate passed through many hands. Buck rode in a wagon, then a truck, then a boat, then a train, and finally a wagon again. For two days and nights this wagon dragged along, and for two days and nights Buck did not eat or drink. His throat and tongue hurt from lack of water. His eyes turned red. He became such an angry beast during

90 this terrible experience that the Judge himself would not have known him.

REREAD
Try to picture this scene in your mind. How is Buck changing?

The deliverymen felt glad to be rid of him when they reached Seattle. They carried the crate into a small back yard. A man in a red sweater came out and signed the driver's book. Buck snarled at the man and pushed against the bars. The man smiled and got an ax and a club.

"You going to take him out now?" the driver asked.

"Sure," the man said. The other four ran to a safe

100 place as he pried the crate open with the ax. Buck banged against the crate and bit the wood.

"Now, you red-eyed devil," the man said when he had made a hole big enough for Buck to fit through. Buck's mouth foamed. He jumped at the man in the red sweater. Just as he was about to bite the man, he felt a shock. He fell to the ground. He had never been struck by a club in his life. He got up and leaped at the man. The shock came again and he fell to the ground. A dozen times he charged. Each time the club

110 smashed him down.

from The Call of the Wild **379**

After the next blow he crawled to his feet. Blood flowed from his nose, mouth, and ears and matted his beautiful fur. The man charged him and hit him harder on the nose. The pain grew worse than ever. Buck roared and ran at the man, but the club caught him under the jaw and flipped him over. For the last time he rushed. The man struck so hard that Buck could do nothing but lie there. He could not even think.

120 "He's no slouch at dog-breaking. That's what I say," one of the men on the wall cried out. Buck's senses came back to him but not his strength. He lay where he had fallen and watched the man in the red sweater.

slouch
(slouch)
lazy person

"Answers to the name of Buck," the man said, reading the saloonkeeper's letter. "Well, Buck, my boy, we've had our little contest. You've learned your place. Be a good dog and all will go well. Be a bad dog, and I'll whale the stuffin' out of you.

130 Understand?"

whale the stuffin' out of you
expression meaning "beat severely"

As he spoke, he patted the head he had pounded. Buck's hair stood on end, but he did not make a sound. Then the man brought Buck water, and Buck lapped it up. Later Buck ate a meal of raw meat from the man's hand. He was beaten, and he knew it, but he was not broken. He saw that he stood no chance against a man with a club. He had learned the lesson,

140 and in all his life he never forgot it. He began to understand primitive law.

primitive
(prĭm' ĭ tĭv)
adj. from an earlier, wilder time

REREAD
What do you think "he was beaten … but he was not broken" means?

THINK IT THROUGH
What did the man in the red sweater teach Buck?

FOCUS _____

> Buck gets two new owners. Read to see what happens.

As the days went by, other dogs came. Some came in crates and others at the ends of ropes. Some came easily. Some came roaring as he had come. The man in the red sweater broke them all. Now and then other men came and talked to the man in the red sweater. Money passed between them, and they took one or more of the dogs away with them. Buck did not know where they went, for they never came back.
150 He began to fear his own future.

Soon his time came. A man with a wrinkled face arrived. He spoke in a strange way that Buck did not always understand. When he saw Buck he said, "What a bully dog! How much?"

> **bully**
> (boŏl′ ē)
> slang for
> "wonderful"

"Three hundred, and a good deal at that, Perrault," said the man in the red sweater. Perrault knew dogs. When he looked at Buck he knew this dog was one in a thousand. Perrault delivered dispatches for
160 the Canadian government. Buck could help him bring the messages more quickly.

> **dispatches**
> (dĭ spăch′ ĭz)
> official reports
> that are sent
> quickly

Buck saw money pass between Perrault and the man in the red sweater. Soon Perrault led him away, along with Curly, an easy-going Newfoundland. That was the last he saw of the man in the red sweater. He and Curly ended up on a ship called the *Narwhal*. As they looked back at the city of Seattle, they did not know
170 they would never see the Southland again.

> **Newfoundland**
> (noō′ fən lənd)
> breed of large
> dog, developed in
> Newfoundland,
> Canada

Perrault turned the dogs over to a dark-skinned giant called François. He took Buck and Curly down to a lower deck of the boat to join two other dogs.

The dogs knew a change was coming. François leashed them and brought them on deck.

One of them tried to steal Buck's food, but François's whip stopped him. The other dog, Dave, kept to himself. When the boat rolled and bucked, they all yelped in fear, but Dave just yawned and went to sleep again.

Buck grew to respect Perrault and François. They
180 were both fair, calm men, but they knew dogs too well to be fooled by them. They tended to the dogs during the long voyage. Each day was just like the next, only colder. Finally the ship stopped moving and grew still. The dogs knew a change was coming. François leashed them and brought them on deck. At the first step onto the cold deck, Buck's feet sank into a white mushy something very much like mud. He sprang back with a snort. More of this white stuff was falling through the air. He shook himself, but
190 more of it fell upon him. He sniffed it, then licked some of it on his tongue. It bit like fire then was gone. This puzzled him. Everyone watching Buck began to laugh. He felt ashamed. He did not know why, for it was his first snow.

THINK IT THROUGH
How do Buck's new owners compare to the man in the red sweater?

Chapter II: **The Law of Club and Fang**
Summary

Buck soon learns the ways of the dogs. They all fight for food and for survival. He sees the dog named Curly killed by the pack for trying to make friends with a mean husky. As Curly begins to die, the other dogs pounce on her and eat her.

200   *Buck obeys the commands of the men out of fear of being whipped. The weather is cold, and there is never enough food. No longer living with people who love him, he listens to his own instincts and quickly becomes wild.*

FOCUS _____

François and Perrault's dog team includes Spitz (the lead dog), Joe, Billee, Sol-leks, Dave, Dub, Dolly, and Pike. How does Buck get along with the team?

Chapter III: **The Dominant Beast**

The wish for dominance was strong in Buck. In this fierce new life, it grew and grew. His new cunning gave him a sense of control.

dominance
(dŏm′ ə nəns)
n. power over others

He did not pick fights, even with Spitz. On the other hand, Spitz, who saw him as a
210 dangerous enemy, bullied him whenever he could. He kept trying to start a fight that could only end in the death of one or the other.

REREAD
What do you think will happen between the dogs?

One snowy night, Perrault and François lit their fire and set up camp on the ice of a lake. Buck made his nest under a rock. He hated to leave the warm nest to eat his dinner. When he did, he came back to find Spitz inside the nest. Now the beast in him roared. Buck sprang upon Spitz in a fury. François rushed

220 out to see what happened. He cheered Buck on and said, "Get that thief!" Spitz looked eager to fight as Buck circled around him. Just then, a pack of more than a hundred starving huskies crept into camp to watch the fight. Perrault and François swung clubs at them, but the wild dogs fought back. They were crazed by the smell of the food. Perrault found one with his head in the grub box. He hit the dog and the box spilled onto the ground. Twenty hungry brutes rushed to get the bread and bacon.

230 Clubs fell upon them. They howled but kept eating until the last crumb was gone.

brutes
(brŏŏts)
beasts

As soon as the team dogs came out of their nests, the wild dogs attacked them. Never had Buck seen such dogs. Their hides barely hung on their bones. Their eyes blazed. Drool dripped from their fangs. The hunger-madness made them terrifying. There was no stopping them. The wild dogs drove the team dogs against the cliff. Three huskies attacked Buck and cut his head and shoulders. Billee cried. Dave and Sol-leks

240 fought bravely side by side. Joe broke one dog's leg and then Pike leaped upon the injured dog and broke its neck. Buck turned and sank his teeth into the throat of another dog. The warm taste of blood made him fearless. He flung himself upon another. At the same time he felt teeth sink into his own throat. It was Spitz, attacking from the side.

REREAD
How does Buck act in his first real fight? Why do you think Spitz attacks him now?

Perrault and François had cleaned out their part of the camp. They hurried over to save their

250 sled dogs, swinging their clubs. The wave of beasts rolled back, and Buck shook himself free. Then the men went back to chase more huskies away from the grub, leaving the team dogs alone again. Billee, scared

into bravery, sprang through the circle and ran away over the ice. Pike and Dub followed, with the rest behind. Buck braced himself, for he saw Spitz rushing upon him. Once off his feet, he knew there was no hope for him. But after the shock of Spitz's charge, he joined the fight out on the lake.

THINK IT THROUGH

Find at least three challenges from the other dogs that Buck has faced so far.

FOCUS

The injured team goes on. Read to see how rough the trail is for them.

260   Later, the nine team-dogs gathered together in the forest. Every one of them was hurt in four or five places. Some were hurt badly. Dub had a broken hind leg. Dolly had a torn throat. Joe had lost an eye. The good-natured Billee, with an ear chewed to pieces, cried through the night. At daybreak, they limped back to camp. They found the two men angry and brooding. Half their food supply was gone. The huskies had chewed through the sled lashings . Nothing edible had

270   escaped them. They had eaten Perrault's moose-hide moccasins , chunks out of the leather traces, and even the end of François's whip. He turned away from the whip to look over his wounded dogs.

"Ah, my friends," he said softly. "Maybe it make you mad dogs, those many bites. Maybe all mad dog. What you think, eh, Perrault?"

lashings
(lăsh' ĭngz)
straps that bind the sled together

edible
(ĕd' ə bəl)
adj. able to be eaten

moccasins
(mŏk' ə sĭnz)
soft leather shoes

The courier shook his head. With four hundred miles of trail between him and Dawson, he could not afford to have mad dogs. Within two hours, the men made some repairs and got the team on its way.

The dogs struggled painfully over the hardest part of the trail they had yet covered.

The Thirty Mile River was wide open. Its wild water would not freeze, except in the quiet places. It took six days to cover those thirty miles. Every step brought risk of life to dog and man. A dozen times, Perrault broke through the ice bridges. He pulled himself out by his pole each time. But a cold snap was on, and it fell to fifty degrees below zero. So each time he broke through he had to build a fire and dry his clothes to save his own life.

Nothing stopped him. That's why he had been chosen as a government courier. He took risks, struggling on from dawn until dark. He sometimes took the sled along rim ice that bent under foot. Once, the sled broke through, with Dave and Buck. They were half-frozen and almost drowned by the time they were dragged out. It took a warming fire to save them. They had to run around the fire, sweating and thawing, close to the flames.

At another time Spitz fell through. Most of the team was dragged in, all the way up to Buck. He dug his paws into the slippery ice and pulled back with all his strength. The only escape was up a cliff. Perrault climbed it and then hoisted the dogs up by rope. François came last with the sled and load. Then they had to use the ropes to lower the dogs safely onto the other side. It took all day to go a quarter of a mile.

courier
(kŏŏr′ ē ər)
someone who delivers dispatches

REREAD
What makes the trail so difficult for men and dogs?

By the time they got to the next town, the dogs were all tired. But Perrault wanted to make up for lost time. They covered thirty-five to forty miles a day for the next few days.

Buck's feet were not as hard as the feet of the huskies. All day he limped in pain. At night, he could not move, and François had to bring him his fish. He also rubbed Buck's feet each night after supper. He
320 even cut off the tops of his moccasins to make four moccasins for Buck. This was a great relief. One morning, when François forgot to put them on him, Buck lay on his back, waving his feet in the air. Even Perrault had to grin. Once Buck's feet finally grew used to the trail, they threw the foot-gear away.

THINK IT THROUGH
Describe two or three major hardships faced by the dogs and men.

FOCUS
Read to learn how Buck begins to challenge Spitz.

One day as they were getting ready to leave, Dolly suddenly went mad. She let out a long wolf howl, then sprang for Buck. He had never seen a dog go mad, yet he knew enough to run away from her. He
330 raced with the panting Dolly, who was one leap behind him. He ran fast out of fear. She ran fast out of madness. He went through the woods and crossed the river to first one island, then another. François called to him and he looped back, hoping the man would save him. François held the ax in his hand. As Buck shot past him, the ax crashed down upon mad Dolly's head.

Buck slumped against the sled, sobbing for breath. Now Spitz saw his chance. He sprang upon Buck, tearing the flesh to the bone. But he did not get any farther. François's lash fell upon Spitz, who got the worst whipping of any dog yet.

"He's one devil, that Spitz," said Perrault. "Some day him kill that Buck."

"That Buck two devils," François replied. "Some fine day him get mad and chew that Spitz all up and spit him out on the snow. Sure. I know."

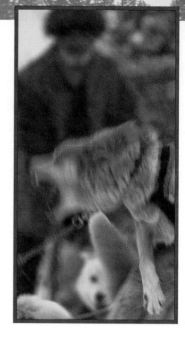

From then on it was war between them. Buck was not soft like other Southland dogs Spitz had known. The club of the man in the red sweater had made Buck cunning. He was willing to wait for just the right moment to take Spitz's place as leader. He wanted it because it was his nature. He had been gripped by the pride of the trail and trace. It was the pride that makes dogs willing to die joyfully in the harness and breaks their hearts if they are cut out of the harness. This was the pride of Dave as wheel-dog and of Sol-leks as he pulled with all his strength. It was the pride that made Spitz thrash the dogs who were lazy or slow. It was this pride that made him fear Buck as a lead dog. And this was Buck's pride too.

Buck tried to protect the other dogs and become their leader. When Pike hid one morning, Spitz searched all over, snarling with anger until he found

pride of the trail and trace
pride in being a sled dog

REREAD
Why does Buck want to be the leader?

thrash
(thrăsh)
punish

him. Buck flew in between them so Spitz could not punish Pike. François had to beat Buck to turn him away from the fight. In the days that followed, Buck continued to come between Spitz and the other dogs, but only when François was not around. Soon the dogs did not want to do as they were told. The team went from bad to worse. There was trouble coming, and at the bottom of it was Buck.

380   Finally they reached Dawson one afternoon. Here were many men and dogs, all at work. The dogs hauled cabin logs and firewood. They took loads to the mines. They did the work that horses did in the Santa Clara Valley. Here and there Buck met Southland dogs, but they were mostly the wild wolf-husky breed. Every night they howled an eerie chant, and Buck loved to join in the song.

> **eerie**
> (îr′ ē)
> *adj.* creating a feeling of mystery and fear

   The aurora borealis flamed coldly
390 overhead. The stars leaped in a frost dance. The land froze under its cloak of snow. This song of the huskies might have been life breaking through the cold. But they sang it in a pleading, sad key, with long wails and sobs. So it seemed more like a song of the struggle for survival. It was an old song, as old as the breed itself. Buck felt stirred when he moaned and sobbed it. He sang of the pain of living that was the pain of his wild fathers. His
400 fears were their fears. The song stirred some part of him that remembered the age of fire and roof. He knew the raw beginnings of life in the howling ages.

> **aurora borealis**
> (ə rôr′ ə bôr′ ē ăl′ ĭs)
> curtains of light that appear in the night sky near the North Pole

> **REREAD**
> This song reminds Buck of past ages when humans and animals lived in the wild.

THINK IT THROUGH
In what ways does Buck challenge Spitz?

Read to see how the war between the two dogs ends.

A week after they pulled into Dawson, they dropped down to the Yukon Trail and turned toward the ocean. Perrault was carrying dispatches even more important than those he had brought in. Also, the travel pride had gripped him. He wanted to make the record trip of the year. It looked as though he could.
410 The dogs had rested for a week. The trail was hard packed. And the police had placed supplies of grub along the way, so they could travel light.

They made good time, but not without trouble. The revolt led by Buck had destroyed the unity of the team. The dogs no longer worked together as a team. And no longer did the dogs fear Spitz.

REREAD
Why do you think the dogs no longer fear Spitz?

Pike robbed him of half a fish one night and gulped it down with Buck as his guard. Another night Dub and Joe fought
420 Spitz. Even Billee was less good-natured with Spitz. As for Buck, he never came near Spitz without growling. In fact, he acted like a bully.

The dogs also argued amongst themselves more. François lashed them, but it did no good. While he backed up Spitz, Buck backed up the rest of the team. He knew Buck was behind the problems, yet Buck worked hard in the traces and never got caught making trouble. He loved his work pulling the sled almost as much as he loved starting fights among his mates.
430 One night after supper, Dub found a rabbit. He tried to catch it but missed. In a second, the whole team was in full chase. Fifty police dogs from a nearby camp heard and joined them. The rabbit sped down the river, turned off into a small creek, and went up the frozen bed. It ran over the snow while

the dogs chased behind. Buck led the pack of sixty around bend after bend.

440 There is a joy that marks the peak of life. It comes to the artist as he paints. It comes to the soldier, war-mad on a field. It came to Buck leading the pack, sounding the old wolf-cry, chasing down the food that was alive and that fled before him in the moonlight. He was calling out to his animal instincts, those that went back to the dawn of Time. He felt the surging of life, the perfect joy of each muscle and joint, of everything that was not death.

surging
(sûr′ jĭng)
rising up

REREAD
How does the chase make Buck feel?

It was all aglow and moving. It was flying under the stars and over the face of dead matter that did 450 not move.

Meanwhile, Spitz left the pack and took a shortcut. Buck did not know this, and as he rounded the bend, the rabbit still flitting before him, he saw another larger animal leap from a high bank into the path of the rabbit. It was Spitz. The rabbit could not turn. As the white teeth broke its back in midair, it screamed as loudly as a man would scream. At the sound of this, the cry of Life plunging down into the grip of Death, the full pack raised its cry.

460 Buck did not cry out. He drove in upon Spitz, shoulder to shoulder, so hard that he missed the throat. They rolled over and over in the snow. Spitz got back on his feet, slashing Buck down the shoulder and leaping clear. Twice his teeth clipped together, like the steel jaws of a trap.

In a flash Buck knew it. The time had come. It was to the death. Calm came over the whiteness. Nothing moved. Not a leaf shook. The breaths of the dogs rose slowly in the frosty air. They had made short

470 work of the rabbit, these wolflike dogs. They, too, were silent as they drew into a circle.

Spitz was a practiced fighter. He never rushed until he was ready to receive a rush. When Buck tried to sink his teeth into the neck of the big white dog, fang clashed against fang, and lips were cut and bleeding. Time and time again he tried for the snow-white throat. Each time Spitz slashed him and got away.

Spitz was untouched, while Buck was bloody and panting hard. All the while, the silent, wolfish circle
480 waited to finish off whichever dog went down. As Buck grew winded, Spitz took to rushing. Once Buck went over but caught himself in midair. But Buck had a quality that made for greatness—imagination. He rushed for the shoulder, but in the end swept low and in. His teeth closed on Spitz's left foreleg. There was a crunch of breaking bone, and the white dog faced him on three legs. Three times he tried to knock him over.
490 Then he repeated the trick and broke the right foreleg. Despite the pain, Spitz struggled to keep up. He saw the silent circle closing in upon him. He had seen the same thing many times before, only this time he was the one who was beaten.

winded
(wĭn′ dĭd)
out of breath

foreleg
(fôr′ lĕg′)
front leg of an animal

REREAD
Try to see the fight in your mind. What will happen if either dog is knocked down?

There was no hope for him. The circle came in until he could feel their breath on him. Buck could see their eyes fixed upon him. A pause seemed to fall. Every animal stood still as though turned to stone. Spitz

500 staggered back and forth, growling as if to scare off his own death. Then Buck sprang in and out, knocking him down. The dark circle became a dot on the moon-flooded snow as Spitz disappeared from view. Buck stood and looked on, the beast who had finally made his kill.

THINK IT THROUGH

1. What happens to Spitz at the end? How does Buck defeat him?
2. What qualities help Buck become the leader of the dogsled team?
3. What do you think the title *The Call of the Wild* means?
4. Where in the story do you think Buck feels "the call of the wild"? Give examples to support your answer.

Everyone makes fun of Talmadge. If Meg becomes his friend, the class will pick on her too. Will she go against the crowd?

The Valentine

by Emily Crofford

Connect to Your Life

Have you or someone you know been picked on by others? Tell a partner about it.

Key to the Story

Some of the conversation in this story is written in dialect. **Dialect** is the distinct way in which people speak in a certain region of the country. Talmadge, a character in the story, is from eastern Tennessee, which was first settled by people from England and Scotland. Some of the words and phrases that Talmadge uses reflect this background.

Vocabulary Preview

Words to Know

twinge	meekness
commenced	embarrassment
vow	

 Reading Coach CD-ROM selection

The Valentine **395**

My first thought when the new boy came into the classroom was that we girls had wasted a lot of time fussing with our hair.

"Class," Miss Gibson said, "this is Talmadge McLinn. His family just moved here from eastern Tennessee."

"From Wild Hog Holler, to be exact," Talmadge said.

Maxine giggled and others sniggered. I didn't, although I had never heard anyone talk like he did, and Wild Hog Holler was
10 a funny name.

> **sniggered**
> (snĭg' ərd)
> laughed in a
> partly stifled way

Miss Gibson glared at us; the room became quiet. I figured Maxine, who giggled about everything, was probably choking herself.

Talmadge's feet were so big, they called even more attention to his clubbed right foot. Clubfeet were not unusual, but I had never seen one like his. His weight came down on the outside of his little toe so that his heel was raised up about two inches from the
20 floor even when he stood still. He was wearing high-top work shoes—without socks, despite the January cold. His shabby overalls stopped before they reached the tops of his shoes. His smile stretched from one side of his face to the other, offering us his friendship, asking for ours.

> **clubfeet**
> (klŭb' fēt')
> feet that are
> curled or twisted
> at the ankles,
> heels, and toes

"Which cheer ye want I should set in?" Talmadge asked Miss Gibson, and Stinky Sterret burst
30 out laughing. Miss Gibson sent him out into the hall.

> **cheer**
> (chîr)
> dialect form of
> *chair*

Stinky, I thought, had forgotten that when he first came from Oklahoma the other boys had ragged him until he'd turned mean and earned the name Stinky.

> **ragged**
> (răgd)
> teased

THINK IT THROUGH

What about Talmadge makes the others laugh at him?

FOCUS —————

What do you think will happen when everyone goes out for the first recess? Read to find out.

At recess we girls talked about Talmadge. "I feel sorry for him," Josie said.

Maxine went into a fit of giggles. "But do you want
40 him for a boyfriend?"

Josie tossed her head. "I have more boyfriends now than I know what to do with. I just said I feel sorry for him."

"Me too," I said. "Stinky is going to make his life miserable."

Stinky did, too, beginning that very recess. He ran by Talmadge, grabbed his cap, and threw it to Raymond. Talmadge seemed to think it was a game and kept grinning and trying to recapture his cap
50 while other boys joined in to keep it away from him.

We girls didn't think it was very funny, except for Maxine. We kept watching, though, waiting to see what would happen.

The smile on Talmadge's face held even when Stinky caught the cap, pinched it on his nose, and blew. That's when Miss Gibson, who had been standing close to the door talking to another teacher, stepped in. Walking fast, her head thrust forward like

a snapping turtle's, she charged into the middle of the
60 group and snatched the cap away from Stinky.

You shouldn't have done that, Miss Gibson, I
thought. *From now on, Stinky will make Talmadge
his enemy.*

Talmadge knew that, too. Wiping his cap
on the dead grass, he said, "Hit don't
make no never mind." He settled the cap
back on his head. "They was just funnin',
Miss Gibson."

> **hit**
> (hĭt)
> dialect form of *it*

Stinky might have been funning before. Now his
70 mouth turned down at the corners in hate.

THINK IT THROUGH
Talmadge has a friendly nature. Why does Stinky start to hate
him?

FOCUS _____
Talmadge starts to change. What does Meg learn about him
that surprises her?

In class Talmadge grew quieter and quieter during
the next two weeks. His hand stopped shooting up to
answer questions; he stayed in during recess and read
rather than go outside.

John Edward, the boy I liked best, didn't act mean to
Talmadge, but he didn't make friends with him.
Nobody did. I stayed away from him too until Mother
sent a note one day that I had had an earache the night
before and couldn't go outside to play. At first Miss
80 Gibson was in the room with Talmadge and me, then
she left. Her feet were still tapping down the
hall when Talmadge sidled into a desk in
the next row from mine.

> **sidled**
> (sīd'ld)
> moved closer

"I'm sorry ye're feeling poorly, Meg," he said.

"Oh, I'm all right," I said. "I had an earache last night. It's gone except for a twinge now and then."

> **twinge**
> (twĭnj)
> *n.* sharp, sudden pain

"My sister gits earaches," he said. "They must be awful." He looked so 90 concerned I fidgeted.

"Ye ever read this here book?" he asked me.

> I glanced at the door and listened hard to see if any of the kids were hanging around in the hall. The only sounds were the muted squeals and laughter from the school grounds.

> **REREAD**
> Why is Meg worried about other kids being around?

"I don't think so," I said, and turned my head to the side to read the title. *Bob, Son of Battle,* it said. There was a picture of a collie dog's face under the title.

100 Talmadge turned from his place at about the middle of the book to the front pages and handed it to me. "It's hard to read," I said after a minute.

"At first it is," he said, "but ye'd soon git the hang of it. I ain't never lent it out before, but ye kin borry it when I'm done this time." He read aloud:

> **borry**
> (bôr' ē)
> dialect form of *borrow*

> *"Ay, the Gray Dogs, bless 'em!" the old man was saying.*
> *"Yo canna beat 'em not nohow. Known 'em ony*
> 110 *time this sixty year, I have, and niver knew a bad un yet."*

It sounded like music when Talmadge read it. "You talk kind of like that," I said.

He nodded. "The Thorntons—my mother was a Thornton—come from the Dalelands." He turned sideways in the desk. "Dalesmen air from England. My dad's people was from across the border—in Scotland.

Fer back the Thorntons and the McLinns spilt blood feudin' one with t'other. So when my mother and father got married, neither side would have aught to do with them. Mother used to cry about it. The feudin' ain't never quit, albeit my father says can't any two people tell the same tale about why it commenced in the first place."

"Oh," I said. I didn't know what else to say. It seemed so important to him that I added, "They were mean to treat your mother and father that way."

Talmadge stroked the book with his fingertips. "I got this here book fer Christmas when I was but a tyke. I'm just now gittin' to the point I can read it good."

There was something I wanted to know. "Talmadge—aren't you going to fight Stinky?"

A week ago, in front of the whole class, Stinky had challenged Talmadge to come behind the ditchbank and fight. Since then Stinky and the three boys who hung around with him had made remarks about Talmadge being yellow.

Talmadge closed the book and shook his head. "We come here to git away from fightin' much as to make a livin'. I seen enough fightin' to last me a lifetime." He traced his finger around the picture of the dog's face on the front of the book. "I've took a vow not to never fight agin." Glancing at me, he said, "I ain't told nobody else except John Edward."

"I won't tell," I said. "John Edward won't either."

aught
(ôt) old term for *anything*

albeit
(ôl bē' ĭt) although

commenced
(kə mĕnst') *v.* began; past tense of *commence*

vow
(vou) *n.* strong promise

THINK IT THROUGH
Why won't Talmadge fight Stinky?

FOCUS

What do you think will happen if Talmadge is pushed too far?

The bell rang; I grabbed my science book and
150 pretended to be studying. Talmadge started back
toward his desk. Too late. Maxine was standing in the
doorway, her bird eyes darting from one of us to the
other. She and Bonnie Lou walked by my desk and
Bonnie Lou said, "Looks like Meg has a new
sweetheart." Maxine bent over from the waist, she
giggled so hard.

After that, I avoided Talmadge. I didn't want the
others to think there was any truth in what Bonnie
Lou and Maxine had said about my liking him. Then
160 one day after the last bell rang I went outside and saw
Talmadge in a circle of other boys.

I saw immediately what had happened. Stinky had
come up behind Talmadge and yanked his *Bob, Son
of Battle* book out of his hand. For the first time since
he had started at our school, all of the
meekness went out of Talmadge.

"Give it back," he said, his voice so
commanding that Stinky blinked, and I
thought he was going to hand the book
170 to Talmadge. But the other boys were
nudging Stinky, saying things like "Git
him, Stinky!" "Make him show his
yellow streak."

> **meekness**
> (mēk′ nĭs)
> *n.* timid quality

> **REREAD**
> What causes the
> change in
> Talmadge?

John Edward didn't do that, but he didn't make a
move to stop it like he had other times either. He
licked his lips, glancing from Stinky to Talmadge.

Although he was taller than Stinky, Talmadge had
the bad foot. I didn't figure he had a chance.

Stinky dropped the book and kicked it to the side.
180 "You want it, hillbilly, pick it up!" he said.

A tremor passed through Talmadge, but because of our conversation I realized that it didn't come from fear. It came from fighting within himself. It struck me that John Edward knew that too.

THINK IT THROUGH

What does Meg realize about Talmadge?

FOCUS

If Talmadge breaks his vow, what might happen?

In one move, Talmadge shucked his coat, took a step forward, and hit Stinky high on the jaw. Stinky staggered and the people watching gasped with surprise. Stinky recovered quickly, though,
190 lowered his head, and charged, swinging hard. Talmadge moved in a circle, ducking and swaying to dodge Stinky's fists. Even when Stinky's blows landed they were short or glancing. Talmadge didn't move his head back enough once, though, and his nose began to dribble blood.

200   Kids from other classes were there now too, some silent, some shouting to stop it, others egging them on. Talmadge had only thrown one punch, but suddenly his fist

shot out again. He hit Stinky in the same place on his jaw. Stinky went down. Talmadge took a couple of long awkward steps and straddled him, pinning his

210 shoulders to the ground. He had won!

And then Talmadge did a terrible thing. He started to cry. Holding his arm over his eyes and his bleeding nose, he got up off Stinky, picked up his book, and walked away.

> **REREAD**
> Who won? Why does Talmadge start to cry?

Some of the crowd, led by Stinky's friends, were shouting "Go back to Wild Hog Holler!" I took a few steps toward Talmadge. *You did the right thing,* I wanted to tell him. *You had to stand up for yourself.*

220 The kids were all staring at me. "Go back to Wild Hog Holler!" I yelled.

THINK IT THROUGH
If Meg thinks Talmadge did the right thing, why does she join the other kids?

FOCUS
Read to see how the class reacts to Talmadge after the fight.

Generally a fight was the topic of conversation the next day, but nobody mentioned the one between Talmadge and Stinky. It was like we all wanted to forget about what had happened. I kept thinking about John Edward, and the way he had licked his lips when Talmadge and Stinky were about to fight. I finally worked it out. He hadn't been excited about the possibility of their fighting, but about whether or

230 not Talmadge could stick to his vow. I decided I liked another boy, Tom Garrity, better than I did John Edward.

I didn't want to talk with Talmadge after that day, though. He was too different; he didn't belong. John Edward looked through him. Nobody included him, or bothered him. He had become an outcast. When I knew he was looking at me, I pretended to be busy with my schoolwork. When he walked beside me as we were leaving
240 the building, I answered him politely and hurried away as soon as I could.

REREAD

How does Meg treat Talmadge? Why?

"It's just politeness," I said to my friend Grace as we walked home in a drizzling rain. "Mother and Daddy have drummed being polite and kind into me since I was born, so I can't help it."

Gentle Grace didn't answer. We had walked another quarter of a mile before she said, "Meg, you ain't being honest. You really like Talmadge."

250 "I don't like him! I can't stand him!"

Grace shrugged and said nothing more.

Finally, I broke the silence. "You know good and well that if I showed that I liked him, the other kids would peck me raw."

With Valentine's Day coming up, I began to get especially
260 nervous about Talmadge. If he brought me a mushy valentine I would just die.

Mother had never liked valentine boxes, not even for first grade, much less sixth. Considering that, I should have known better than to fuss about having to make my own valentines.

"You can either make them from the wallpaper book or forget it. And if you make one, you have to make them for every person in the class."

270   The next morning I hesitated before approaching the box, considering holding out Stinky's and Bonnie Lou's and Maxine's and Talmadge's. *Oh, what the heck*, I decided. *I might as well end it by giving a valentine to everybody.* I dropped all my envelopes through the slot.

Miss Gibson didn't hand out the valentines until the last period, and by that time I was a wreck. I had started imagining that I would get only four or five. I got 13. Josie and John Edward got more, but I didn't

280   feel too bad. The one from Tom Garrity was store-bought with an elephant on the front. "I've got a trunkful of love for you, Valentine," it said.

I felt sorry for Talmadge and was glad I had made a valentine for him. Mine had been one of the three he received. I had just printed "Happy Valentine's Day" in red and signed my name. There was no way the kids could make something of that.

THINK IT THROUGH

What are Meg's feelings about Talmadge? Find two or three details in the story that let you know.

FOCUS _____

Read to learn what happens when Talmadge visits Meg.

Talmadge did though. He caught up with me on the front steps as we were leaving school.

290   "Shore makes a feller feel good to git a valentine from a blossom-eyed gal like you,

shore
(shôr)
dialect form of
sure

Meg," he said. "I hope hit don't fret ye that I didn't give you one. I didn't give nary one—couldn't git around to making any."

fret
(frĕt)
worry

"That's all right," I said quickly and, turning my back to him, started talking to Josie.

Saturday morning, our house smelled of burning wood and the gingerbread Mother had baked. Cozy and happy, I was helping her quilt when Brownie gave 300 a warning growl from the porch. At that moment, I heard a call: "Hello!" My head jerked up, and I looked through the front window. There, beside the road, stood Talmadge.

I slid off the stool, and one of those miserable burning blushes I couldn't do a thing about raced from my neck right up to my hairline. "It's the new boy in our class," I said.

Daddy went to open the door, his face crinkling with amusement at my 310 embarrassment. "Come on in," he called, which also let Brownie know that the visitor was welcome.

embarrassment
(ĕm băr′ əs mənt)
n. feeling of shame when others see your weakness

Talmadge came up the boardwalk, scraped the road mud off his shoes on the front steps, and came inside, nodding and smiling.

"This is Talmadge," I said stiffly. "He moved here from Tennessee."

"From Wild Hog Holler, to be exact," Talmadge said, smiling all over his face.

320 Daddy chuckled with a merriment that matched Talmadge's and said, "I know your father. Fine man."

"Take Talmadge's coat for him, Meg," Mother said. There was a puzzled note in her voice, as if she didn't understand why I seemed to have forgotten the art of making welcome.

"I believe I'll keep it on awhile," Talmadge said. "I'm chilled to the marrow ."

> **marrow**
> (măr′ ō)
> inner part of the bones

Just then my brothers Bill and Correy came bursting in from the yard, puffing
330 and laughing.

"Talmadge!" Bill exclaimed.

"Hi, Bill," Talmadge said.

It didn't surprise me that Bill knew Talmadge—kids in the lower grades often knew the ones above them. It did surprise me that Talmadge knew Bill.

Correy was staring at Talmadge's clubfoot.

"That's Correy," Bill and I said at the same time, his tone proud and cheerful, mine forced. Talmadge squatted down, one knee up, one down, man-fashion,
340 so he would be eye level with Correy.

"Hi, Correy." He pointed at his foot. "Hit were like that when I come into this world." He winked. "Don't slow me down none, though."

THINK IT THROUGH
How does Meg's family treat Talmadge when he comes to visit?

FOCUS
Read to see how Meg reacts to what Talmadge brings her.

Then he came straight over to me, reached into his left overcoat pocket, took out a big white envelope, and handed it to me.

"I walked up the highway and hitched a ride into town and bought this," he said.

Fumbling, I opened the envelope.

350 "Hit's a valentine," Talmadge said. "Since Valentine's Day has done passed, I got it for half

price. With money I saved up myself."

The valentine was beautiful, lacy with delicate flowers and hearts on the front. Inside it said, "To My Sweetheart."

360 "I was goin' to git one that said 'To My Friend,'" Talmadge said nervously, "but they didn't have none like that."

Despite his bad foot, he had walked miles in bitter weather to bring a valentine to me. As I continued to gaze silently at it, I could tell that he was waiting for me to say something. Mother and Daddy and Bill and Correy were waiting too.

370 I relaxed. If the kids at school found out about Talmadge bringing the valentine, I would laugh and say, "I thought I would die!"

"It's the prettiest valentine I ever saw," I said. "Thank you very much."

Talmadge's ears turned red.

Smiling, I asked, "Would you like to have some gingerbread and buttermilk with us?"

REREAD
Why is Meg suddenly being friendly?

"Shore is a temptation," Talmadge said, "but I've 380 got to git on home. Been gone so long."

"At least take a piece with you," Mother said. She went quickly into the kitchen and came back with a big square of the cake.

We watched out the window as Talmadge started up the road eating the gingerbread. The snow had almost fizzled out, and the sun was sparkling around the edges of broken clouds.

"I'm proud of you," Daddy said to me in a soft, pleased voice. "Proud that you choose your friends
390 according to what's inside them. I've heard about the way the lad's been shunned."

I stared at the floor, too ashamed to lift my head. I could see Talmadge sitting hunched in his desk, his eyes pleading with me to be his friend; I could hear myself shouting, "Go back to Wild Hog Holler!"

shunned
(shŭnd) treated as an outcast by everyone

"It took courage not to go along with the crowd," Daddy said and reached out to touch me.

"Don't—please." My words came out choked.
400 I hurried into my room and scrambled into my coat, then ran blindly outside to the barn and climbed up to the loft. The fragrant, loose hay gave under my weight, cradling me when I sank down into it, muffling the sound when I said, "Talmadge, I'm sorry," and let the tears burst free.

THINK IT THROUGH

1. Why does Meg cry at the end?
2. Why do you think that Talmadge still wants to be Meg's friend?
3. What words would you use to describe Talmadge? Would you want him for a friend? Why or why not?
4. How do you think Meg will treat Talmadge in the future?

Jamie doesn't believe in luck. Then a streak of bad luck hits. Will it ruin his life?

The STREAK

by Walter Dean Myers

Connect to Your Life

Do you believe in luck? Talk over with a partner a time when you felt lucky or unlucky. What happened?

Key to the Story

In "The Streak," Jamie and his friends use a lot of slang and sports terms as they talk. You may not always know what each term means. But you can often use clues in the story to guess what the character is saying. And when the streak hits, the characters have a lot to say!

Vocabulary Preview

Words to Know

finesse   swollen

resign   strutting

Reading Coach CD-ROM selection

Jamie is having one of those really bad days. Read to find out what has happened.

Okay, so my name is Jamie, Jamie Farrell. Remember that, in case I get famous or something.

My main man, my ace, the Jack who's got my back, is Froggy Williams. Froggy is definitely for real. Only thing is that he doesn't know scratch about ball.

REREAD
Put into your own words what Jamie is saying about Froggy.

"So you missed a shot," Froggy said. "Big deal."

"So we lost to Powell Academy," I said. "We're the
10   only team uptown that has lost to Powell."

"So what happened?"

"The game was down to fifteen seconds and we're losing by a point," I said. "Tommy Smalls steals the ball and they all jump up into his face. Me, I see Tommy cop the pill and I'm running down the court. My man is trying to double-team Tommy and so I'm free as I want to be and standing under the basket."

cop the pill
slang for "steal the ball"

"Tommy didn't see you?"

20   "No, he sees me, jumps up, and gets me the ball with like two seconds to go."

"Yeah?"

"Then I blow the layup," I said.

"Why you do that?" Froggy asked.

"How do I know?" I said. "I was free, I didn't rush it, I banked it soft off the backboard just like in practice, and it rolled around the rim and fell off!"

blow the layup
miss a shot made from almost under the basket

"So you want to go by my crib and
30   listen to some jams?" Froggy asked.

crib
house

"Man, the whole school is on my case for blowing the game to dumb old Powell Academy and you talking about listening to some jams," I said. "What am I going to listen to, the Death March?"

"Yo, just forget it ever happened," Froggy said. "Life goes on."

40 "No, it doesn't," I said. "That was the first thing that happened today. Then I go into the locker room and all the guys are giving me the evil eye because I blew the game, right?"

"Yeah?"

"So I try to finesse it off and I'm sitting there drinking a bottle of WonderAde, okay?" I said, thinking maybe I shouldn't even tell him.

finesse
(fə nĕs')
v. pretend not to be bothered by something

50 "WonderAde is cool," Froggy said.

"It was until I dropped the bottle, it broke on the floor, and everybody had to pussyfoot around the floor so they wouldn't get cut by the broken glass," I said.

pussyfoot
(pŏŏs' ē fŏŏt')
slang for "walk carefully"

"Oh." That's what Froggy said.

Okay, so I go on home and I'm feeling miserable. When I go to bed what fills up my dreams? Tommy throwing me the ball and me blowing the layup. Only 60 in my dreams when the ball falls off the rim it breaks up on the floor and everybody on my team gets cut.

THINK IT THROUGH
Whom or what does Jamie blame for his day?

When I get up in the morning I don't even want to go to school, but I go. You know, do the right thing and all that.

Froggy and I have biology together. All the way down the hall to class people were giving me dirty looks. We stopped to look at the posters for the junior dance and a girl gave me a bump in the back. I gave her a look and she gave me a look back.

70 "How you blow that layup?" she said. "You taking bribes or something?"

When she left I turned my attention back to the junior dance. "I'm thinking about asking Celia to the dance," I told Froggy.

"Celia *Evora?*" he asked.

"Yeah." Celia was from the Dominican Republic and the | finest chick | in the school.

"Man, you are never in all your days going to | pull that girl |," Froggy said. "You
80 probably couldn't even pull her in a dream."

That got my jaw a little tight, but I didn't say anything. I just went on in and sat through the longest biology class I have ever had in my life. I thought the bell would never ring, but it finally did.

"Okay, class, let's wrap it up," Mr. Willis said. "This slide project is going to count as twenty-five percent of your final grade so I want the slides labeled with your name, class, and—"

90 My hands must have been sweaty. Maybe I caught a cramp in my fingers, I don't know. All I remember was a sick feeling to my stomach when the slide

> **finest chick**
> slang for "best-looking girl"

> **pull that girl**
> slang for "get her to go out with you"

slipped out of my hand. I went to grab it and almost had it before it hit the ground. I looked up and Mr. Willis was looking down at me and shaking his head.

100 I had to explain to Mr. Willis how I didn't break the slide on purpose and he didn't believe a word of it. The man just looked at me and kept shaking his head. He picked up his marking book and I saw him write down a big red 0 next to my name.

"I'm giving up," I said to Froggy. "I'm going home, getting under my bed, and staying there until the year 3000. Maybe things won't be going so bad by then."

"You could be a streaker," Froggy said.

110 "A what?"

"A streaker," he said. "I read in this book that some people do things in streaks. You ever hear about a baseball player who gets a lot of hits in a row, then he stops and they don't get any more touchdowns?

"You mean base hits?" I said.

"Whatever," Froggy shrugged. "Anyway, some people go through their whole lives like that. All of a sudden something really bad happens to you and then you do a bunch of bad things in a row. Or something good

120 happens and you do a bunch of good things in a row. You lost the ball game, you broke the bottle in the locker room, then you just broke your slide in biology."

THINK IT THROUGH

How does Froggy explain the bad things that are happening to Jamie?

The Streak **415**

"I don't believe in luck or streaks or whatever else you're talking about," I said. We were taking a break in the cafeteria. I was having a soda and Froggy was drinking milk like he always did. "I don't believe in astrology, either."

astrology
(ə strŏl′ ə jē)
belief that the motions of the sun, moon, and planets can affect human life

130 Froggy kept on talking about this streak stuff but I wasn't into it. The next bell rang and we got up to leave. I dropped my soda can carefully into the garbage can. Then I grabbed Froggy's milk container and tossed it into the center of the can. I said center because I meant center. I don't know how it hit the edge of the can and bounced off into Maurice DuPre's lap.

REREAD
What other bad luck does Jamie have?

Maurice DuPre is six feet high, six feet wide, and has more fingers and toes than he has points on his IQ. I watched as the last drops of milk fell onto Maurice's lap.

140 Then I watched as he looked up at me with his little squinty, bloodshot eyes. Then I watched as he stood up with his fist in a ball. Then I ran out the cafeteria as fast as I could.

I spent all day sneaking around the halls and slipping into classrooms so Maurice wouldn't find me. I mean, I wasn't worried about fighting him, because I knew how it would come out. What I was worried about was if I would ever wake up when the fight was over.

When school was over I didn't even go to my locker
150 to get my stuff. I just told Froggy to walk down the hall and if he saw Maurice to call out my name and point in some direction away from where I was sneaking out of a side door. Froggy didn't understand sports, but he understood me not wanting to get my

butt kicked and so he went along with it. Last thing I heard in school was that Maurice was chasing Froggy around the gym.

THINK IT THROUGH
What evidence supports Froggy's idea about "streaks"?

FOCUS
Can things get any worse? Read to find out!

I got to the block thinking about Froggy and Maurice and the streak. I stopped on the corner
160 where I live and bought some potato wedgies and a soda from the burger joint. I got the wedgies first and started munching on them while the lady behind the counter poured my soda. Then I remembered I had taken my wallet out of my pocket and put it in my locker after lunch.

"These wedgies don't taste right!" I called out.

"They're going to taste a whole lot worse with a
170 broken jaw," the manager called out. "So you just better pay up and eat them."

I knew by the time he got around the counter I could get away. All he got was one little whack at the back of my head that didn't even hurt.

REREAD
What has happened to Jamie here?

Right home. Up the stairs, close the door and lock it, then cool out. Life was just wrong! The phone rang and I started not to answer it, but then the way things
180 were working out I figured maybe it was somebody

warning me that a killer was coming up the stairs to get me. I rushed to the phone, stopping just long enough to hit my ankle into a dumbbell. You ever hear that sound your anklebone makes when it hits steel? You ever see them little stars that go off in your head?

dumbbell
(dŭm′ bĕl′)
metal bar with weights on either end

"Hello?"

"Jamie?" the voice on the phone asked.

"It depends," I said. "Who's this?"

"This is Mr. Bradley," ...
"I just wanted to let you know you failed your English test big-time.

190   "This is Mr. Bradley," came the answer. "I just wanted to let you know you failed your English test big-time. You're about a hair from failing the course. I just wanted to warn you."

about a hair from
slang for "very close to"

"Oh, thank you, sir. You have made my day with your kindness," I said.

By the time I got to the refrigerator to get some ice for my ankle I was crying. No, I don't mean no sad look—I mean some right out boo-hooing with tears

200 running down my face. My ankle was throbbing, my feelings were hurt, and I was ready to give it all up and resign from the human race.

resign
(rĭ zīn′)
v. quit

I put the ice on my ankle, which was bruised and swollen and a little bloody. Then I sat down, put my leg up on the kitchen table, and called Froggy.

swollen
(swō′ lən)
adj. grown larger

"Froggy, I give up, man," I said. "I'm on a death streak and I know I'm probably headed right on out 210 the world."

"No, man, the streak is going to end," Froggy said.
"Yeah, when I'm dead."
"No," Froggy said. "Just like you missed the shot and lost the baseball game—"
"Basketball game," I said.
"Whatever. Anyway, something dramatic can happen and the whole thing will turn around. Then you'll have as much good luck as you had bad luck."

> **REREAD**
> What hope does Froggy offer to Jamie?

220 "What you mean by dramatic?" I asked.
"Hey, when it happens," Froggy said, "you'll know it."

THINK IT THROUGH
Find details that tell you Jamie finally believes in streaks.

FOCUS
What will it take to change Jamie's luck? Maybe his sister knows.

Ellen is my sister. She's twelve and has a fast mouth. She also has braces that cost a whole bunch of money and I can't pop her when she's running her weak girl game.

> **has a fast mouth**
> slang for "talks a lot"

"What happened to you?" she said when she came home. "I heard somebody was chasing you down the 230 street?"
"Nothing," I said.
"Why don't you tell me who was chasing you so I can go tell them you're here?" she said.

"Why don't you shut up?" I answered.

"What happened to your leg?"

"Nothing."

She went to the refrigerator and took out the eggs. She took one egg out and handed it to me.

"Here," she said. "If nothing happened to your ankle
240 you must have an egg under your skin it's sticking up so much. Here's another egg for your other leg."

Man, I just wanted to punch her right smack in her wire braces. She went waltzing out the kitchen and had the nerve to stick out her tongue at me. That's when I lost it. I tossed that egg toward the sink and started to get up but then the pain started throbbing in my leg and I sat back down real quick. I saw this movie once where this guy got shot in the leg and they had to cut it off. They gave him a drink of
250 whiskey and a bullet to bite on. There was some soda in the fridge and I eased my leg down real slow and went for that. That's when I saw it.

> Okay, wrap your brain around this. I got one hand on the refrigerator door when my mind hit the sink. I looked at the sink and there wasn't any egg in it. Then I looked at the carton of eggs on the counter and there were twelve eggs in the carton.

REREAD
What has happened to the egg that Jamie threw?

"Yo! Ellen! Come in here, quick!"

260 Ellen took her sweet time getting to the kitchen. Then she stood in the doorway with her hand on her skinny little hip. "What?" . . .

"Did you hand me an egg or did you not hand me an egg?" I asked.

"Yeah, you had an egg," she said. "Just don't get violent on me. You seeing any purple rabbits running around or things like that?"

"Check this out," I said. I knew I was excited. "I threw the egg over here and it landed in the
270 egg carton!"

"Isn't that sweet."

"No, you don't understand," I said. "First the telephone was ringing and then I hit my leg on the dumbbell and then I failed English, see?"

"You really enjoy yourself when you're alone, huh?"

Okay, so the girl was seriously stupid. But I knew who would understand and I called Froggy back and told him what happened.

THINK IT THROUGH
What does Jamie believe has happened?

FOCUS —
Find out what Froggy thinks about the turn in Jamie's luck.

"How many bad things happened to you?"
280 Froggy asked.

"A thousand," I said.

"No, exactly how many bad things happened to you?" he said. "We need the exact number."

I started counting. I missed the shot in the basketball game, that was the first thing. Then I broke the bottle in the locker room. The third thing was when I broke the slide in biology.

"Then you dumped milk on Maurice DuPre," Froggy said. "He's still looking for you."

290 "Right, then I left my wallet in school and couldn't pay for my potato wedgies. Then when I got home I banged up my ankle and found out that I flunked my English test."

"Seven things," Froggy said. "Now you have seven pieces of good luck coming your way."

"Seven things," Froggy said. "Now you have seven pieces of good luck coming your way."

"Wait a minute," I said. "I just found out that I failed the English test. I didn't actually fail it at that time."

"When did you take it?"

"Just before the . . . just before the basketball
300 game," I said.

"Okay, now you just had one piece of good luck because you threw the egg toward the sink and it landed in the carton," Froggy said. "You have six to go."

"I'm going for the top right away," I said. "I'm asking Celia to the dance."

"Hey, go for it."

THINK IT THROUGH

How does Froggy figure out that Jamie has six more pieces of good luck?

FOCUS

Read to learn what Jamie's good luck streak brings him.

I figured I'd see Celia in school and pop the question. The whole scene was in my mind. Celia would be coming down the hall with one of those short little
310 skirts she wears, looking tan and sweet and with those fine legs of hers strutting like she owned the world. Then I would call her name and say, "Hey, we *are* going to the dance together?" and she would just kind of go into a

> **strutting**
> (strŭt' ĭng)
> *adj.* walking in a very proud way

half swoon and maybe giggle a little and it would be all set.

> **half swoon**
> almost a faint

When I got to school I was feeling good. Math was the first class and we had one of Galicki's famous pop quizzes. I was sitting in the back of the room where I always sit and dreaming about laying some serious lip on Celia when I heard Mr. Galicki calling my name.

> **laying some serious lip**
> slang for "kissing"

"Yeah, wazzup?"

"I said"—Mr. Galicki raised his voice—"that I'm really surprised that you did so well on the pop quiz. You really understand parallelograms."

> **parallelograms**
> (pär′ ə lĕl′ ə grămz′) rectangles with slanted sides, commonly taught in math classes

Hey, what can I tell you? I met Froggy, who was coming from band practice, and told him the good news.

"That's two things," he said. "You got five left."

"That wasn't luck," I said.

"Math?" Froggy said. "You're good in math?"

It was luck. I had to be careful. I needed to get a yes from Celia before I used up my streak. I stopped right there in the hallway and told myself to calm down.

"Calm down and think hard, my Nubian selfhood."

> **Nubian**
> *Nubian* refers to Jamie's African background

I needed a soda. I went to the cafeteria, looked around to see if Maurice was there, saw he wasn't, and went and dropped a quarter in the machine.

"Yo, it ain't working!" Tommy from the ball team called to me. "It takes your money, but you don't get a soda!"

I had only put in a quarter, but the machine was whirring and humming. Then a bottle of soda came down.

The guys came over and started pounding on the machine, but nothing happened for them. That was my third lucky thing on my streak. I had four to go.

THINK IT THROUGH
What three things have happened so far on Jamie's good-luck streak?

FOCUS
Read to find out why Jamie's good luck makes him nervous.

Okay, I had to go for the big time. Celia was from Santiago, DR. Just looking at her made me want to move to the Dominican Republic. I decided to go the whole nine with her, flowers and everything. The plan was this. I buy some roses, take them over to her house, which is up on 153rd and Broadway, give her the roses, and ask her to the dance. There's a guy on 135th who sells roses, so I bought six. A dozen sounds good but six is cool.

Then I get a little nervous. Celia can make you nervous because she is so fine. Anyway, girls make me a little uptight. But I'm working on the streak so everything is everything. I buy the roses, and I come home. Ellen is checking me out and I tell her to mind her business. Then I call Celia's number, which I had gotten from Ramona Rodriguez, who is also fine, but she goes with Paco, and nobody messes with Paco.

> **whole nine**
> shorter version of *whole nine yards,* meaning "to do everything one can"

> **everything is everything**
> slang meaning "everything is going all right"

"Hello? Mrs. Evora? This is Jamie Farrell. Is Celia there?"

"Who?"

"Jamie Farrell," I repeated. "I go to school with Celia."

"Oh, she had to go to the doctor," Mrs. Evora said. "She has an allergy to certain flowers and she has to take treatments."

"Roses?" I asked.

"She told you?"

"Something like that," I said. "Will you tell her Jamie called?"

'Yes, Gamie called to find out about her allergy," she said.

Right. Gamie called to find out about her allergy. I gave the flowers to my mother. That was four good things that happened. But the flowers cost me a lot and if I was going to take Celia to the dance I'd at least need money to stop for something to eat afterward and a taxi to get her home.

My streak was running low and I was getting nervous. I still hadn't actually asked Celia to go to the dance with me.

"So just do it," Froggy said. "Walk up to her and say, 'Hey, mama, let's you and me start working on the lambada so we look good for the natives at the dance.'"

> lambada
> (ləm bä' də)
> a type of Latin
> American dance

"What's the lam—what did you call it?"

"Call the chick quick," Froggy said.

So I'm lying in bed listening to the news, which sounds like the same thing they've been telling us for the last year, so I don't see why it's news, when there's a knock on my door. I figure it's Ellen coming to borrow something, so I don't say anything. Then the door opens and it's my dad and he flicks the light on.

"Can I talk to you?" he asks.

"Yeah, sure," I say. I'm wondering if he ever dated
410 a Dominican fox.

"Son, I want to talk to you about drugs."

He never dated a Dominican fox, I think. . . .

Then my dad breaks into this whole rap about how bad drugs are and it's like we're making a television commercial or something. All the time I'm wondering how I'm going to get the money to take Celia home in a taxi and if I could make a move on her in the back of the taxi.

"I know that so many young men living
420 in the inner city feel deprived of the better things in life," my dad was saying. "Son, I'm going to give you this hundred dollars so you won't feel that way. And I'm asking you, in return, to come and talk to me about anything that bothers you. You seem so depressed lately. I won't push it, though. I'll wait for you."

That was the fifth thing in the streak. My dad giving me a hundred dollars just when I needed money. I was in desperate trouble.

THINK IT THROUGH
Why is Jamie worried about the number of lucky things happening to him?

FOCUS
How does Jamie try to control his luck?

430 I had to concentrate on Celia. . . . I was in love with her and I had this one shot, this one streak to

get her to go to the dance with me. Concentrate. Concentrate on Celia.

I called Froggy.

"You're in trouble," he said. "Your streak is jumbling up on you."

"What's that mean?" I asked.

"It's out of control," he said. "You're probably just naturally lucky, so your luck is coming too fast."

440   Nothing. That was what I was going to do until I got Celia on the phone and asked her to the dance. Nothing. Lie on the bed. Nothing. I wasn't even going to think of anything. I got a sheet of paper and wrote down all the good things that had happened to me. Then I realized that I was doing something that could result in good luck. I was lying on the bed and lifted my head until I could see my wastebasket. I tossed a high, arcing shot toward the basket.

> **REREAD**
>
> What is Jamie trying to do by doing nothing?

450   Panic! I dove for the paper to knock it away! I didn't want this to be my next lucky thing. I hit it up in the air just before it went into the basket. Then the door opened and knocked the paper against the wall just over my Malcolm X poster, against the side of my dresser, and into the wastebasket.

"What is wrong with you?" Ellen stood in the doorway. "Are you, like, freaking out or something?"

I called Froggy.

"Did you want the paper to go into the basket?"
460   he asked.

"Not when I realized it was going to be my sixth lucky thing," I said.

"But when you threw it, you did, right?" Froggy asked.

I hung up and made a note to myself that I did not like Froggy.

Okay, get the picture. I'm in school and I'm running out of luck. I've got one shot left in my streak.

And my school, Ralph Bunche, is playing against Carver. We're not supposed to beat Carver. But I'm worried and I tell the coach that my ankle is hurt and I can't play. He looks at the ankle and it's still swollen and he says okay. I'm on the bench.

Carver is supposed to kill us. They've got guys on that team that are fifteen, maybe sixteen feet tall. But somehow our team stays with them and I'm praying that us winning with me not even playing is not my last lucky event. I figured no way that could happen. But then our guys, really going all out, are playing Carver so tough that the game is just about even. But some of our key guys are fouling out. It gets down to the end of the game and the coach turns to me.

"Either you play or we only have four players and we lose for certain," he said.

Just don't shoot, I think.

THINK IT THROUGH

In your opinion, is Jamie taking his streak too seriously?

FOCUS

Read to learn if Jamie's good luck runs out before he can talk to Celia.

I remembered how this whole thing began. Fifteen seconds to go against Powell Academy and me running toward the basket and then missing the shot. I want us to win this game but I want to go to a dance with Celia even more.

I looked up at the clock. Nine seconds. I looked up at the scoreboard. Carver 47, Ralph Bunche 46. Don't

shoot, I said to myself. Just don't shoot. Think of
Celia. Dark eyes. Short skirt. Beautiful teeth. . . .

"We've got one chance in a million," the coach
said. "We'll go with the thirty-four play to Tommy.
Jerry inbounds the ball to Tommy and everybody else
blocks out their man the best they can.

"Good choice, Coach," I said.

Jerry inbounded the ball or, at least, he tried to
500 inbound the ball. A Carver guy knocked it away and
it came to me. I picked it up and saw Tommy sliding
inside. Two huge dudes from Carver came after me. I
needed to get the ball to Tommy and threw it over
their outstretched fingers. The ball went up, and up,
and up. The buzzer went off as the ball went down
and the referee pointed to it. The last shot of the
game. Only it wasn't a shot. It really wasn't a shot. It
really, really, *really* wasn't a shot even as it came
down through the net.

510 They carried me off the court and, to tell the truth,
it felt pretty good. But I had blown my one chance
with Celia.

The next day in school everybody was talking about how I had won the game and everything and how cool I was with it. What I was waiting for was my new streak to begin. So I'm walking down the hall and who's coming down the hall with two of her girlfriends but none other than Celia Evora, Her Loveliness.

REREAD
What does Jamie expect to happen?

520   "Nice game," she says to me. Her teeth are like sparkling and her eyes are like flashing and my heart is beating like crazy but I know the score.

"It was luck," I said.

"My mom told me you called," she said.

"Just wanted to see how you were doing," I said. "Your mom said you had an allergy."

"Yes, and I wanted to talk to you about something," she said.

"What?"

530   "You going with anybody to the junior dance?" she asked.

"I hadn't thought about it," I said.

"You want to go with me?" she asked.

"Sure," I said.

"I *knew* you would say yes," she said. "I just knew it."

"You did?"

"Sure. This is my lucky week. Figure it out. The hospital finally figured out what I'm allergic to, and 540 I passed every test I took in school. Then, just after my mom said I couldn't go to the dance because she didn't trust any of the boys, you called to find out about my allergy and she said you had to be the nicest boy in the school and if I went with you I could go. Am I lucky or what?"

REREAD
How are Celia's ideas about luck similar to Jamie's?

"It sounds like you're on a streak," I said.

"I hope it never ends!" she said. "Pick me up early for the dance."

550 Celia turned her head, flashed those dark eyes at me, and danced her way down the hall.

Froggy saw me standing in the hallway leaning against the wall.

"What happened?" he asked. "You okay?"

"I just figured out that the whole world is on a streak," I said.

"What does that mean?" Froggy asked.

Froggy went on about what the word *streak* meant. I really didn't care anymore. It was all good.

THINK IT THROUGH

1. Jamie uses up all his lucky chances. How does he end up going to the dance with Celia?
2. Think of two or three bad things that happen to Jamie. Which are due to bad luck? Which are due solely to his own actions? Explain your answer.
3. What do you think is the writer's attitude about people and their luck? Give examples from the story to support your answer.

Student Resources

Active Reading Strategies

Good readers think while they read. Every so often they stop and check their understanding. They predict what might happen next. They question what they're reading. After they finish, they think about what they read. Each strategy below happens in a good reader's mind while he or she is reading.

CONNECT
Think about your own life when you read something. Think of something similar that you have gone through, seen, or heard.

VISUALIZE
Make a picture in your mind of what the text says. Imagine you are looking at what is described.

PREDICT
Try to guess what will happen next in the story or article. Then read on to find out if your guess was correct.

QUESTION
Let questions come to your mind when you read. If something doesn't make sense, don't pass it by. Ask or write a question to yourself. Look for answers as you read.

CLARIFY
Slow down and make sure you understand what you're reading. Reread something to make sure you understood what it meant. As you read farther, expect to understand or to find out more.
These are ways you can clarify your understanding:
- Sum up what happened in your own words, or summarize.
- Identify the main idea of the paragraph, especially in nonfiction.
- Make inferences about what the author meant but didn't say. Read between the lines and use your own experience to figure it out.

EVALUATE
Form opinions about what you read as you read it. Evaluate again after you read it.

The examples on the pages that follow show how each strategy works. The examples are from "Baseball Saved Us," by Ken Mochizuki. During World War II, a Japanese-American boy and his family have to stay in a prison camp. The boy and the others play baseball in order to keep their spirits up.

CONNECT

Think about your own life when you read something. Think of something similar that you have gone through, seen, or heard.

> Back in school, before Camp, I was shorter and smaller than the rest of the kids. I was always the last to be picked for any team when we played games.

READER CONNECTS: I know how he feels. I'm almost always picked last for basketball games, and it's embarrassing. Everybody makes noises and says, "Okay, I guess I'll take you. Nobody else is left."

VISUALIZE

Make a picture in your mind of what the text says. Imagine you are looking at what is described.

> This Camp wasn't anything like home. It was so hot in the daytime and so cold at night. Dust storms came and got sand in everything, and nobody could see a thing. We sometimes got caught outside, standing in line to eat or to go to the bathroom.

READER VISUALIZES: In my mind I see gold sand blowing in a swirl, everything hazy like a fog. There is a line of people that you can barely see because the dust is blowing so hard. It's almost like a blizzard but it's dust.

PREDICT

Try to guess what will happen next in the story or article. Read on to find out if your guess was correct.

> Once Dad asked Teddy to get him a cup of water.
> "Get it yourself," Teddy said.
> "What did you say? " Dad snapped back.
> The older men stood up and pointed at Teddy. "How dare you talk to your father like that!" one of them shouted.
> Teddy got up, kicked the crate he was sitting on, and walked away. I had never heard Teddy talk to Dad that way before.

READER PREDICTS: I bet Teddy's dad is going to hit him, especially since he talked back to him in front of other people.

> That's when Dad knew we needed baseball. We got shovels and started digging up the sagebrush in a big empty space near our barracks.

READER CHECKS PREDICTION: Guess I was wrong. He didn't get mad at Teddy. He figured out that Teddy was acting that way because of the place.

QUESTION

Let questions come to your mind when you read. If something doesn't make sense, don't pass it by. Ask or write a question to yourself.

> Then, a few months ago, it got worse. The kids started to call me names and nobody talked to me, even though I didn't do anything bad. At the same time the radio kept talking about some place far away called Pearl Harbor.

READER QUESTIONS: Why are they calling him names and picking on him? And what does this Pearl Harbor have to do with anything? I wonder if it has something to do with the war. He's a Japanese American, and Japan was our enemy. I still don't quite understand. I'll look for answers as I read.

CLARIFY

Slow down and make sure you understand what you're reading. Reread something to make sure you understood what it meant. As you read farther, expect to understand or to find out more.

> All the time I practiced, the man in the tower watched. He probably saw the other kids giving me a bad time and thought that I was no good. So I tried to be better because he was looking.

READER CLARIFIES: Why is this guy watching? Who is he? Oh, maybe he's the guard. It must be creepy to be watched all the time. And the narrator knows he's watching and it makes him feel like he's being judged.

EVALUATE

Form opinions about what you read. Think about something as you read it and then again after you read it.

> But it wasn't as if everything were fixed. Things were bad again when we got home from Camp after the war. Nobody talked to us on the street, and nobody talked to us at school, either. Most of my friends from Camp didn't come back here. I had to eat lunch by myself.

READER EVALUATES: That doesn't seem right. Not only did the Japanese Americans have to stay in a camp, but then people were still mad at them after the war. They didn't do anything! People shouldn't have been so mean.

Fiction

A work of fiction is a story that the writer made up. It could be based on a real event, or it could be totally imagined. The **elements of fiction** are the most important parts of fiction. They are the **characters, setting, plot,** and **theme.** These elements make up the skeleton of the story.

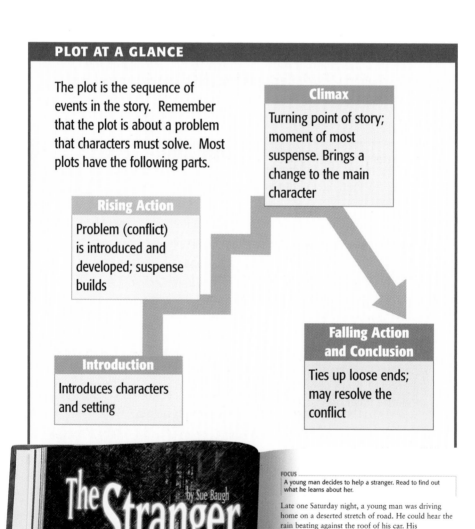

PLOT AT A GLANCE

The plot is the sequence of events in the story. Remember that the plot is about a problem that characters must solve. Most plots have the following parts.

Climax

Turning point of story; moment of most suspense. Brings a change to the main character

Rising Action

Problem (conflict) is introduced and developed; suspense builds

Introduction

Introduces characters and setting

Falling Action and Conclusion

Ties up loose ends; may resolve the conflict

The Stranger

by Sue Baugh

If you saw someone standing by the road on a cold, rainy night, would you stop to help?

One young man does   and gets a real surprise!

FOCUS
A young man decides to help a stranger. Read to find out what he learns about her.

Late one Saturday night, a young man was driving home on a deserted stretch of road. He could hear the rain beating against the roof of his car. His headlights cut through a cold mist that clung to the trees on either side of the road. In the flashes of lightning, tree branches seemed like ghostly hands grasping for his car. He could feel the steady drumroll of thunder. What a night to be out! He
10 shivered and wished he were safe at home.

Suddenly, as he rounded a curve, his headlights lit up a young woman standing by the side of the road. Her hair and white dress were soaked from the rain. She

clung
(klŭng)
v. held on to something; past tense of *cling*

TERMS IN FICTION

- **Characters:** the people or animals in the story
- **Setting:** where and when the story happens
- **Plot:** what happens. The plot grows around a problem, or conflict. The story is about how the characters deal with this problem.
- **Conflict:** the struggle between two forces. **External conflict** happens between a character and an animal, nature, or a person. **Internal conflict** happens in a character's mind, such as a hard choice or a guilty conscience.
- **Theme:** the message the writer wants to share with the reader
- **Narrator:** the voice telling the story to the reader
- **Point of view:** the way the narrator is telling the story

   First person point of view: The narrator is part of the story.

   Third person point of view: The narrator is not part of the story, but is reporting it.
- **Suspense:** the feeling of growing tension and excitement

TYPES OF FICTION

- **Short story:** a short work of fiction that can be read at one sitting. It has a few main characters and a single conflict.
- **Folk tale:** a story that was told over and over by word of mouth. The characters may be animals or people.
- **Historical fiction:** a story set in the past. It may refer to real people or events. The dialogue is usually made up.
- **Myth:** a very old story that was told by ancient people to explain the unknown. The characters often include gods or heroes.
- **Novel:** a long story that usually cannot be read at one sitting. A novel usually has many characters. The plot is complicated. A novel excerpt is one part of the novel.
- **Legend:** a story about a hero that has been told over and over. Most legends are based on a real person or event.
- **Horror story:** a short story that is meant to scare the reader

Nonfiction

Nonfiction is writing about real people, places, and events. It is mostly based on facts.

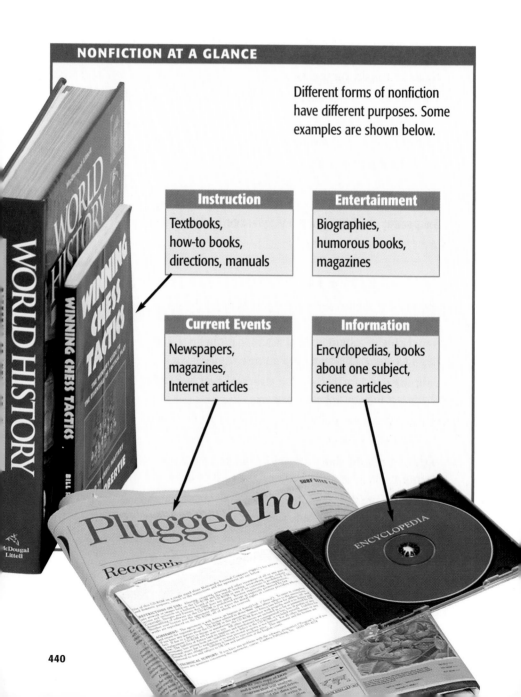

NONFICTION AT A GLANCE

Different forms of nonfiction have different purposes. Some examples are shown below.

Instruction

Textbooks,
how-to books,
directions, manuals

Entertainment

Biographies,
humorous books,
magazines

Current Events

Newspapers,
magazines,
Internet articles

Information

Encyclopedias, books
about one subject,
science articles

TERMS IN NONFICTION

- **Facts:** statements that can be proved to be true
- **Opinions:** statements of personal belief that cannot be proved
- **Chronological order:** the order or sequence in which events happen in time
- **Cause and Effect:** The cause is the reason something happens. The effect is the result, or what happens due to the cause.
- **Visuals:** diagrams, maps, charts, photos, and pictures that are part of an article. They give facts by means of pictures and sketches, with just a few words.

TYPES OF NONFICTION

- **Biography:** a true story about someone's life, written by someone else. It can cover the whole life or just one part.
- **Autobiography:** the true story of a person's life, written by that person
- **Feature Article:** an article that gives facts about a current subject. It is often found in a newspaper or a magazine. Most include visuals.
- **Informative Article:** an article that gives facts about a subject. The article might be from an encyclopedia, textbook, or book.
- **Interview:** a conversation between two people. One asks the other questions. The answers are written in the form of an interview.
- **Essay:** a piece of writing about one subject. The writer might share an opinion or make a point.
- **True Account:** an article about a real event that is told as a story
- **Narrative Nonfiction:** an article about a real event told in chronological order. It is often historical.
- **Anecdote:** the true story of a small event, usually from the teller's life. An anecdote might be funny (to entertain) or might make a point.

Drama

A drama, or play, is a story that is meant to be acted out. Actors present the play onstage. They act out the story for an audience.

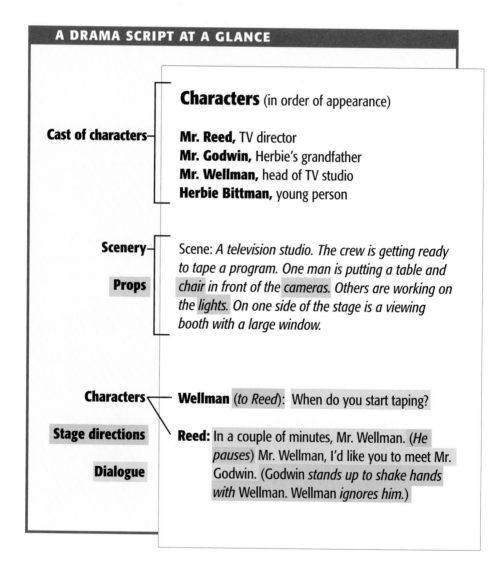

A DRAMA SCRIPT AT A GLANCE

Cast of characters—

Characters (in order of appearance)

Mr. Reed, TV director
Mr. Godwin, Herbie's grandfather
Mr. Wellman, head of TV studio
Herbie Bittman, young person

Scenery—
Props

Scene: *A television studio. The crew is getting ready to tape a program. One man is putting a table and chair in front of the* cameras. *Others are working on the* lights. *On one side of the stage is a viewing booth with a large window.*

Characters
Stage directions
Dialogue

Wellman (*to Reed*): When do you start taping?

Reed: In a couple of minutes, Mr. Wellman. (*He pauses*) Mr. Wellman, I'd like you to meet Mr. Godwin. (Godwin *stands up to shake hands with* Wellman. Wellman *ignores him.*)

TERMS IN DRAMA

- **Stage:** the platform on which the actors perform
- **Script:** the written words for the play. This is what everyone reads in order to perform the play.
- **Cast of Characters:** the list of people who play a part in the story
- **Dialogue:** the words the characters say
- **Stage Directions:** the directions to the actors and stage crew. These words tell how people should move and speak. They describe the scenery—the decoration onstage.
- **Acts and Scenes:** the parts of a play. These usually change when the time or the place changes.
- **Props:** the objects used onstage in the play, such as a telephone
- **Scenery:** the background art or structures onstage to help show the setting

A Stage

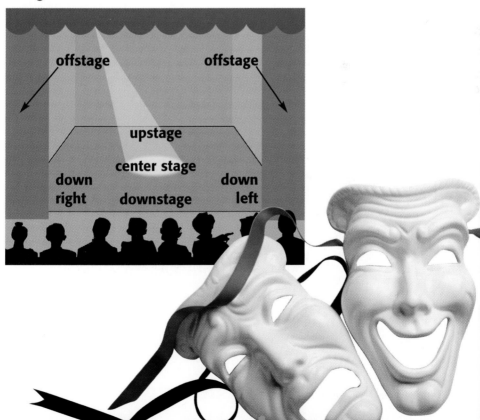

Poetry

Poetry is literature that uses a few words to tell about ideas, feelings, and images. The poet crafts the look of the poem and chooses words for their sound and meaning. Most poems are meant to be read aloud. Poems may or may not rhyme.

POETRY AT A GLANCE

Some People

By Rachel Field

Isn't it strange some people make — **line**
    You feel so tired inside, **stanza**
Your thoughts begin to shrivel up
    Like leaves all brown and dried! **rhyming words**

But when you're with some other ones,
    It's stranger still to find
Your thoughts as thick as fireflies **simile**
    All shiny in your mind! **visual imagery**

Some

People

By Rachel Field

Some people make you feel good and some people don't. Do you know someone who belongs in this poem?

Some People

By Rachel Field

Isn't it strange some people make
    You feel so tired inside,
Your thoughts begin to shrivel up
    Like leaves all brown and dried!

5   But when you're with some other ones,
    It's stranger still to find
Your thoughts as thick as fireflies
    All shiny in your mind!

TERMS IN POETRY

- **Form:** the way a poem looks on the page; its shape
- **Lines:** Poets arrange words into lines. The lines may or may not be sentences.
- **Stanzas:** groups of lines in traditional poetry
- **Free verse:** poems that usually do not rhyme and have no fixed rhythm or pattern. They are written like conversation.
- **Rhyme:** sounds that are alike at the end of words, such as *make* and *rake.* Some poems have rhyming words at the end of lines. Some poems have rhymes in the middle of lines too.
- **Rhythm:** the beat of the poem. Patterns of strong (´) and weak (˘) syllables make up the beat.
- **Repetition:** the repeating of sounds, words, phrases, or lines in a poem
- **Imagery:** words and phrases that appeal to the five senses—sight, hearing, smell, taste, and touch. Poets often use imagery to create pictures, tastes, or feelings in the reader's mind. For example, "The smell of sizzling bacon filled the air."
- **Figurative language:** words and phrases that help readers picture things in new ways. For example, "Snow crystals displayed a rainbow of colors in the sun."

    Simile: a comparison of two things using the words *like* or *as.* For example, "Confetti fell like rain."

    Metaphor: a comparison of two things without the words *like* or *as.* For example, "His face is a puzzle."

    Personification: a description of an animal or an object as if it were human or had human qualities. For example, "The dog smiled joyfully."
- **Speaker:** the voice that talks to the reader
- **Theme:** the message the poet gives the reader through the poem

A

abruptly (ə brŭpt′ lē) *adv.* suddenly
abruptamente *adv.* repentinamente

accumulated (ə kyōōm′ yə lā′ tĭd) *v.* piled up; past tense of *accumulate*
acumuló *v.* juntó; pasado de *accumulate/acumular*

adopted (ə dŏp′ tĭd) *adj.* made part of a family by legal means
adoptivo *adj.* pariente por adopción

ancestors (ăn′ sĕs′ tərz) *n.* family members from long ago
antepasados *s.* familiares que vivieron hace tiempo

ancient (ān′ shənt) *adj.* from a time long past
antiguo *adj.* de hace mucho tiempo

antibiotics (ăn′ tĭ bī ŏt′ ĭks) *n.* medicines that kill infections
antibióticos *s.* medicinas que matan infecciones

artifacts (är′ tə făkts′) *n.* objects created by humans, such as tools, weapons, or jewelry
artefactos *s.* objetos creados por seres humanos, como herramientas, armas o jollas

B

barracks (băr′ əks) *n.* houses built for military purposes
barracas *s.* casas para militares

barrier (băr′ ē ər) *n.* something that blocks the way
barrera *s.* algo que bloquea el paso

barrio (bä′ rē ō′) *n.* mainly Spanish-speaking neighborhood in a U.S. city
barrio *s.* en los Estados Unidos, un vecindario de latinos

biological (bī′ ə lŏj′ ĭ kəl) *adj.* related by birth
biológico *adj.* pariente por nacimiento

bleachers (blē′ chərz) *n.* outdoor stands or benches for watching games
gradas *s.* bancas al aire libre para ver partidos

braced (brāst) *v.* got ready for danger or pain; past tense of *brace*
preparó *v.* fortaleció para recibir un dolor o mala noticia; pasado de *brace/preparar*

C

calculus (kăl′ kyə ləs) *n.* branch of mathematics beyond algebra
cálculo *s.* rama de las matemáticas más avanzada que el álgebra

callouses (kăl′ ə sĭz) *n.* small areas of hard, thick skin
callo *s.* área de piel espesa y escabrosa

captivity (kăp tĭv′ ĭ tē) *n.* state of being locked up
cautiverio *s.* falta de libertad

cautiously (kô′ shəs lē) *adv.* carefully, in order to avoid danger
cautelosamente *adv.* cuidadosamente a fin de evitar un peligro

celebrated (sĕl′ ə brā′ tĭd) *v.* marked an event with special food, games, and music; past tense of *celebrate*
celebró *v.* festejó una ocasión con comida, juegos, música; pasado de *celebrate/celebrar*

censored (sĕn′ sərd) *v.* inspected and stopped; past tense of *censor*
censuró *v.* inspeccionó y paró; pasado de *censor/censurar*

chef (shĕf) *n.* cook
chef *s.* cocinero

clamor (klăm′ ər) *n.* noise made by many people
clamor *s.* ruido de mucha gente

cleverness (klĕv′ ər nĭs) *n.* brightness, smartness, or quick-wittedness
astucia *s.* inteligencia, ingenio

clung (klŭng) *v.* held on
se agarró *v.* se sujetó

coincidence (cō ĭn′ sĭ dəns) *n.* accidental happening where two events occur at the same time
coincidencia *s.* situación en que dos cosas ocurren al mismo tiempo por azar

collapsed (kə lăpst′) *v.* fell down; past tense of *collapse*
se desplomó *v.* se cayó; pasado de *collapse/desplomarse*

commenced (kə mĕnst′) *v.* began; past tense of *commence*
comenzó *v.* empezó; pasado de *commence/comenzar*

concentrate (kŏn′ sən trāt′) *v.* pay close attention
concentrarse *v.* prestar atención

concentric (kən sĕn′ trĭk) *adj.* having a common center, such as one circle inside another circle
concéntrico *adj.* que tiene un centro común, como un círculo dentro de otro

condition (kən dĭsh′ ən) *n.* disease
afección *s.* enfermedad

condolences (kən dō′ lən sĭz) *n.* statement of sympathy and concern
condolencias *s.* pésame

conscious (kŏn′ shəs) *adj.* aware
consciente *adj.* enterado

coping (kō′ pĭng) *n.* handling successfully
arreglándoselas *v.* manejar con buenos resultados

courtesy (kûr′ tĭ sē) *n.* polite behavior
cortesía *s.* demostración de respeto o afecto

craved (krāvd) *v.* needed very badly; past tense of *crave*
anhelaba *v.* necesitaba con urgencia; pasado de *crave/anhelar*

current (kûr′ ənt) *n.* steady flow of water
corriente *s.* movimiento constante del agua

D

decline (dĭ klīn′) *v.* refuse; say no
rehusar *v.* rechazar; decir que no

deftly (dĕft′ lē) *adv.* skillfully and effortlessly
diestramente *adv.* hábilmente

desperate (dĕs′ pər ĭt) *adj.* suffering from extreme need
desesperado *adj.* que tiene una aguda necesidad

destination (dĕs′ tə nā′ shən) *n.* place to which one is going
destino *s.* lugar a donde se dirige algo

detain (dĭ tān′) *v.* stop someone from leaving a place
detener *v.* no dejar ir

determined (dĭ tûr′ mĭnd) *adj.* firm in pursuing a goal
resuelto *adj.* decidido

devastated (dĕv′ ə stā′ tĭd) *v.* completely destroyed; past tense of *devastate*
devastado *v.* completamente destruido; pasado de *devastate/devastar*

diagnosed (dī′ əg nōst′) *v.* identified as having a disease; past tense of *diagnose*
diagnosticó *v.* identificó una enfermedad; pasado de *diagnose/diagnosticar*

dignity (dĭg′ nĭ tē) *n.* self-respect and pride
dignidad *s.* amor propio y orgullo

directory (dĭ rĕk′ tə rē) *n.* book with names grouped in some way
directorio *s.* libro de nombres agrupados en cierto orden

disguised (dĭs gīzd′) *adj.* dressed to look like another person
disfrazado *adj.* vestido como otra persona

dominance (dŏm′ ə nəns) *n.* power over others
dominación *s.* poder sobre otros

dredge (drĕj) *n.* machine used to bring up objects from the bottom of rivers and lakes
draga *s.* máquina que saca objetos del fondo de ríos y lagos

drought (drout) *n.* time of little or no rain
sequía *s.* época en que no llueve

E

edible (ĕd′ ə bəl) *adj.* able to be eaten
comestible *adj.* que se puede comer

eerie (îr′ ē) *adj.* creating a feeling of mystery and fear
misterioso *adj.* que da una sensación de extrañeza o miedo

embarrassment (ĕm băr′ əs mənt) *n.* feeling of shame when others see your weakness
vergüenza *s.* molestia cuando otros ven tus faltas

empire (ĕm′ pīr) *n.* large area ruled by a king or emperor
imperio *s.* extensa región gobernada por un rey o emperador

endured (ĕn dŏŏrd′) *v.* put up with; past tense of *endure*
aguantó *v.* soportó; pasado de *endure/aguantar*

excavate (ĕk' skə vāt') *v.* uncover by digging
  excavar *v.* descubrir al hacer agujeros en la tierra

excuse (ĭk skyōōs') *n.* made-up reason
  excusa *s.* razón inventada

exhausted (ĭg zôs' tĭd) *adj.* extremely tired or without energy
  agotado *adj.* muy cansado o sin energía

exterminator (ĭk stûr' mə nā' tər) *n.* person who kills insects, rats, and other pests for a living
  exterminador *s.* persona que trabaja matando ratas, insectos, y otras plagas

F

finesse (fə nĕs') *v.* pretend not to be bothered by something
  disimular *v.* aparentar que algo no molesta

flourished (flûr' ĭsht) *v.* grew very well; past tense of *flourish*
  prosperó *v.* se desarrolló muy bien; pasado de *flourish/prosperar*

foresight (fôr' sīt') *n.* ability to look or plan ahead
  previsión *s.* capacidad de planear para el futuro

fortress (fôr' trĭs) *n.* large place that is strong and secure
  fortaleza *s.* lugar grande, fuerte y seguro

fracture (frăk' chər) *n.* break in a bone
  fractura *s.* rompimiento de un hueso

G

glinting (glĭn' tĭng) *v.* sparkling
  destellando *v.* brillando

gore (gôr) *v.* stab with a horn
  cornear *v.* herir con un cuerno

graveyard (grāv' yärd') *n.* place where dead people are buried
  cementerio *s.* lugar donde se entierra a los muertos

grudging (grŭj' ĭng) *adj.* unwilling
  maldispuesto *adj.* reacio, desinclinado

H

handicapped (hăn' dē kăpt') *adj.* having a physical or mental problem
discapacitado *adj.* que tiene un problema físico o mental

headstone (hĕd' stōn') *n.* stone placed at the head of a grave
lápida *s.* piedra que se coloca en la cabecera de una tumba

honorable (ŏn' ər ə bəl) *adj.* worthy of trust and respect
honorable *adj.* que merece confianza y respeto

hostile (hŏs' təl) *adj.* unfriendly or belonging to an enemy
hostil *adj.* poco amistoso, de un enemigo

hover (hŭv' ər) *v.* hang above something
flotar *v.* estar suspendido

humiliation (hyōō mĭl' ē ā' shən) *n.* loss of self-respect and dignity
humillación *s.* herida al respeto y la dignidad

I

identical (ī dĕn' tĭ kəl) *adj.* exactly alike
idéntico *adj.* exactamente igual

immune (ĭ myōōn') *adj.* protected against an illness
inmume *adj.* protegido de una enfermedad

indignantly (ĭn dĭg' nənt lē) *adv.* angrily
con indignación *adv.* con furia

infamous (ĭn' fə məs) *adj.* having a bad reputation
infame *adj.* de mala reputación

infection (ĭn fĕk' shən) *n.* germs invading a wound
infección *s.* invasión de microbios

inject (ĭn jekt') *v.* force a liquid into the body, usually with a needle
inyectar *v.* introducir un líquido al cuerpo con una aguja

intrigued (ĭn trēgd') *v.* made curious; past tense of *intrigue*
intrigó *v.* dio curiosidad; pasado de *intrigue/intrigar*

investigating (ĭn vĕs' tĭ gā´ tĭng) *n.* examining closely and carefully
investigando *s.* examinando con atención

J

jeering (jîr' ĭng) *adj.* mocking or shouting insults
mofándose *adj.* gritando insultos

K

kayak (kī' yăk) *n.* small, one-person boat
kayak *s.* bote pequeño para una persona

L

lunged (lŭnjd) *v.* moved forward suddenly; past tense of *lunge*
arremetió *v.* se movió hacia adelante de repente; pasado de
lunge/arremeter

M

matadors (măt' ə dôrz') *n.* bullfighters
matadores *s.* toreros

mediocre (mē' dē ō' kər) *adj.* ordinary
mediocre *adj.* ordinario

meekness (mēk' nĭs) *n.* timid quality
mansedumbre *s.* timidez

mentor (mĕn' tôr') *n.* someone who teaches and guides another
mentor *s.* persona que enseña o guía a otra.

misjudging (mĭs jŭj' ĭng) *v.* judging wrongly
errando v. juzgando mal

missionaries (mĭsh' ə nĕr' ēz) *n.* people who are sent to teach religion
to others
misioneros *s.* personas que van a otra parte a enseñar religión

momentum (mō mĕn' təm) *n.* force and speed
impulso *s.* fuerza y velocidad

mysterious (mĭ stîr' ē əs) *adj.* unable to be explained
misterioso *adj.* que no se puede explicar

N

navigator (năv′ ĭ gā′ tər) *n.* person who directs the course of an airplane
navegante *s.* persona quien dirige el curso de un avión

notorious (nō tôr′ ē əs) *adj.* well-known for bad deeds
notorio *adj.* famoso por sus malas acciones

O

opportunity (ŏp′ ər tōō′ nĭ tē) *n.* chance to do or have something
oportunidad *s.* chance de hacer o tener algo

optician (ŏp tĭsh′ ən) *n.* person who makes and sells eyeglasses
óptico *s.* persona que hace y vende gafas

P

pale (pāl) *adj.* without much color, as if ill
pálido *adj.* sin color

panic (păn′ ĭk) *n.* sudden fear that cannot be controlled
pánico *s.* miedo repentino e incontrolable

phobia (fō′ bē ə) *n.* strong and unreasonable fear of something
fobia *s.* miedo fuerte y sin razón a algo en especial

physics (fĭz′ ĭks) *n.* science of matter and energy
física *s.* ciencia de la materia y la energía

pierced (pîrst) *v.* touched deeply; past tense of *pierce*
penetró *v.* tocó a fondo; pasado de *pierce/penetrar*

pneumonia (nōō mōn′ yə) *n.* serious disease in which the lungs become inflamed and sore
neumonía *s.* inflamación y dolor de pulmones

prejudiced (prěj′ ə dĭst) *adj.* judging unfairly usually based on outward appearance
mostrando prejuicio *adj.* juzgando injustamente por las apariencias

primitive (prĭm′ ĭ tĭv) *adj.* from an earlier, wilder time
primitivo *adj.* de una época remota

protruding (prō trōō′ dĭng) *adj.* sticking out
saliente *adj.* que se destaca

R

raw (rô) *adj.* cold and damp
crudo *adj.* frío y húmedo

realm (rĕlm) *n.* kingdom
reino *s.* dominio

rebellions (rĭ bĕl′ yənz) *n.* internal wars meant to overthrow a ruler
rebeliones *s.* levantamientos para tumbar a un gobernante por la fuerza

recipe (rĕs′ ə pē′) *n.* directions for making a certain food
recetas *s.* instrucciones para preparar un platillo

reflexes (rē′ flĕk′ sĭz) *n.* reactions
reflejos *s.* reacciones

refugees (rĕf′ yōō jēz′) *n.* people who flee a country to find protection from war or political oppression
refugiados *s.* gente que abandona su país para escapar de una guerra o opresión política

relics (rĕl′ ĭks) *n.* objects that are important for their age and historic interest
reliquias *s.* objetos de importancia por su antigüedad e interés histórico

resemblance (rĭ zĕm′ bləns) *n.* likeness in appearance
parecido *s.* apariencia similar

reservation (rĕz′ ər vā′ shən) *n.* land set aside by the U.S. government where Native Americans have to live
reserva *s.* tierra apartada por el gobierno para que vivan los indígenas

resign (rĭ zīn′) *v.* quit
renunciar *v.* dejar un trabajo

resort (rĭ zôrt′) *n.* place people go to have fun and relax
lugar de veraneo *s.* sitio para descansar

restaurant (rĕs′ tər ənt) *n.* place people go to eat
restaurante *s.* negocio que vende comidas

resumes (rĭ zo͞omz′) *v.* begins again
continúa *v.* vuelve a empezar

riveted (rĭv′ ĭ tĭd) *v.* fastened firmly; past tense of *rivet*
remachó *v.* unió firmemente; pasado de *rivet/remachar*

route (ro͞ot) *n.* path
ruta *s.* camino

rubble (rŭb′ əl) *n.* broken bits of something that is destroyed
escombros *s.* pedazos de algo destruido

S

savoring (sā′ vər ĭng) *adj.* enjoying and appreciating fully
saboreando *adj.* disfrutando a fondo

scattered (skăt′ ərd) *adj.* thrown about
regado *adj.* tirado alrededor

scholarship (skŏl′ ər shĭp′) *n.* money awarded to a student to use for going to school
beca *s.* dinero donado a un estudiante para sus estudios

scorched (skôrcht) *adj.* burned on the surface
chamuscado *adj.* quemado en la superficie

sedately (sĭ dāt′ lē) *adv.* in a slow, dignified way
tranquilamente *adv.* con calma y dignidad

sensation (sĕn sā′ shən) *n.* big success with the public
sensación *s.* gran éxito

shield (shēld) *n.* something that guards or protects
escudo *s.* algo que protege

siblings (sĭb′ lĭngz) *n.* brothers and sisters
hermanos y hermanas *s.* hijos de los mismos padres

sidetrack (sīd′ trăk′) *v.* turn away from the main goal
desviar *v.* alejarse de la meta

siege (sēj) *n.* military blockade meant to cut off supplies and aid
sitio *s.* bloqueo militar para que no entren suministros a un lugar cerrado, como un castillo

sinews *s.* tendones

site (sīt) *n.* place where something, such as a building, was once located
sitio *s.* lugar donde se construyó algo

situations (sĭch' ōō ā' shənz) *n.* events that happen at a certain time and place
situaciones *s.* cosas que pasan en cierto momento y lugar

skeletons (skĕl' ĭ tnz) *n.* bones that support the human body
esqueletos *s.* conjunto de huesos del cuerpo

solo (sō' lō) *adj.* alone
solo *adj.* sin compañía

spectacle (spĕk' tə kəl) *n.* colorful public event
espectáculo *s.* función para el público

stable (stā' bəl) *adj.* steady
estable *adj.* firme

stance (stăns) *n.* pose or position of the body
postura *s.* pose o posición del cuerpo

statement (stāt' mənt) *n.* message presented through a sign or a symbol
declaración *s.* mensaje presentado por medio de un símbolo

strutting (strŭt' ĭng) *v.* walking in a very proud way
pavonéandose *v.* caminando con mucho orgullo

suspicious (sə spĭsh' əs) *adj.* distrusting or doubting
suspicaz *adj.* desconfiado o receloso

swollen (swō' lən) *adj.* grown larger
hinchado *adj.* que se ha abultado

symptoms (sĭm' təmz) *n.* physical or mental signs of an illness
síntomas *s.* señales físicas o mentales de enfermedad

T

tolerate (tŏl' ə rāt') *v.* put up with
tolerar *v.* soportar

transferred (trăns fûrd′) *v.* carried from one place to another
transferido *v.* llevado de un lugar a otro

transparent (trăns pâr′ ənt) *adj.* so thin it can be seen through
transparente *adj.* que deja pasar la luz

twinge (twĭnj) *n.* sharp, sudden pain
punzada *s.* dolor agudo

U

unmistakable (ŭn′ mĭ stā′ kə bəl) *adj.* very clear
inconfundible *adj.* muy claro

V

venom (vĕn′ əm) *n.* poison
veneno *s.* ponzoña

venture (vĕn′ chər) *n.* risky adventure
aventura *s.* empresa arriesgada, negocio arriesgado

victorious (vĭk tôr′ ē əs) *adj.* having won a game or struggle
victoriosamente *adj.* salir victorioso

vow (vou) *n.* strong promise
juramento *s.* promesa

W

wake (wāk) *n.* trail
estela *s.* rastro

warily (wâr′ ĭ lē) *adv.* cautiously
cautelosamente *adv.* con cuidado

wielding (wēl′ dĭng) *adj.* waving
meneando *adj.* ondeando

Index of Authors and Titles

Acknowledgments

Literature

UNIT ONE

Lee & Low Books: *Baseball Saved Us* by Ken Mochizuki. Text copyright © 1993 by Ken Mochizuki. Illustrations copyright © 1993 by Dom Lee. Permission granted by Lee & Low Books, Inc., New York.

McIntosh and Otis: "The Day the Sun Came Out" by Dorothy M. Johnson, originally published as "Too Soon a Woman" in *Cosmopolitan*, 1953. Copyright © 1953 by Dorothy M. Johnson. Reprinted by permission of McIntosh and Otis, Inc.

Clarion Books/Houghton Mifflin Company and Stoddart Publishing Company: *The Dragon's Pearl*, retold by Julie Lawson. Text copyright © 1993 by Julie Lawson. Illustrations copyright © 1993 by Paul Morin. Reprinted by permission of Clarion Books/Houghton Mifflin Company and Stoddart Publishing Company Limited, Toronto. All rights reserved.

Hyperion Books for Children: Excerpt from *Elena* by Diane Stanley. Text copyright © 1996 by Diane Stanley. Reprinted by permission of Hyperion Books for Children.

UNIT TWO

Doris Holmes Eyges: "Rhyme of Rain" by John Holmes. Reprinted by permission of Doris Holmes Eyges.

Marian Reiner, Literary Agent: "Pigeons," from *I Thought I Heard the City* by Lilian Moore. Copyright © 1969 by Lilian Moore, renewed © 1997 by Lilian Moore Reavin. Used by permission of Marian Reiner for the author.

Alfred A. Knopf: "City," from *Collected Poems* by Langston Hughes. Copyright © 1994 by the Estate of Langston Hughes. Reprinted by permission of Alfred A. Knopf, a division of Random House, Inc.

Richard García: "The City Is So Big," from *Selected Poetry* by Richard García. Copyright © 1973 by Richard García. Reprinted by permission of the author.

BOA Editions: "In the Inner City," from *Good Woman: Poems and a Memoir, 1969–1980* by Lucille Clifton. Copyright © 1987 by Lucille Clifton. Reprinted with the permission of BOA Editions, Ltd.

UNIT THREE

Multimedia Product Development: "Forty-Five Seconds Inside a Tornado," from *Incredible True Adventures* by Don L. Wulffson. Copyright © 1986 by Don L. Wulffson. Reprinted by permission of Multimedia Product Development, Inc., Chicago, Ill.

NTC/Contemporary Publishing Group: "Trapped by Fear," from *The Contemporary Reader*, Vol. 1, No. 3. Copyright © 1994 by Contemporary Books, Inc. Used with permission from NTC/Contemporary Publishing Group, Inc.

"Typhoid Mary," from *The Wild Side: Crime and Punishment* by Henry Billings and Melissa Billings. Copyright © 1996 by NTC/Contemporary Publishing Group, Inc. Used with permission from NTC/Contemporary Publishing Group, Inc.

HarperCollins Publishers: "Whatif," from *A Light in the Attic* by Shel Silverstein. Copyright © 1981 by Evil Eye Music, Inc. Used by permission of HarperCollins Publishers.

Nickelodeon Magazine: Excerpt from "Sca-a-a-a-a-ry Jobs" by Robin Sayers, originally published in *Nickelodeon Magazine*, October 1997. Copyright © 1997 by Nickelodeon Magazine. Reprinted by permission of Nickelodeon Magazine.

UNIT FOUR

Dial Books for Young Readers: *My Man Blue* by Nikki Grimes, illustrated by Jerome Lagarrigue. Text copyright © 1999 by Nikki Grimes. Illustrations copyright © 1999 by Jerome Lagarrigue. Used by permission of Dial Books for Young Readers, an imprint of Penguin Putnam Books for Young Readers, a division of Penguin Putnam Inc.

International Publishers: Adaptation of "Little Things Are Big," from *A Puerto Rican in New York and Other Sketches* by Jesus Colon. Copyright © 1961 by Masses & Mainstream, © 1982 by International Publishers. Reprinted by permission of International Publishers, New York.

New Directions Publishing Corporation: "Puerto Ricans in New York," from *By the Waters of Manhattan* by Charles Reznikoff. Copyright © 1959 by Charles Reznikoff. Reprinted by permission of New Directions Publishing Corporation.

Arlene Erlbach: "Never Home Alone!" originally published as "Elizabeth, Jeff, Sam, Kelly, and Mike: Ages 15, 14, 12, 11, and 10" in *The Families Book* by Arlene Erlbach. Copyright © 1996 by Arlene Erlbach. Reprinted by permission of the author.

Houghton Mifflin Company and Editorial de la Universidad de Puerto Rico: "Goodbye, Falcon," English translation of *Adiós falcón* by Wenceslao Serra Deliz, from *Explore* in *Houghton Mifflin Reading: Invitations to Literacy* by J. David Cooper, John J. Pikulski, et al. Copyright © 1985 by Wenceslao Serra Deliz, Universidad de Puerto Rico. English translation

© 1993, 1996 by Houghton Mifflin Company. Reprinted by permission of Houghton Mifflin Company and Editorial de la Universidad de Puerto Rico. All rights reserved.

UNIT FIVE

Encore Performance Publishing: Excerpt from *Scars and Stripes* by Thomas Cadwaleder Jones. Copyright © 1994 by Thomas Cadwaleder Jones. All rights reserved. Reprinted by permission of Encore Performance Publishing (http://www.encoreplay.com), holder of all rights worldwide.

H. W. Wilson Company and David Higham Associates: "Westwoods" by Eleanor Farjeon (in *The Little Bookroom* [Oxford University Press, 1955; Godine, 1984]), adapted by Aaron Shepard, from *Stories on Stage: Scripts for Reader's Theater*, pp. 132–145. Copyright © 1993 by Aaron Shepard. Reproduced with permission of the H. W. Wilson Company and David Higham Associates Limited.

UNIT SIX

Writers House: "Victor" by James Howe. Copyright © 1995 by James Howe. Reprinted by permission of Writers House, LLC.

Scholastic: "The Cage" by Martin Raim, published in *Literary Cavalcade*, October 1960. Copyright © 1960, 1988 by Scholastic Inc. Reprinted by permission of Scholastic Inc.

"The Jigsaw Puzzle," from *Tales for the Midnight Hour: Stories of Horror* by J. B. Stamper. Copyright © 1977 by Judith Bauer Stamper. Reprinted by permission of Scholastic Inc.

UNIT SEVEN

Lee & Low Books: *Richard Wright and the Library Card* by William Miller. Text copyright © 1997 by William Miller. Permission granted by Lee & Low Books, Inc.

Clarion Books/Houghton Mifflin Company: *El Chino* by Allen Say. Copyright © 1990 by Allen Say. Reprinted by permission of Clarion Books/Houghton Mifflin Company. All rights reserved.

Weigl Educational Publishers: "Amelia Earhart: American Pilot," from *Explorers* by Carlotta Hacker. Copyright © 1998 by Weigl Educational Publishers Limited. All rights reserved. Reprinted by permission of Weigl Educational Publishers.

UNIT EIGHT

Franklin Watts: "I Prove Myself a Hunter," from *Wise Words of Paul Tiulana: An Inupiat Alaskan's Life* by Vivian Senungetuk. Copyright © 1998 by Vivian Senungetuk. Reprinted by permission of Franklin Watts, a division of Grolier Publishing Company.

Scholastic: "Gail Devers" by Zoë Kashner, from *Scholastic Action*, February 21, 2000. Copyright © 2000 by Scholastic Inc. Reprinted by permission of Scholastic Inc.

Carol D. Spelius: "The Swimmer's Chant" by Carol D. Spelius. Copyright © 1995 by Carol D. Spelius. Reprinted by permission of the author.

Dell Publishing: Excerpt from *Brian's Return* by Gary Paulsen. Copyright © 1999 by Gary Paulsen. Used by permission of Dell Publishing, a division of Random House, Inc.

UNIT NINE

Boyds Mills Press: "I Never Said I Wasn't Difficult," from *I Never Said I Wasn't Difficult* by Sara Holbrook. Text copyright © 1996 by Sara Holbrook. Published by Boyds Mills Press, Inc. Reprinted by permission.

Harcourt: "Phizzog," from *Good Morning, America* by Carl Sandburg. Copyright © 1928 and renewed 1956 by Carl Sandburg. Reprinted by permission of Harcourt, Inc.

James Houston: "Eastern Eskimo Song," from *Songs of the Dream People: Chants and Images from the Indians and Eskimos of North America*, edited and illustrated by James Houston. Published by Atheneum, New York. Copyright © 1972 by James Houston. Reprinted by permission of the author.

Scholastic: "Old Snake," from *This Big Sky* by Pat Mora. Published by Scholastic Press, a division of Scholastic Inc. Copyright © 1998 by Pat Mora. Reprinted by permission of Scholastic Inc.

Luis Alberto Ambroggio: "Aprender el inglés"/"Learning English" by Luis Alberto Ambroggio. Copyright © Luis Alberto Ambroggio. Reprinted by permission of the author.

Naomi Long Madgett: "Midway," from *Star by Star* by Naomi Long Madgett. Copyright © 1965, 1970 by Naomi Long Madgett. Reprinted by permission of the author.

UNIT TEN

J. Weston Walch, Publisher: "Jaime Escalante: Math Teacher," from *16 Extraordinary Hispanic Americans* by Nancy Lobb. Copyright © 1995 by J. Weston Walch, Publisher. Used with permission of J. Weston Walch, Publisher. Further reproduction prohibited.

Scholastic: "Patches," from *Dog to the Rescue: Seventeen True Tales of Dog Heroism* by Jeannette Sanderson. Copyright © 1993 by Jeannette Sanderson. Reprinted by permission of Scholastic Inc.

The Creative Company: *Chief Joseph of the Nez Perce* by Matthew G. Grant. Copyright © Creative Education. Reprinted by permission of Creative Education, Mankato, MN, USA.

UNIT ELEVEN

Childrens Press: Excerpt from *Archaeology* by Dennis B. Fradin. Copyright © 1983 by Regensteiner Publishing Enterprises, Inc. Reprinted by permission of Childrens Press, a division of Grolier Publishing Company.

Random House Children's Books: "The Sacred Well," from *True-Life Treasure Hunts* by Judy Donnelly. Copyright © 1984 by Random House, Inc. Reprinted by permission of Random House Children's Books, a division of Random House, Inc.

Franklin Watts: Excerpt from *Castles* by Jenny Vaughan. Copyright © 1984 by Franklin Watts Ltd. Reprinted by permission of Franklin Watts, a division of Grolier Publishing Company.

Harcourt: "Matajuro's Training," from *Sword of the Samurai: Adventure Stories from Japan* by Eric A. Kimmel. Copyright © 1999 by Eric A. Kimmel. Reprinted by permission of Harcourt, Inc.

Henry Holt and Company: "The Cow-Tail Switch," from *The Cow-Tail Switch and Other West African Stories* by Harold Courlander and George Herzog. Copyright © 1947, 1974 by Harold Courlander. Reprinted by permission of Henry Holt and Company, LLC.

UNIT TWELVE

Carolrhoda Books: "The Valentine," from *Stories from a Blue Road* by Emily Crofford. Text copyright © 1992 by Emily Crofford. Published by Carolrhoda Books, Inc., a division of the Lerner Publishing Group. Used by permission of the publisher. All rights reserved.

Random House Children's Books: "The Streak," from *145th Street: Short Stories* by Walter Dean Myers. Copyright © 2000 by Walter Dean Myers. Used by permission of Random House Children's Books, a division of Random House, Inc.

Art Credits

COVER

city Copyright © Christian Michaels/FPG International/PictureQuest; *Mackinac bridge* Copyright © W. Cody/Corbis; *microbes* Digital Imagery copyright © 2001 PhotoDisc, Inc; *aerial view of farm* Copyright © Sunset Avenue Productions/Artville/PictureQuest; *runners* Digital Imagery copyright © 2001 PhotoDisc, Inc.; *canoeing* Copyright © Tom Bean/Corbis; *face* Wolff/Graphistock; *dock* Digital Imagery copyright © 2001 PhotoDisc, Inc.; *Chichen Itzen* Copyright ©Cosmo Condina/Stone; *crowd* Copyright © Leo Mason. Split Second/Image Bank.

UNIT ONE

4 *Baseball Saved Us* (1993), Illustrations copyright © Dom Lee. Lee & Low Books, Inc., New York; **8** *Baseball Saved Us* (1993), Illustrations copyright © Dom Lee. Lee & Low Books, Inc., New York; **11** *Baseball Saved Us* (1993), Illustrations copyright © Dom Lee. Lee & Low Books, Inc., New York; **12** *Baseball Saved Us* (1993), Illustrations copyright © Dom Lee. Lee & Low Books, Inc., New York; **13** Digital Imagery copyright © 2001 PhotoDisc, Inc.; **14–15** *bottom* Copyright © Kevin R. Morris/Corbis; **14–15** *top* Copyright © Robert Frerck/Stone; **16–17** Digital Imagery copyright © 2001 PhotoDisc, Inc.; **18** Copyright © Phyllis Picardi/Stock South/PictureQuest; **20** Copyright © Rocky Weldon/Stock Photography/PictureQuest; **24** Selected illustrations from *The Dragon's Pearl* by Julie Lawson. Illustrations copyright © 1993 by Paul Morin. Reprinted by permission of Clarion Books/Houghton Mifflin Co. All rights reserved; **25** Selected illustrations from *The Dragon's Pearl* by Julie Lawson. Illustrations copyright © 1993 by Paul Morin. Reprinted by permission of Clarion Books/Houghton Mifflin Co. All rights reserved; **28** Selected illustrations from *The Dragon's Pearl* by Julie Lawson. Illustrations copyright © 1993 by Paul Morin. Reprinted by permission of Clarion Books/Houghton Mifflin Co. All rights reserved; **31** Selected illustrations from *The Dragon's Pearl* by Julie Lawson. Illustrations copyright ©1993 by Paul Morin. Reprinted by permission of Clarion Books/Houghton Mifflin Co. All rights reserved; **32** Selected illustrations from *The Dragon's Pearl* by Julie Lawson. Illustrations copyright © 1993 by Paul Morin. Reprinted by permission of Clarion Books/Houghton Mifflin Co. All rights reserved; **34** Selected illustrations from *The Dragon's Pearl* by Julie Lawson. Illustrations copyright © 1993 by Paul Morin. Reprinted by permission of Clarion Books/Houghton Mifflin Co. All rights reserved; **36–37** Copyright ©Sergio Dorantes/Corbis. **37** *right* Copyright © Andre Jenny/Focus Group/PictureQuest; **41** *background* Copyright © Sergio Dorantes/Corbis; **41** *foreground* Copyright © Corbis/Bettmann; **43** Digital Imagery copyright © 2001 PhotoDisc, Inc.; **46** Proprietary property of MapQuest.com. Unauthorized use, including copying, of this product, is expressly prohibited; **49** Copyright © Andre Jenny/Focus Group/PictureQuest.

UNIT TWO

51 Copyright © Words & Pictures/PictureQuest; **51** Copyright © Joanne Dugan Photography/Graphistock; **51** *background* Digital Imagery copyright ©2001 PhotoDisc, Inc.; **52** *foreground* Copyright © Joanne Dugan Photography/Graphistock; **54** *background* Copyright © Words & Pictures/PictureQuest; **54** *foreground* Copyright © Image Farm/PictureQuest; **56**

background Digital Imagery copyright © 2001 PhotoDisc, Inc.; **56** *foreground* Copyright © Christian Michaels/FPG International/PictureQuest; **56** *top* Digital Imagery copyright © 2001 PhotoDisc, Inc.; **58** *The Brooklyn Bridge: Variations on an Old Theme* (1939) Joseph Stella. Oil on canvas, 70″ x 42″. Collection of Whitney Museum of American Art, New York. Photograph Copyright ©2000: Whitney Museum of American Art; **60** Orchard Street (1972) David Levine. Watercolor, 11″x14″. Collection of the Artist. Courtesy Forum Gallery, New York; **60** Copyright ©Digital Stock/Corbis.

UNIT THREE

63 Copyright © USDA/Science Source/Photo Researchers, Inc.; **64** Digital Imagery copyright © 2001 PhotoDisc, Inc.; **64–65** *background* Copyright © Alan R. Moller/Stone; **65** *left* Copyright © Texian Press, Waco, TX; **65** *right* Copyright © Texian Press, Waco, TX; **69** *bottom* Copyright © Texian Press, Waco, TX; **69** *top* Copyright © Texian Press, Waco, TX; **70** Copyright © Texian Press, Waco, TX; **72** *bottom* Copyright © Color Day Production/Image Bank; **72** *left* Digital Imagery copyright © 2001 PhotoDisc, Inc.; **72** *right* Digital Imagery copyright © 2001 PhotoDisc, Inc.; **72–73** *background* Copyright © W. Cody/Corbis; **73** *left* Copyright © Robert Dowling/Corbis; **73** *right* Digital Imagery copyright © 2001 PhotoDisc, Inc.; **74** Copyright © W. Cody/Corbis; **77** *bottom* Copyright © Robert Dowling/Corbis; **77** *top* Copyright © Color Day Production/Image Bank; **80** Copyright ©Dover Publications; **80–81** *background* Digital Imagery copyright © 2001 PhotoDisc, Inc.; **81** Copyright ©Corbis/Bettmann; **88** *background* Digital Imagery copyright © 2001 PhotoDisc, Inc.; **88** *bottom* Copyright ©USDA/Science Source/Photo Researchers, Inc.; **88** *left* Copyright © USDA/Science Source/Photo Researchers, Inc.; **88** *top* Copyright © USDA/Science Source/Photo Researchers, Inc.; **88–89** *foreground* Copyright © Suzanne L. Collins & Joseph T. Collins/Photo Researchers, Inc.; **89** *top* Copyright ©Martin B. Withers; Frank Lane Picture Agency/Corbis; **91** AP/Wide World Photos; **93** Copyright © Martin B. Withers; Frank Lane Picture Agency/Corbis.

UNIT FOUR

96 from *My Man Blue* by Nikki Grimes, illustrated by Jerome Lagarrigue. Illustrations copyright © 1999 by Jerome Lagarrigue. Used by permission of Dial Books for Young Readers, an imprint of Penguin Putnam Books for young readers, a division of Penguin Putnam Inc; **103** from *My Man Blue* by Nikki Grimes, illustrated by Jerome Lagarrigue. Illustrations copyright © 1999 by Jerome Lagarrigue, permission of Dial Books for Young Readers, an imprint of Penguin Putnam Books for young readers, a division of Penguin Putnam Inc.; **107** from *My Man Blue* by Nikki Grimes, illustrated by Jerome Lagarrigue. Illustrations copyright © 1999 by Jerome Lagarrigue. Used by permission of Dial Books for Young Readers, an imprint of Penguin Putnam Books for young readers, a division of Penguin Putnam Inc.; **112** *Wow Car* (1997) Colleen Browning. Oil on canvas. Southern Alleghenies Museum of Art, Loretto, Pennsylvania; **112–113** Copyright © Form and Function, San Francisco; **115** *Libra* (1977) Colleen Browning. Oil on canvas. Harmon-Meek Gallery, Naples, Florida. Collection of the Artist; **117** Digital Imagery copyright © 2001 PhotoDisc, Inc.; **118** Digital Imagery copyright © 2001 PhotoDisc, Inc.; **118** *bottom* Copyright © PictureQuest; **118** *right* Copyright © Form and Function, San Francisco; **118** *top* Copyright © S.J. Carrera; **119** *left* Copyright © Form and Function, San Francisco; **121** Digital Imagery copyright © 2001 PhotoDisc, Inc.; **124** Copyright © Image Club/EyeWire Inc.; **126** *bottom* Copyright © Perry Conway/Corbis; **126** *top* Copyright © Brian Vikander/Corbis; **126–127** *background* Copyright © Stephanie Maze/Corbis; **128** Copyright © Stephanie Maze/Corbis; **133** Digital Imagery copyright © 2001 PhotoDisc, Inc.; **133** Digital Imagery copyright © 2001 PhotoDisc, Inc.

UNIT FIVE

135 Copyright © Andrea Pistolesi/Image Bank; **136** *background* Copyright © Andrea Pistolesi/Image Bank; **136** *foreground* Copyright © Guido Archive Holdings Inc. Alberto Rossi/Image Bank; **137** *bottom* Digital Imagery copyright © 2001 PhotoDisc, Inc.; **137** *top* Copyright © Guido Archive Holdings Inc. Alberto Rossi 03RROG/Image Bank; **139** Digital Imagery copyright © 2001 PhotoDisc, Inc.; **142** 1959 Harley Davidson Sportster. Photo by Garry Stuart; **145** Copyright © Andrea Pistolesi/Image Bank; **147** Copyright © Kevin Fleming/Corbis; **148** Illustration by Emily Thompson; **148** Illustration by Emily Thompson; **149** Illustration by Emily Thompson; **154** Illustration by Emily Thompson; **156** Illustration by Emily Thompson; **159** Illustration by Emily Thompson; **161** Illustration by Emily Thompson; **164** Illustration by Emily Thompson.

UNIT SIX

170 Digital Imagery copyright © 2001 PhotoDisc, Inc.; **172** Copyright © Storm Pirate Productions/Artville/PictureQuest; **174** Illustration by Bill Cigliano; **174** Digital Imagery copyright © 2001 PhotoDisc, Inc.; **174** *background* Digital Imagery copyright © 2001 PhotoDisc, Inc.; **178** Copyright © Sunset Avenue Productions/Artville/PictureQuest; **181** Digital Imagery copyright © 2001 PhotoDisc, Inc.; **185** Illustration by Bill Cigliano; **188–189** Copyright © Stephen Derr/Image Bank; **188–189** *top* Digital Imagery copyright © 2001 PhotoDisc, Inc.; **190** Copyright © Image Farm/PictureQuest; **193** Copyright © Stephen Derr/Image Bank; **194** Digital Imagery copyright © 2001 PhotoDisc, Inc.; **196** Digital Imagery copyright © 2001 PhotoDisc, Inc.; **196** *background* Copyright © Dover Publications, Inc.; **196** *foreground* Copyright © Paramount/PictureQuest; **203** Digital Imagery copyright © 2001 PhotoDisc, Inc.; **205** Copyright © Paramount/PictureQuest; **206** Copyright © Paramount/PictureQuest; **207** Copyright © Harriet Zucker/Photonica.

UNIT SEVEN

209 Copyright © Carin Krasner/Stone; **210** *bottom* Copyright © Digital Stock/Corbis; **210** *top* AP/Wide World Photos; **211** *background* Copyright © Digital Stock/Corbis; **211** *foreground* Memphis/Shelby County Archives, Memphis/Shelby County Public Library & Information Center; **213** Memphis/Shelby County Archives, Memphis/Shelby County Public Library &

Information Center; **217** Copyright © Image Farm/PictureQuest; **218** from *El Chino* (1990), Allen Say. Reprinted by Permission of Clarion/Houghton Mifflin Co. All rights reserved; **218** Digital Imagery copyright © 2001 PhotoDisc, Inc.; **220** from *El Chino* (1990), Allen Say. Reprinted by Permission of Clarion/Houghton Mifflin Co. All rights reserved; **221** Copyright © Dorling Kindersley Ltd.; **222** from *El Chino* (1990), Allen Say. Reprinted by Permission of Clarion/Houghton Mifflin Co. All rights reserved; **226** from *El Chino* (1990), Allen Say. Reprinted by Permission of Clarion/Houghton Mifflin Co. All rights reserved; **228** from *El Chino* (1990), Allen Say. Reprinted by Permission of Clarion/Houghton Mifflin Co. All rights reserved; **230** Copyright © Carin Krasner/Stone; **231** Courtesy of the George S. Bolster collection of the Historical Society of Saratoga Springs, NY; **233** Copyright © Christopher Thomas/Stone; **234** Copyright © Underwood & Underwood/Corbis; **235** Copyright © Bettmann/Corbis; **235** Copyright © Bettmann/Corbis; **236** Copyright © Bettmann/Corbis; **237** Copyright © Bettmann/Corbis; **241** Copyright © Bettmann/Corbis.

UNIT EIGHT

243 AP/Wide World Photos; **243** Illustration by Bill Cigliano; **244** Hubbard Photo Collection, Santa Clara University Archives; **244–245** *background* Digital Imagery copyright © 2001 PhotoDisc, Inc.; **249** Copyright © Chris Arend/Alaska Stock Images; **252** Copyright © AFP/Corbis; **252** Copyright © AFP/Corbis; **252–253** Digital Imagery copyright © 2001 PhotoDisc, Inc.; **254** AP/Wide World Photos; **257** Copyright © Mike Powell/Allsport USA; **262** AP/Wide World Photos; **264** *foreground* Copyright © Duomo/Corbis; **264–265** Digital Imagery copyright © 2001 PhotoDisc, Inc.; **268** Illustration by Bill Cigliano; **268** Copyright © Tom Bean/Corbis; **268–269** AP/Wide World Photos; **274** Illustration by Bill Cigliano; **277** Illustration by Bill Cigliano.

UNIT NINE

279 Digital Imagery copyright © 2001 PhotoDisc, Inc.; **284** Jeremy Wolff/Graphistock **286** Copyright © Clark James Mishler/Alaska Stock; **288** Copyright © Stockart.com; **290** Photo by Sharon Hoogstraten; **294** Copyright © 2001 Brad Holland/Theispot.

UNIT TEN

298 Copyright © Shelley Gazin/Corbis; **301** Digital Imagery copyright © 2001 PhotoDisc, Inc.; **302** AP/Wide World Photos; **305** Warner Brothers/Shooting Star; **306** *background* Copyright © Roine Magnusson/Stone; **306** *foreground* Copyright © Ulrike Schanz/Animals Animals; **308** Digital Imagery copyright © 2001 PhotoDisc, Inc.; **308** Digital Imagery copyright © 2001 PhotoDisc, Inc.; **313** Photo courtesy of Heinz Ken-L Ration; **314** Copyright © Bettmann/Corbis; **314–315** Digital Imagery copyright © 2001 PhotoDisc, Inc.; **315** detail of *Sunset of a Dying Race* (ca. 1913) Photo by Joseph Kossuth Dixon. William Hammond Mathers Museum, Indiana University; **316** Digital Imagery copyright © 2001 PhotoDisc, Inc.; **320** *Sunset of a Dying Race* (ca. 1913) Photo by Joseph Kossuth Dixon. William Hammond Mathers Museum, Indiana University; **323** Photo courtesy Rudy Shebala/Nez Perce Horse Registry; **326** Photo By Sharon Hoogstraten.

UNIT ELEVEN

327 Copyright © Maria Stenzel/NGS Image Collection; **329** Courtesy of the Egypt Exploration Society, London; **331** Copyright © Tom Nebbia/Corbis; **331** Copyright © Maria Stenzel/NGS Image Collection; **331** Copyright © Charles & Josette Lenars/Corbis; **332** Copyright © Dorling Kindersley Ltd.; **332** Copyright © Dorling Kindersley Ltd.; **333** Copyright © Form and Function, San Francisco; **334** Copyright © Cosmo Condina/Stone; **334** Copyright © Superstock; **334** Copyright © Will & Deni McIntyre/Stone; **334** Digital Imagery copyright © 2001 PhotoDisc, Inc.; **334** Photo by Sharon Hoogstraten; **336** Copyright © Cosmo Condina/Stone; **339** Photograph by A. Tozzer. Peabody Museum, Harvard University; **339** Photograph by Hillel Burger. Peabody Museum, Harvard University; **340** Photograph by Hillel Burger. Peabody Museum, Harvard University; **341** J.J. Foxx/NYC; **342** Bibliotheque Nationale, Paris/The Bridgeman Art Library; **345** Copyright © Angelo Hornak/Corbis; **346** Copyright © English Heritage Photo Library; **349** Illustration by the studio of Wood Ronsaville Harlin, Inc., Annapolis MD; **351** Copyright © Michael Nicholson/Corbis; **354** Copyright © Dave Bartruff/Corbis; **354–355** Digital Imagery copyright © 2001 PhotoDisc, Inc.; **355** Werner Forman Archive/Art Resource, New York; **358** Copyright © Michael S. Yamashita/Corbis; **360** Copyright © Honeychurch Antiques, Ltd./Corbis; **362** Werner Forman Archive/Art Resource, New York; **363** *Tajima the Arrow-cutter.* The Manchester Museum, The University of Manchester; **364** from *The Cow-Tail Switch and Other West African Stories.* Drawing copyright © Madye Lee Chastian. Used by permission of Henry Holt and Co.; **369** Copyright © Dorling Kindersley, London.; **370** from *The Cow-Tail Switch and Other West African Stories.* Drawing copyright © Madye Lee Chastian. Used by permission of Henry Holt and Co.

UNIT TWELVE

373 Copyright © Image Club/EyeWire Inc.; **374** Copyright © Mark Newman/Index Stock Imagery/PictureQuest; **376** Digital Imagery copyright © 2001 PhotoDisc, Inc.; **378** Copyright © Media Rights; **388** Copyright © Carol Kohen/Image Bank; **392** Copyright © David Falconner/Words & Pictures/PictureQuest; **394** Copyright © Bettmann/Corbis; **396** Digital Imagery copyright © 2001 PhotoDisc, Inc.; **402** Copyright © Hulton Getty/Getty Images; **404** Copyright © Bettmann/Corbis; **408** Copyright © Bettmann/Corbis; **410** Digital Imagery copyright © 2001 PhotoDisc, Inc.; **410** Copyright © Leo Mason. Split Second/Image Bank; **411** Digital Imagery copyright © 2001 PhotoDisc, Inc.; **413** Digital Imagery copyright © 2001 PhotoDisc, Inc.; **413** Copyright © Image Club/EyeWire Inc.; **415** Digital Imagery copyright © 2001 PhotoDisc, Inc.; **417** Copyright © Burke & Triolo/Artville/PictureQuest; **418** Copyright © Corbis; **424** Digital Imagery copyright © 2001 PhotoDisc, Inc.; **426** Photo by Sharon Hoogstraten; **429** Copyright © Leo Mason. Split Second/Image Bank.